NURSING and INFORMED CONSENT

A Case Study Approach

by Elizabeth Hogue, Esquire

(NHP) NATIONAL HEALTH PUBLISHING
A Division of Rynd Communications

Contents

How To Use This Book

1.   The cases appearing in this book are actual court decisions. However, they were extensively edited in order to make them easier to read. The editing included deletion of portions of the body of each case, all footnotes and all citations to cases made within a decision. If the readers wish to read any case in its entirety, they should first check with a public library to see if legal publications are available. Most public libraries do not have these cases, so, in most instances, readers must go to a law library to obtain the entire case.

2.   A chart entitled, "How to Read a Citation," is provided at the end of this book. This chart may be helpful to readers who wish to review the entire text of a case because the citation tells you where a case is located. It may also be useful for those readers who are curious about what the letters and numbers following the name of a case are all about.

3.   A glossary of legal terms is also provided. The purpose of this glossary is to assist readers to better understand the legal terminology which inevitably "peppers" even the edited versions of court decisions. Readers should refer to this glossary whenever they encounter legal words and phrases they do not understand.

4.   Finally, readers should try to remember that it is not essential to understand all of the procedural aspects of these decisions or all of the legal language in order to derive value from them. It is also important to understand that the more court decisions read, the easier it becomes for lawyers and nonlawyers to understand them. In short, practice is essential.

Foreword

Historically, physicians were legally responsible to obtain informed consent because they performed all surgical and technical procedures. During the last fifteen years the increased utilization of nurse practitioners, nurse anesthetists, and nurse midwives has expanded the types of primary care providers. As primary care providers, these practitioners have increasingly greater obligations in the area of informed consent. In addition, as nurses continue to lobby for changes in their Nurse Practice Acts in order to gain more autonomy in their practices, they will be faced with the responsibility of obtaining informed consent from their patients.

There is a growing tendency among consumers to be more involved in health care decisions. Necessary to the promotion of health and prevention of illness is a highly developed sense of personal responsibility for decisions related to health care. Personal responsibility for health-related decisions is possible only if practitioners provide thorough, complete information to patients in language patients can understand so that intelligent choices can be made. This is the essence of informed consent. As facilities, wellness centers, birthing centers, hospice programs and home health care programs grow in number, nurses and nurse practitioners will have even greater responsibility for providing information to their patients.

Elizabeth E. Hogue has shown an astute understanding of the unique role of the nurse. Her background in health care law as well as her interest in the promotion of nurses as health care providers is reflected in the focus of this book. Her commentaries are easy to understand and apply to situatiohs nurses frequently encounter. She has assisted many nurses in acquiring the necessary knowledge to prepare for nursing on the cutting edge of the health care delivery system by offering the support, encouragement and legal perspective needed to step into nursing of the future—which is one of health, education and prevention.

Maryann Burman Thayer, RN, MSN, CPNP

Introduction

Consent by the patient to routine and non–routine medical care is required prior to rendering treatment. The most important principle governing consent is that individuals have the right to control their bodies. The clearest expression of this principle appears in *Schloendorff v. Society of New York Hospitals*, 211 N.Y. 125, 105 N.E. 92 (1914) *overruled on other grounds*, and *Bing v. Thunig*, 2 N.Y.2d656, 143 N.E.2d 3, 163 N.Y.S.2d 3 (1957), a case concerning consent to surgery. In the decision in *Schloendorff*, Justice Cardozo stated:

> Every human being of adult years and sound mind has a right to determine what shall be done with his own body and a surgeon who performs an operation without his patient's consent commits an assault for which he is liable in damages...

More specifically, consent requires the presence of three elements: 1) capacity; 2) information; 3) voluntariness. All three requirements must be met in order to obtain the consent of the patient. Historically, health professionals have focused almost all of their attention on the evidence that information about treatment was conveyed to the patient: the consent form. Every nurse has seen these forms which are signed by the patient and then become part of the patient's medical record. The traditional attitude is that everything with regard to consent to treatment is "OK" as long as the patient signs the form and it appears in the chart.

In fact, this attitude results in a completely false sense of security. Practitioners must redirect their attention from the consent form which functions as evidence that information concerning treatment was conveyed to the actual process of conveying information. In other words, the consent form will protect providers from liability only if it is a reflection of a dialogue between treating professional and patient. If no discussion or an incomplete exchange occurred, the execution of the consent form is absolutely meaningless because a crucial element of consent is missing. Information regarding treatment was not actually given to the patient.

The importance of the process of providing information to the patient as opposed to the execution of a consent form may be clearer to providers when they realize that the law recognizes oral consent to treatment. In order to meet the requirements of the law, the patient is not required to sign a consent form. When practitioners give patients all of the information required by the law, they have already met their legal obligations. The consent form evidences that all obligations were met in case questions about consent are raised later. When viewed in this light, a tape recording of the conversation with the patient may substitute for a consent form. A witness may also serve as a useful substitute for execution of the form.

Practically speaking, healthcare institutions should routinely have each patient sign at least two consent forms. The first form, giving consent to routine, relatively non-invasive procedures, should be signed upon admission. This consent to routine treatment may cover the drawing of blood by the usual method and in customary amounts, a chest x-ray, etc. One or more additional consent forms should be signed by the patient to cover any non-routine invasive treatment including surgery, diagnostic testing, and radiological procedures.

Consent to non-routine treatment may be signed only *after* the patient has received the information necessary to make an intelligent choice. At a minimum, the procedure must be described to the patient along with anticipated risks and benefits. Alternative treatments must also be discussed. The patient must be given an opportunity to ask questions, and all questions must be answered as completely and truthfully as possible. Patients must also be told that they can withdraw their consent at any time without prejudicing further treatment.

Since the purpose of the form is to serve as evidence that this information was given to the patient, this information, specific to the treatment given each patient, must appear on the consent form. General consent forms will not fulfill the requirements of the law because they do not accurately reflect the discussion which must occur with regard to specific treatment. If a patient is being treated for an ingrown toenail and signs a consent form which says she consents to additional procedures as necessary and understands that one or more may result in sterility, the surgeon cannot perform a hysterectomy based upon this form. Despite what the form says, the patient was not given proper information concerning a hysterectomy.

Nurses becoming familiar with court cases involving consent to treatment have correctly observed that almost all of the cases involve physicians. This is true because, traditionally, treating physicians, not nurses, were required to convey the information necessary to obtain informed consent. The reason for this requirement is that, theoretically, only physicians had enough knowledge of the procedure or treatment involved to give the patient all necessary information. Consequently, law suits involving consent are almost always brought against physicians.

As a result, nurses may well wonder why they need to be knowledgeable about this area of the law. If informed consent is physicians' responsibility, let them handle the whole issue. However, this point of view fails to account for several practical aspects of nurses' roles. First, getting consent forms signed is often a part of a nurse's job. Nurses must, therefore, be knowledgeable about the improper aspects of this extremely common practice so that it can be corrected. While nurses themselves may not be liable for failure to obtain consent, their employers may experience severe adverse consequences of a failure to abide by the law which may ultimately adversely affect nurses directly. Second, the role of nurses, particularly those in so-called expanded roles, has changed dramatically to include diagnosis, prescription, and treatment. These are areas of practice which once belonged exclusively to physicians. When nurses perform these functions, they are treating professionals themselves. As such, it is likely that they have a legal obligation to get consent from patients for the treatment they render themselves. Consequently, nurses need to understand the law of informed consent.

Nurses have also correctly observed that a number of the court cases involving informed consent are not very recent. The primary reasons for this fact are that: (1) The legal principles governing informed consent have been well-established for a number of years, and (2) Because courts base their decisions on precedent or previously decided cases consistent with the principles of *stare decisis*, it is essential to turn to older cases in order to find a thorough discussion of well-established principles. Nurses should be assured that despite the chronological age of some of the cases in this book, the principles are relevant to nursing practice today.

Even when practitioners fully understand their obligations in the area of consent, many of them resist. Their resistance is often based on arguments that getting informed consent from each patient takes too much time and that consent forms involve too much paperwork. At the same time, practitioners express dismay concerning the number of malpractice suits initiated by dissatisfied patients. Practitioners must realize that there is a direct relationship between informed consent and liability. If valid consent is not obtained from the patient prior to treatment, the treating physician(s) may be liable for 1) battery and/or 2) negligence. In order to prove battery, the patient must prove that the physician 1) intended 2) to touch the patient in 3) a manner unauthorized by the patient. In order to establish negligence, the patient must show that 1) the physician had a duty of care to the patient which 2) the physician breached 3) causing 4) injury or damage to the patient. Thus, obtaining informed consent must be viewed as a tool of risk management.

In addition to a lot of discussion about the "nuts and bolts" of avoiding liability, much lip service is paid to the idea that the most important thing practitioners can do to avoid liability is to develop a positive, healthy relationship with their patients. The dialogue between provider and patient required in order to obtain informed consent enhances relationships with most patients, thereby providing additional protection from liability. If practitioners are serious about avoiding liability and establishing satisfactory relationships with their patients, they must participate in and support the process required to obtain truly informed consent.

ELEMENTS OF CONSENT

Capacity, Information, and Voluntariness

In terms relevant to consent:

A. Capacity. Capacity is defined with respect to: 1) a person's age (Generally, persons over the age of majority, as defined by state statutes, are legally permitted to make various decisions on their own behalf.); and 2) a person's competence. Individuals are competent when they have the mental ability to make choices and understand the consequence of their decisions. Although the trend is away from this approach, the law often makes a blanket determination of competency or incompetency. A person is completely competent or incompetent for all purposes. An example of an individual who lacks competency is someone who is profoundly mentally retarded.

Practically speaking, there are two groups of patients whose competency to make decisions concerning medical treatment may be difficult to determine: the elderly and the mentally disabled. Elderly patients are often "confused." In addition, many family members seem to be willing, and even eager, to assume lack of competency on the part of elderly relatives. The cognitive functions of the mentally disabled may be diminished by their illnesses. Nonetheless, nurses must guard against assuming a lack of legal capacity to give informed consent. Only individuals adjudicated incompetent by a court lack capacity for the purposes of informed consent; patients must be presumed to be competent unless they are adjudicated incompetent. Commitment to an institution for the mentally ill does not mean that a patient is incompetent. This determination must be made in a separate court proceeding.

B. Information. Many court decisions governing consent focus on the element of disclosure of relevant information. The key issue has been the standard used to determine whether sufficient information has been imparted to the patient.

One group of cases requires a *professional* standard of care. Applying this standard, a physician is obliged to disclose to the patient information which a reasonable medical practitioner would have disclosed under the same or similar circumstances. In another group of cases, the courts rejected a professional standard of care in favor of a "lay" standard. According to these decisions, a physician's disclosure is governed by the patient's need for information. The appropriate standard is not what the physician in the exercise of his medical judgment thinks a patient should know; the focus is on what data a particular individual needs in order to make an informed choice. For example, if a patient is a concert violinist, the professional standard requires that the person be given that information which most physicians would give to most patients undergoing the same treatment. The "lay" standard requires that the patient be given any and all information relevant to a particular concern, the effect of any treatment upon the use of the concert violinist's hands. While this information may not be important for all patients, under the "lay" standard of disclosure it is particularly important to the violinist and, therefore, must be given to the patient. In recent years, many courts have rejected a professional standard of disclosure in favor of the "lay" standard. An attorney in your state can tell you which standard is applied to cases in your area.

C. Involuntariness. Individuals act voluntarily when they exercise freedom of choice without force, fraud, deceit, duress, over-reaching, or any other form of constraint or coercion. When hospital admitting personnel insist that the patient sign a consent form at the time of admission with no prior exchange of information between physician and patient or else be refused admission, consent is invalid because force and duress were applied to the patient. The patient did not act voluntarily.

The courts have also recognized less obvious constraints upon the voluntariness of patients' actions such as an institutional environment and the effects of long-term hospitalization. The suggestion is made that patients who are institutionalized for long periods of time may lose the ability to act voluntarily because they become accustomed to responding almost exclusively to the demands of institutional regimens and relatively powerful caretakers.

PRACTITIONERS LIABLE FOR FAILURE TO DISCLOSE RISKS OF SURGERY

Although it was decided a number of years ago, *Canterbury v. Spence*, 464 F.2d 772 (D.C. Cir. 1972) cert. denied, 409 U.S. 1064 (1972) is an extremely important case in the area of informed consent. For one thing, it contains a discussion of many of the basic principles governing consent and the reasoning which serves as the basis for the principles. *Canterbury* also includes practical information about consent which is helpful to practitioners. For example, the court discusses the amount and type of information which must be shared with the patient. The court makes it clear that "full" disclosure is not required; practitioners cannot be expected to tell a patient about every possible risk of a procedure. Rather, according to *Canterbury*, providers must tell patients everything material to their decisions. This requirement is based on the court's conclusion that providers of healthcare are in a better position to know their patients than other professionals. Surely, nurses are in the best position of all to meet this expectation since they have sustained contact with patients. *Canterbury* also makes it clear that risks that are material but generally known, such as the risk of infection from surgery, need not be disclosed to patients.

Canterbury is also important to practitioners because of the discussion it contains about causation. One of the consequences of failing to obtain informed consent is liability for negligence. In order to prove negligence, the plaintiff must prove that 1) the defendant had a legal duty to the plaintiff, 2) the defendant breached this legal duty owed to the plaintiff, and 3) the defendant's breach caused injury to the plaintiff. *Canterbury* explains what the plaintiff must show regarding causation when claiming negligence due to lack of informed consent. That is, plaintiffs must show that if proper information had been given, they would not have undergone the treatment which caused injury.

Canterbury v. Spence, 464 F.2d 772 (D.C. Circ. 1972)
United States Court of Appeals

. . . The record we review tells a depressing tale. A youth troubled only by back pain submitted to an operation without being informed of a risk of paralysis incidental thereto. A day after the operation he fell from his hospital bed after having been left without assistance while voiding. A few hours after the fall, the lower half of his body was paralyzed, and he had to be operated on again. Despite extensive medical care, he has never been what he was before. Instead of the back pain, even years later, he hobbled about on crutches, a victim of paralysis of the bowels and urinary incontinence. In a very real sense this lawsuit is an understandable search for reasons.

At the time of the events which gave rise to this litigation, appellant was nineteen years of age, a clerk-typist employed by the Federal Bureau of Investigation. In December, 1958, he began to experience severe pain between his shoulder blades. He consulted two general practitioners, but the medications they prescribed failed to eliminate the pain. Thereafter, appellant secured an appointment with Dr. Spence, who is a neurosurgeon.

Dr. Spence examined appellant in his office at some length but found nothing amiss. On Dr. Spence's advice appellant was x-rayed, but the films did not identify an abnormality. Dr. Spence then recommended that appellant undergo a myelogram—a procedure in which dye is injected into the spinal column and traced to find evidence of disease or other disorder—at the Washington Hospital Center.

Appellant entered the hospital on February 4, 1959. The myelogram revealed a "filling defect" in the region of the fourth thoracic vertebra. Since a myelogram often does no more than pinpoint the location of an aberration, surgery may be necessary to discover the cause. Dr. Spence told appellant that he would have to undergo a laminectomy— the excision of the posterior arch of the vertebra—to correct what he suspected as a ruptured disc. Appellant did not raise any objection to the proposed operation nor did he probe into its exact nature.

Appellant explained to Dr. Spence that his mother was a widow of slender financial means living in Cyclone, West Virginia, and that she could be reached through a neighbor's telephone. Appellant called his mother the day after the myelogram was performed and, failing to contact her, left Dr. Spence's telephone number with the neighbor. When Mrs. Canterbury returned the call, Dr. Spence told her that the surgery was occasioned by a suspected ruptured disc. Mrs. Canterbury then asked if the recommended operation was serious and Dr. Spence replied, "not anymore than any other operation." He added that he knew Mrs. Canterbury was not well off and that her presence in Washington would not be necessary. The testimony is contradictory as to whether during the course of the conversation Mrs. Canterbury expressed her consent to the operation. Appellant himself apparently did not converse again with Dr. Spence prior to the operation.

Dr. Spence performed the laminectomy on February 11 at the Washington Hospital Center. Mrs. Canterbury traveled to Washington, arriving on that date but after the operation was over, and signed a consent form at the hospital. The laminectomy revealed several anomalies: a spinal cord that was swollen and unable to pulsate, an accumulation of large tortuous and dilated veins, and a complete absence of epidural fat which normally surrounds the spine. A thin hypodermic needle was inserted into the spinal cord to aspirate any cysts which might have been present, but no fluid emerged. In suturing the wound, Dr. Spence attempted to relieve the pressure on the spinal cord by enlarging the dura—the outer protective wall of the spinal cord—at the area of swelling.

For approximately the first day after the operation appellant recuperated normally, but then suffered a fall and an almost immediate setback. Since there is some conflict as to precisely when or why appellant fell, we construct the events from the evidence most favorable to him. Dr. Spence left orders that appellant was to remain in bed during the process of voiding. These orders were changed to direct that voiding be done out of bed, and the jury could find that the change was made by hospital personnel. Just prior to the fall, appellant summoned a nurse and was given a receptacle for use in voiding, but was then left unattended. Appellant testified that during the course of the endeavor he slipped off the side of the bed, and that there was no one to assist him, or side rail to prevent the fall.

Seven hours later, appellant began to complain that he could not move his legs and that he was having trouble breathing; paralysis seems to have been virtually total from the waist down. Dr. Spence was notified on the night of February 12, and he rushed to the hospital. Mrs. Canterbury signed another consent form and appellant was again taken into the operating room. The surgical wound was reopened and Dr. Spence created a gusset to allow the spinal cord greater room in which to pulsate.

Appellant's control over his muscles improved somewhat after the second operation but he was unable to void properly. As a result of this condition, he came under the care of several specialists, and at all times was under the care of several specialists and at all times was under the care of a urologist while still in the hospital. In April, following a cystoscopic examination, appellant was operated on for removal of bladder stones, and in May was released from the hospital. He re-entered the hospital the following August for a 10-day period, apparently because of his urologic problems. For several years after his discharge he was under the care of several specialists, and at all times was under the care of a urologist. At the time of the trial in April, 1968, appellant required crutches to walk, still suffered from urinal incontinence and paralysis of the bowels, and wore a penile clamp.

In November, 1959, on Dr. Spence's recommendation, appellant was transferred by the F.B.I. to Miami where he could get more swimming and exercise. Appellant worked three years for the F.B.I. in Miami, Los Angeles, and Houston, resigning finally in June, 1962. From then until the time of the trial, he held a number of jobs, but had constant trouble finding work because he needed to remain seated and close to a bathroom. The damages appellant claims include extensive pain and suffering, medical expenses, and loss of earnings . . .

. . . The testimony of appellant and his mother that Dr. Spence did not reveal the risk of paralysis from the laminectomy made out a prima facie case of violation of the physician's duty to disclose which Dr. Spence's explanation did not negate as a matter of law . . .

. . . The root premise is the concept, fundamental in American jurisprudence, that "(e)very human being of adult years and sound mind has a right to determine what shall be done with his own body . . ."

True consent to what happens to one's self is the informed exercise of a choice, and that entails an opportunity to evaluate knowledgeably the options available and the risks attendant upon each. The average patient has little or no understanding of the medical arts, and ordinarily has only his physician to whom he can look for enlightenment with which to reach an intelligent decision. From those almost axiomatic considerations springs the need, and in turn the requirement, of a reasonable divulgence by physician to patient to make such a decision possible . . .

. . . The context in which the duty of risk–disclosure arises is invariably the occasion for decision as to whether a particular treatment procedure is to be undertaken. To the physician, whose training enables a self–satisfying evaluation, the answer may seem clear, but it is the prerogative of the patient, not the physician, to determine for himself the direction in which his interests seem to lie. To enable the patient to chart his course understandably, some familiarity with the therapeutic alternatives and their hazards becomes essential . . .

. . . Once the circumstances give rise to a duty on the physician's part to inform his patient, the next inquiry is the scope of the disclosure the physician is legally obliged to make. The courts have frequently confronted this problem, but no uniform standard defining the adequacy of the divulgence emerges from the decisions. Some have said "full" disclosure, a norm we are unwilling to adopt literally. It seems obviously prohibitive and unrealistic to expect physicians to discuss with their patients every risk of proposed treatment––no matter how small or remote––and generally unnecessary from the patient's viewpoint as well. Indeed, the cases speaking in terms of "full" disclosure appear to envision something less than total disclosure, leaving unanswered the question of just how much . . .

. . . In our view, the patient's right of self–decision shapes the boundaries of the duty to reveal. That right can be effectively exercised only if the patient possesses enough information to enable an intelligent choice. The scope of the physician's communications to the patient, then, must be measured by the patient's need, and that need is the information material to the decision. Thus the test for determining whether a particular peril must be divulged is its materiality to the patient's decision: all risks potentially affecting the decision must be unmasked . . .

. . . The topics importantly demanding a communication of information are the inherent and potential hazards of the proposed treatment, the alternatives to that treatment, if any, and the results likely if the patient remains untreated. The factors contributing significance to the dangerousness of a medical technique are, of course, the incidence of injury and the degree of the harm threatened. A very small chance of death or serious disablement may well be significant; a potential disability which dramatically outweighs the potential benefit of the therapy or the detriments of the existing malady may summon discussion with the patient.

There is no bright line separating the significant from the insignificant; the answer in any case must abide a rule of reason. Some dangers––infection, for example–– are inherent in any operation; there is no obligation to communicate those of which persons of average sophistication are aware. Even more clearly, the physician bears no responsibility for discussion of hazards the patient has already discovered, or those having no apparent materiality to the patient's decision on therapy . . .

. . . Two exceptions to the general rule of disclosure have been noted by the courts. Each is in the nature of a physician's privilege not to disclose, and the reasoning underlying them is appealing. Each, indeed, is but a recognition that, as important as is the patient's right to know, it is greatly outweighed by the magnitudinous circumstances giving rise to the privilege. The first comes into play when the patient is unconscious or otherwise incapable of consenting, and harm from a failure to treat is imminent and outweighs any harm threatened by the proposed treatment. When a genuine emergency of that sort arises, it is settled that the impracticality of conferring with the patient dispenses with need for it . . .

The second exception obtains when risk–disclosure poses such a threat of detriment to the patient as to become unfeasible or contraindicated from a medical point of view. It is recognized that patients occasionally become so ill or emotionally distraught on disclosure as to foreclose a rational decision, or complicate or hinder the treatment, or perhaps even pose psychological damage to the patient. Where that is so, the cases have generally held that the physician is armed with a privilege to keep the information from the patient, and we think it clear that portents of that type may justify the physician in action he deems medically warranted. The critical inquiry is whether the physician responded to a sound medical judgment that communication of the risk information would present a threat to the patient's well-being.

The physician's privilege to withhold information for therapeutic reasons must be carefully circumscribed, however, for otherwise it might devour the disclosure rule itself. The privilege does not accept the paternalistic notion that the physician may remain silent simply because divulgence might prompt the patient to forego therapy the physician feels the patient really needs. That attitude presumes instability or perversity for even the normal patient, and runs counter to the foundation principle that the patient should and ordinarily can make the choice for himself. Nor does the privilege contemplate operation save where the patient's reaction to risk information, as reasonably foreseen by the physician, is menacing . . .

. . . (As) in malpractice actions generally, there must be a causal relationship between the physician's failure to adequately divulge and damage to the patient.

A causal connection exists when, but only when, disclosure of significant risks incidental to treatment would have resulted in a decision against it. The patient obviously has no complaint if he would have submitted to the therapy notwithstanding awareness that the risk was one of its perils. On the other hand, the very purpose of the disclosure rule is to protect the patient against consequences which, if known, he would have avoided by foregoing the treatment. The more difficult question is whether the factual issue on causality calls for an objective or a subjective determination . . .

. . . (W)hen causality is explored at a post-injury trial with a professedly uninformed patient, the question whether he actually would have turned the treatment down if he had known the risks is purely hypothetical: "Viewed from the point at which he had to decide, would the patient have decided differently had he known something he did not know?" And the answer which the patient supplies hardly represents more than a guess, perhaps tinged by the circumstances that the uncommunicated hazard has in fact materialized.

In our view, this method of dealing with the issue on causation comes in second–best. It places the physician in jeopardy of the patient's hindsight and bitterness. It places the factfinder in the position of deciding whether a speculative answer to a hypothetical question is to be credited. It calls for a subjective determination solely on testimony of a patient–witness shadowed by the occurrence of the undisclosed risk.

Better it is, we believe, to resolve the causality issue on an objective basis: in terms of what a prudent person in the patient's position would have decided if suitably informed of all perils bearing significance. If adequate disclosure could reasonably be expected to have caused that person to decline the treatment because of the revelation of the kind of risk or danger that resulted in harm, causation is shown, but otherwise not. The patient's testimony is relevant on that score of course but it would not threaten to dominate the findings. And since that testimony would probably be appraised congruently with the factfinder's belief in its reasonableness, the case for a wholly objective standard for passing on causation is strengthened. Such a standard would in any event ease the fact–finding process and better assure the truth as its product . . .

. . . Reverse and remand for a new trial.

o **Recap of the Case**. In *Canterbury v. Spence*, the court decided that the plaintiff was entitled to a new trial. Recognizing a duty on the part of practitioners to disclose certain information to patients prior to rendering treatment, the court ordered a new trial to determine whether this duty to disclose information was met by practitioners treating the plaintiff. However, even if these practitioners failed to disclose necessary information, the patient will not win the case unless he can show that he would have refused surgery if he had been properly informed.

NO LIABILITY WHEN PATIENT EXPERIENCES COMPLICATIONS DUE TO RISKS OF TREATMENT

Cobbs v. Grant is another important case in the area of informed consent because it also clearly states many basic principles governing consent and the reasons for these requirements. In addition, *Cobbs* also draws a helpful distinction between conduct resulting in liability for battery and actions leading to a claim of negligence based upon lack of informed consent. Practitioners who render treatment which the patient never consented to at all are liable for battery. For example, if the patient consents to an appendectomy and a surgeon removes a kidney, the surgeon is liable for battery, not negligence. By the same token, practitioners are liable for negligence due to lack of consent when a potential risk which was never disclosed to the patient occurs. The court in *Cobbs* suggests that this distinction between battery and negligence is important primarily because liability for battery may include punitive damages, an additional type of damages available to the plaintiff if the defendant's behavior was especially gross, which are unavailable in a suit for negligence.

Cobbs v. Grant,
8 Ca.3d 229, 104 Cal.Rptr. 505, 502 P.2d 1 (1972)
Supreme Court of California

. . . Plaintiff was admitted to the hospital in August 1964 for treatment of a duodenal ulcer. He was given a series of tests to ascertain the severity of his condition and, though administered medication to ease his discomfort, he continued to complain of lower abdominal pain and nausea. His family physician, Dr. Jerome Sands, concluding that surgery was indicated, discussed prospective surgery with plaintiff and advised him in general terms of the risks of undergoing a general anesthetic. Dr. Sands called in defendant, Dr. Dudley F. P. Grant, a surgeon, who after examining plaintiff, agreed with Dr. Sands that plaintiff had an intractable peptic duodenal ulcer and that surgery was indicated. Although Dr. Grant explained the nature of the operation to plaintiff, he did not discuss any of the inherent risks of the surgery.

A two–hour operation was performed the next day, in the course of which the presence of a small ulcer was confirmed. Following the surgery the ulcer disappeared. Plaintiff's recovery appeared to be uneventful, and he was permitted to go home eight days later. However, the day after he returned home, plaintiff began to experience intense pain in his abdomen. He immediately called Dr. Sands who advised him to return to the hospital. Two hours after his readmission, plaintiff was bleeding internally as a result of a severed artery at the hilum of his spleen. Because of the seriousness of the hemorrhaging and since the spleen of an adult may be removed without adverse effects, defendant decided to remove the spleen. Injuries to the spleen that compel a subsequent operation are a risk inherent in the type of surgery performed on plaintiff and occur in approximately 5 percent of such operations.

After removal of his spleen, plaintiff recuperated for two weeks in the hospital. A month after discharge he was readmitted because of sharp pains in his stomach. X-rays disclosed plaintiff was developing a gastric ulcer. The evolution of a new ulcer is another risk inherent in surgery performed to relieve a duodenal ulcer. Dr. Sands initially decided to attempt to treat this nascent gastric ulcer with antacids and a strict diet. However, some four months later, plaintiff was hospitalized when the gastric ulcer continued to deteriorate and he experienced severe pain. When plaintiff began to vomit blood the defendant and Dr. Sands concluded that a third operation was indicated: a gastrectomy with removal of 50 percent of plaintiff's stomach to reduce its acid-producing capacity. Some time after the surgery, plaintiff was discharged, but subsequently had to be hospitalized yet again when he began to bleed internally due to the premature absorption of a suture, another inherent risk of surgery. After plaintiff was hospitalized, the bleeding began to abate and a week later he was finally discharged . . .

. . . The jury could have found for plaintiff either by determining that defendant negligently performed the operation, or on the theory that defendant's failure to disclose inherent risks of the initial surgery vitiated plaintiff's consent to operate. Defendant attacks both possible grounds of the verdict . . .

. . . [W]hen an undisclosed potential complication results, the occurrence of which was not an integral part of the treatment procedure but merely a known risk, the courts are divided on the issue of whether this should be deemed to be a battery or negligence . . .

. . . Although this is a close question, either prong of which is supportable by authority, the trend appears to be towards categorizing failure to obtain informed consent as negligence. That this result now appears with growing frequency is of more than academic interest; it reflects an appreciation of the several significant consequences of favoring negligence over a battery theory . . . [M]ost jurisdictions have permitted a doctor in an informed consent action to interpose a defense that the disclosure he omitted to make was not required within his medical community. However, expert opinion as to community standard is not required in a battery count, in which the patient must merely prove failure to give informed consent and a mere touching absent consent. Moreover a doctor could be held liable for punitive damages under a battery count, and if held liable for the intentional tort of battery he might not be covered by his malpractice insurance. Additionally, in some jurisdictions the patient has a longer statute of limitations if he sues in negligence.

We agree with the majority trend. The battery theory should be reserved for those circumstances when a doctor performs an operation to which the patient has not consented. When the patient gives permission to perform one type of treatment and the doctor performs another, the requisite element of deliberate intent to deviate from the consent given is present. However, when the patient consents to certain treatment and the doctor performs the treatment, but an undisclosed inherent complication with a low probability occurs, no intentional deviation from the consent given appears; rather, the doctor in obtaining consent may have failed to meet his due care duty to disclose pertinent information. In that situation the action should be pleaded in negligence.

The facts of this case constitute a classic illustration of an action that sounds in negligence. Defendant performed the identical operation to which plaintiff had consented. The spleen injury, development of the gastric ulcer, gastrectomy and internal bleeding as a result of the premature absorption of a suture, were all links in a chain of low probability events inherent in the initial operation.

. . . The thesis that medical doctors are invested with discretion to withhold information from their patients has been frequently ventilated in both legal and medical literature . . . Despite what defendant characterizes as the prevailing rule, it has never been unequivocally adopted by an authoritative source. Therefore we probe anew into the rationale which purportedly justifies, in accordance with medical rather than legal standards, the withholding of information from a patient. Preliminarily we employ several postulates. The first is that patients are generally persons unlearned in the medical sciences and therefore, except in rare cases, courts may safely assume the knowledge of patient and physician are not in parity. The second is that a person of adult years and in sound mind has the right, in the exercise of control over his own body, to determine whether or not to submit to lawful medical treatment. The third is that the patient's consent to treatment, to be effective, must be an informed consent. And the fourth is that the patient, being unlearned in medical sciences, has an abject dependence upon and trust in his physician for the information upon which he relies during the decisional process, thus raising an obligation in the physician that transcends arms-length transactions.

From the foregoing axiomatic ingredients emerges a necessity, and a resultant requirement, for divulgence by the physician to his patient of all information relevant to a meaningful decisional process. In many instances, to the physician whose training and experience enable a self-satisfying evaluation, a particular treatment may seem evident, but it is the prerogative of the patient, not the physician, to determine for himself the direction in which he believes his interests lie. To enable the patient to chart his course knowledgeably, reasonable familiarity with the therapeutic alternatives and their hazards becomes essential.

Therefore, we hold, as an integral part of the physician's overall obligation to the patient, there is a duty of reasonable disclosure of the available choices with respect to proposed therapy and of the dangers inherently and potentially involved in each.

A concomitant issue is the yardstick to be applied in determining reasonableness of disclosure. This defendant and the majority of courts have related the duty to the custom of physicians practicing in the community . . . The majority rule is needlessly overbroad. Even if there can be said to be a medical community standard as to the disclosure requirement for any prescribed treatment, it appears so nebulous that doctors become, in effect, vested with virtual absolute discretion . . . The court in *Canterbury v. Spence* bluntly observed: "Nor can we ignore the fact that to bind the disclosure obligation to medical usage is to arrogate the decision on revelation to the physician alone. Respect for the patient's right of self-determination on particular theory demands a standard set by law for physicians rather than one which physicians may or may not impose upon themselves." Unlimited discretion in the physician is irreconcilable with the basic right of the patient to make the ultimate informed decision regarding the course of treatment to which he knowledgeably consents to be subjected.

A medical doctor, being the expert, appreciates the risks inherent in the procedure he is prescribing, the risks of a decision not to undergo the treatment, and the probability of a successful outcome of the treatment. But once this information has been disclosed, that aspect of the doctor's expert function has been performed. The weighing of these risks against the individual subjective fears and hopes of the patient is not an expert skill. Such evaluation and decision is a nonmedical judgment reserved to the patient alone. A patient should be denied the opportunity to weigh the risks only where it is evident he cannot evaluate the data as, for example, where there is an emergency or the patient is a child or incompetent. For this reason the law provides that, in an emergency, consent is implied . . . and if the patient is a minor or incompetent, the authority to consent is transferred to the patient's legal guardian . . . In all cases other than the foregoing, the decision whether or not to undertake treatment is vested in the party most directly affected: the patient.

The scope of the disclosure required of physicians defies simple definition. Some courts have spoken of "full disclosure" . . . but such facile expressions obscure common practicalities. Two qualifications to a requirement of "full disclosure" need little explication. First, the patient's interest in information does not extend to a lengthy polysyllabic discourse on all possible complications. A mini-course in medical science is not required; the patient is concerned with the risk of death or bodily harm. A medical doctor has a duty to disclose to his patient the potential of death or serious harm; and problems of recuperation. Second, there is no physician's duty to discuss the relatively minor risks inherent in common procedures, when it is common knowledge that such risks inherent in the procedures are of very low incidence. When there is a common procedure a doctor must, of course, make such inquiries as are required to determine if for the particular patient the treatment under consideration is contraindicated—for example, to determine if the patient has had adverse reactions to antibiotics; but no warning beyond such inquiries is required as to the remote possibility of death or serious bodily harm.

However, when there is a more complicated procedure, as the surgery in the case before us, the jury should be instructed that when a given procedure inherently involves a known risk of death or serious bodily harm a medical doctor has a duty to disclose to his patient the potential of death or serious harm and to explain in lay terms the complications that might possibly occur. Beyond the foregoing minimal disclosure, a doctor must also reveal to his patient such additional information as a skilled practitioner of good standing would provide under similar circumstances.

In sum, the patient's right of self–decision is the measure of the physician's duty to reveal. That right can be effectively exercised only if the patient possesses adequate information to enable an intelligent choice. The scope of the physician's communications to the patient, then, must be measured by the patient's need, and that need is whatever information is material to the decision. Thus the test for determining whether a potential peril must be divulged is its materiality to the patient's decision . . .

We point out, for guidance on retrial, an additional problem which suggests itself. There must be a causal relationship between the physician's failure to inform and the injury to the plaintiff. Such causal connection arises only if it is established that had revelation been made consent to treatment would not have been given. Here the record discloses no testimony that had plaintiff been informed of the risks of surgery he would not have consented to the operation . . .

The patient–plaintiff may testify on this subject but the issue extends beyond his credibility. Since at the time of trial the uncommunicated hazard has materialized, it would be surprising if the patient–plaintiff did not claim that had he been informed of the dangers he would have declined treatment. Subjectively he may believe so, with the 20/20 vision of hindsight, but we doubt that justice will be served by placing the physician in jeopardy of the patient's bitterness and disillusionment. Thus an objective test is preferable: i.e., what would a prudent person in the patient's position have decided if adequately informed of all significant perils . . .

Whenever appropriate, the court should instruct the jury on the defenses available to a doctor who has failed to make the disclosure required by law. Thus, a medical doctor need not make disclosure of risks when the patient requests that he not be so informed . . . Such a disclosure need not be made if the procedure is simple and the danger remote and commonly appreciated to be remote. A disclosure need not be made beyond that required within the medical community when a doctor can prove by a preponderance of the evidence he relied upon facts which would demonstrate to a reasonable man the disclosure would have so seriously upset the patient that the patient would not have been able to dispassionately weigh the risks of refusing to undergo the recommended treatment . . .

The judgment is reversed.

o **Recap of the Case**. The patient in the Cobbs case experienced a number of complications and sued the provider.

The court first decided that failure to give informed consent may result in liability for negligence, not assault and battery. The court then found that treating practitioners have a duty to disclose common risks to their patients. The only exceptions to this rule are: 1) an emergency situation exists which requires immediate treatment; 2) the patient is a minor; 3) the patient is incompetent; and 4) the facts show that disclosure of risks would upset the patient so much that the patient would be unable to evaluate the risks of refusing treatment.

Part I

EXCEPTIONS TO THE REQUIREMENT OF CONSENT

Emergencies and Therapeutic Privilege

1

Emergencies

In an emergency, consent from the patient is unnecessary because the law assumes that patients consent to the preservation of their own lives. Lack of consent in an emergency does not constitute battery or provide the basis for a claim of negligence.

It is difficult in many instances to decide whether there is an emergency. The law defines an emergency as a situation where there is an immediate threat to life and/or a threat of permanent impairment of health. If delaying treatment does not increase the risk to the patient's life or health, the situation is probably not an emergency. However, some courts have taken a more liberal view and have allowed emergency treatment without consent in order to alleviate pain and suffering even though no threat to life or of irreparable harm to health exists.

Of course, implicit in the concept of presumed or implied consent to emergency treatment is the inability of the patient to consent and the unavailability of anyone authorized to act on behalf of the patient. A competent adult may refuse medical treatment even if the result is likely to be death or irreparable harm. Therefore, implied consent in emergencies requires the following: 1) the inability of patients or their authorized representatives to give consent, and 2) a situation in which failure to treat will result in death or irreparable harm to the patient.

PRACTITIONERS NOT LIABLE FOR EMERGENCY AMPUTATION WITHOUT PATIENT CONSENT

Despite the fact that it was decided in 1912, *Luka v. Lourie*, is helpful to nurses because of its discussion concerning what constitutes an emergency. In this case, three expert witnesses appeared on the issue of whether the plaintiff's condition was an emergency, thereby permitting the defendant to amputate plaintiff's foot without anyone's consent. The type of questions asked of these three expert witnesses is similar to the examination that would occur today in this type of case.

Practitioners should also give special attention to the court's discussion of the fact that defendant consulted a number of other physicians prior to amputation. From this discussion, practitioners may conclude that one way to avoid liability in situations which are not clearly emergencies is to consult colleagues on questionable cases. If possible, a consensus of opinion should be reached and acted upon.

The court's statements about defendant's attempts to locate other persons who might be available to give consent to the amputation also have practical implications. Another way to avoid liability for emergency treatment rendered without any consent at all is to first make at least some effort to locate substitute decisionmakers and to document these efforts in patients' medical records. Based upon *Luka*, providers should not render emergency treatment first and look for substitute consent later. If time allows, efforts should be made to find those authorized to consent before treatment is rendered.

Luka v. Lourie, 171 Mich.122, 136 N.W. 1106 (1912)
Supreme Court of Michigan

The plaintiff, a boy 15 years of age, while crossing the Michigan Central Railroad track, was knocked down by an engine and in some manner, not clearly shown, was thrown under the wheels of a car. His left foot was mangled and crushed. There was a compound disarticulation of the bones of the foot, and one of the principal bones of the arch, the "scaphoid" bone, was torn away entirely, the flesh was crushed and torn from the top of the foot, leaving the muscles, ligaments and bones exposed. The plaintiff testified: "I could see the bones sticking out. I could see they weren't broken. Don't know how many bones were sticking out; around four or five, something like that." Shortly after his injury, plaintiff was removed to Harper Hospital in an ambulance. He was partially conscious upon his arrival and was able to communicate his name and the name of the street upon which he lived to the attending surgeons. Within 10 or 15 minutes after his arrival, he lapsed into a comatose condition, and later into complete unconsciousness. Efforts to revive him by injections of strychnine and infusion of a saline solution were made, but he remained unconscious until after the operation. Soon after his arrival at the hospital, at 10:15 a.m., plaintiff's foot was examined by four house physicians connected with the hospital. They concluded that prompt surgical treatment was necessary and telephoned to defendant, who is assistant surgeon of the Michigan Central Railroad. Defendant arrived at the hospital at 10:15 a.m. Upon examining the plaintiff, he found him unconscious, with a weak pulse and dilated pupils. The foot was found to be cold and dead, the circulation having been interrupted. Defendant testified that he learned from the surgeon the boy's name and residence street. With reference to the residence, he knew the distance from Harper Hospital and the time it would take to get from there to the hospital; that he inquired of the house surgeon if anyone, any relative, were present, and was informed that no one was present. After a consultation with the four house physicians, it was agreed by all that an immediate amputation was necessary to save the plaintiff's life. The foot was amputated, and the plaintiff recovered. It is the plaintiff's claim that his foot should not have been amputated at all, and particularly without first obtaining his consent or the consent of his parents, who went to the hospital as soon as possible after learning of the accident . . .

The first question presented is whether it was necessary to amputate. Plaintiff offered the evidence of two physicians, Dr. Gottman and Dr. Gibbes, who testified that in their opinion the foot might have been saved. Dr. Gottman, who had been engaged as a general practitioner for 17 years, testified that in his practice he had treated one case like plaintiff's, and that he had never done any amputating of the lower extremities except a toe. He examined the foot the day after it was amputated. Upon cross–examination, he testified in part as follows: "Q. Suppose the injury was so severe that the circulation had ceased, would you clean the wound and leave it? A. If the bone were crushed and the parts all torn and I saw no chance, I would amputate. Q. Would you form your own opinion and judge whether amputation was necessary or not? A. I would call in counsel. I would not rely upon my own judgment. I would talk it over. Other people might see things differently than I did. Surgeons have differences of opinion. With proper consultation, it is a question which is the best course to follow under certain circumstances. I would call at least one surgeon, and if I was not satisfied with his statement, I would call another. We would talk it over and consider it. Q. Would you take their judgment? A. Certainly, we would talk it over and consider it. We are often in doubt in medicine. Q. There are conditions in an emergency where a surgeon is confronted with dirt, and a serious wound to the lower extremities, for instance the foot, where it is a matter of grave doubt, and requires calm judgment as to whether an amputation should be immediately performed or not? A. If the foot is all crushed and the bones crushed and the circulations destroyed, then I would say, perhaps, it would be necessary to amputate, but perhaps not immediately, because there is no immediate hurry in the amputation of a foot of that kind, not within eight or ten hours. I don't think, unless I don't know as I do know of any exception. . . . I would not always want to depend upon my own judgment, when and where and how an amputation should be made in all cases. There are cases where amputation of the leg is necessary. It is for the surgeon to determine whether it is necessary or not, and he bases his determination on his best judgment. Q. It is a matter for the judgment and determination of the surgeon as to what time and in what manner and in what method an amputation shall take place? A. I do not know how to answer it. Q. Question repeated. . . . A. There is only one way to answer it, and that is by, 'Yes.' Q. Your answer is, 'Yes'? A. Yes, sir. Q. A surgeon must determine, must he not, when an amputation shall be performed, and from his judgment all the circumstances of the case? . . . A. I will answer 'Yes.' After he takes all the facts into consideration, then he may be wrong in his judgment. Q. And it is up to him therefore to determine from what he can learn of the case, and what he can see of the injury, to what extent the danger of blood poisoning is imminent? A. Yes, sir."

Dr. Gibbes, a physician and instructor of many years' experience, making a specialty of the study of all forms of disease, examined the foot more than a year after amputation, and gave it as his opinion that the foot <u>might</u> have been saved. Upon cross-examination he testified in part: "Q. Would you venture, from the professional skill that you have had in the years that you have been practicing your profession, an opinion of that kind without knowing the exact conditions of the patient at the time he was brought to the hospital? A. If I was in the fix that I am now, I would. Q. What do you mean by 'fix'? A. With a foot that has been in alcohol for a year, how could I do otherwise. If I could have seen the flesh conditions of the boy's foot when injured, it would have been a different thing. Q. If you knew the conditions of the boy when the operation was performed, that might alter your opinion entirely? A. I cannot tell; it might, of course. Q. Not knowing how the condition was, you still venture an opinion that that foot ought not to have been amputated? A. On the conditions I find there I base my opinion. I say on the conditions I find there, and nothing else. I don't know whether the circulation had entirely stopped in the foot or not. On the condition I saw I am ready to give an opinion. Other conditions might entirely influence my opinion; if I saw the end of the artery was torn out, and the circulation entirely stopped, it might alter it. I don't know whether the bone protruded from the foot after the injury. There is a longitudinal cut there, and I don't know how much was done by the accident. I don't know after the injury, after the boy was taken to the hospital, whether the foot was perfectly cold and the circulation had ceased entirely. If two hours after the injury the foot was still cold I would wait 24 hours, to see whether collateral circulation had set in. Q. That would be for the judgment of the attending surgeon, assuming he was a competent surgeon? A. I suppose so. Q. That is a fact? A. That would depend upon where he was educated. There are a good many competent surgeons, but they look upon things with a different eye. They are not all taught the same. Q. Assuming that the man was a competent surgeon, and he was called in to attend this case, he would have to rely on his best judgment? A. Yes, sir. Q. Taking everything into consideration? A. Yes, sir. . . Q. A surgeon finds himself on the horns of a dilemma, and when he finds himself between a shock killing the patient, and a decision between that and the possibility of dangers which are incurred by delay, he has to use his best judgment? A. No, he calls in two or three more surgeons. Q. Suppose he calls in one or two more, and they all agree? A. Then it is hard on the patient. Q. Then he is doing what seems best? A. Yes, sir. Q. To those who have examined the patient at the time? A. Yes, sir. . . Q. Suppose the boy remained unconscious three-quarters of an hour, what would that indicate? A. It would indicate a certain amount of shock; nothing very serious with the state of the part. Q. Would the three-quarters of an hour unconsciousness, would that indicate pretty severe shock to that boy's system? A. It would mean a shock, but nothing but what he could recover from. Q. Are you sure of that? A. I am not sure of anything. Q. What would the pulse be? A. I don't know. Q. How high a pulse would indicate a rather serious condition as to shock? A. In that boy? Q. We are not talking of any other boy? A. I don't know. I can't say from what I know or from what I have seen of the injury. Q. How high a pulse? A. I don't know what it would be in his case. Q. Could you from your experience tell what pulse would indicate a serious condition? A. No, considering it is about 20 years since I have had a case of that kind. Q. That pulse is a very important matter in the necessity of an operation? A. Yes and no. Q. You could not tell? A. You have to fit in each case that you have. You cannot give a general statement. Q. You are giving a general statement without considering those facts? A. I would not. Q. Do you want to eliminate the question of the boy's pulse in deciding the necessity of the operation? A. I am giving my opinion of what I have seen of the injury and what I have heard of the case. My opinion is not based on anything I don't know. Q. You would have a good deal more faith in your own opinion if you had attended the boy at the time? A. Yes, sir. Q. You would have a good deal more faith in some other competent surgeon's opinion that had attended the boy at the time? A. Than what? Q. Than your own now? A. Of course, a competent surgeon attending it. Q. His opinion would be better than yours? A. Yes, I think it would."

Dr. Childs, a third expert called by plaintiff, testified: "Q. In order for you as a surgeon to come to an intelligent conclusion whether an operation was necessary, would it be necessary to know the condition of the wound, the condition of the pulse, the temperature, the condition of the shock, and to know whether the wound was clean or dirty, how much hemorrhage there had been, and indication of that sort, before you could form a correct conclusion in your own mind what was necessary to do? A. I told you without seeing the case I could not give a positive opinion as to that because there is always other circumstances. An injury might be very small, and for all that it would be absolutely necessary that there should be an amputation for the very fact that there are extraneous matters injected into the wound, and I have had small ones and lost a life, and I have had large ones that you would think it almost impossible to save and saved them, so you cannot go by the magnitude of it. While larger ones always appear most aggravating, you have to take into consideration all the matter connected with it. There is no surgeon competent to give a decision. He is incompetent to decide or give a positive answer whether it is absolutely necessary at the time of that operation or not—indications might be that it was, and indications might be that it was not. The indications that would appear there that would make it absolutely necessary would be extreme. There would be cessation of the circulation, etc., and also extraneous matter. You cannot cleanse the wound any too quickly, and you should always cleanse the wound and tend to that thoroughly. You have to treat each case according to all appearances. Q. If as a skilled surgeon you had seen the patient, seen the foot torn and open, and observed his condition, the shock, the condition of the wound, his pulse, and all that, and you concluded that the operation was immediately necessary, would you feel that your opinion was better and more apt to be correct than that of a surgeon or a doctor who saw the foot after the amputation had taken place? A. That can be answered in this way: That a man that made all those examinations and saw it, he might be as competent after that to judge as someone else who had more experience and had seen those things oftener, and yet he might be absolutely correct, but his chances would be superior undoubtedly to the man who did not see it. Still, although the foot afterwards might not indicate the necessity for amputation so far as that is concerned, but the question would be whether an immediate operation would be necessary; that would be the question. The tarsal and metatarsal bones were dislocated, also the cuneiform bones. The scaphoid bone was gone. That bone is still farther in the rear from the tarsal bones. The flesh was all denuded off the top and simply covered by some tendons—a few tendons here—and the muscular tissues were all gone. Q. There is often, from a severe traumatic injury, an injury from external violence; is there a serious condition from shock? A. Most always, lacerated wounds cause more severe shock. Shock is an interruption of the current of the nerve fluid which produces a reaction upon the circulation. Severe shock produces death many times. Q. Have you found in your practice that shock is continued and is progressive on account of the serious condition of the wound? A. Yes, I have seen it; yes, sir. Q. The fact is what makes surgical attendance immediately necessary? A. Yes, sir; and that is where immediate attention does come in, and sometimes—"

Taking all the testimony on behalf of the plaintiff and considering it broadly, it amounts, at most, to this: That by following a different course, plaintiff's foot *might* have been saved. While they disagree upon some details, they apparently all agree that the proper course for a surgeon to pursue, when confronted by such an exigency, is to consult with another or others, and then exercise the best judgment and skill of which he is capable. This seems to have been the course followed by defendant. The four house surgeons, after consultation with defendant, concluded, with him, that an immediate operation was necessary to save plaintiff's life.

Two experts, Drs. Kennedy and Brodie, surgeons of very wide experience, testified that in their opinion an immediate amputation was necessary to insure the plaintiff's life. It stands uncontradicted upon this record that the circulation in the foot was wholly devitalized; that the plaintiff was in a condition of profound coma from which the attending surgeons were unable to arouse him. It is also uncontradicted that death from shock frequently results from severe traumatic injury.

Taking into consideration the condition in which the plaintiff was when the defendant reached him, we have no hesitation in holding that defendant was amply justified in treating it as a case of emergency, and his conduct should be viewed in the light of the legal principles governing such cases . . .

. . . In an ordinary action for negligence, the fact that defendant has acted according to his best judgment is no defense. His act is to be judged by the standard of conduct of an ordinarily prudent man under the circumstances. In conduct, resting upon judgment, opinion, or theory, however, a different rule has been recognized "The distinction between error judgment and negligence is not easily determined. It would seem, however, that if one, assuming a responsibility as an expert, possesses a knowledge of the facts and circumstances connected with the duty he is about to perform, and, bringing to bear all his professional experience and skill, weighs those facts and circumstances, and decides upon a course of action which he faithfully attempts to carry out, then want of success, if due to such course of action, would be due to error of judgment, and not to negligence. But if he omits to inform himself as to facts or circumstances or does not possess the knowledge, experience, or skill which he professes, then a failure, if caused thereby, would be negligence. 'No one can be charged with carelessness, when he does that which his judgment approves, or where he omits to do that of which he has no time to judge. Such act or omission, if faulty, may be called a mistake, but not carelessness.' ". . .

. . . One reasonable justification for this exception is the elementary principle that when a man acts according to his best judgment in an emergency, but fails to act judiciously, he is not chargeable with negligence. Physicians in the nature of things are sought for and must act in emergencies, and, if a surgeon waits too long before undertaking a certain amputation, he must be held to have known the consequences of such delay, and may be held liable for the resulting damage . . .

It would be unreasonable to hold a properly qualified physician or surgeon responsible for an honest error of judgment, where, as in the instant case, he is called upon to act in an emergency and must choose between two courses of action, either one of which involves the possibility of the gravest hazard to the patient . . .

It is, we think, very clear upon this record that the question presented to the defendant, at the moment he was called upon to act, was one of judgment only. Instant action of some sort was imperative. In reaching a conclusion as to the proper course to be pursued, the attending surgeon must necessarily be influenced by many considerations: the physical character of the wound, the fact that there was a compound dislocation of the bones of the foot, the entire absence of one of these bones, the stripping off of the flesh from the anterior part of the foot leaving the tendons bare and shiny, the fact that the foot had become wholly devitalized, the presence of hemorrhage, the danger from blood poisoning at the time or from future infection, the character and quantity of foreign matter, dirt, cinders, etc., in the wound. To a consideration of these matters must be added a careful attention to the general condition of the patient, the degree and cause of the existing shock, the apparent ability or inability of the patient to resist shock, the condition of the temperature, pulse, and respiration, and the reaction or lack of it produced by the administration of stimulants. Called upon to act under such circumstances and to determine which of two courses (one entailing certain mutilation and the other probable death to the patient) should be followed, it is apparent that the defendant is not bound by the ordinary rules of negligence, but is entitled to insist that, having used his best judgment, he is not liable.

There is nothing in this record to indicate that, had the parents of plaintiff been present at the operating table, they would have refused their consent to the operation. Indeed, it is inconceivable that such consent would have been withheld in the face of the determination of five duly qualified physicians and surgeons that it was necessary to save the plaintiff's life. But defendant testifies, and in this he is not contradicted, that he made inquiry for relatives of the plaintiff and was told that none were in the hospital. Suppose that his informant was in error (which is not certain), the defendant had a right to rely upon the information and to act in the emergency upon the theory that to obtain consent was impracticable . . . "In such event a surgeon may lawfully, and it is his duty to, perform such operation as good surgery demands without such consent". . .

The fact that surgeons are called upon daily, in all our large cities, to operate instantly in emergency cases in order that life may be preserved, should be considered. Many small children are injured upon the streets in large cities. To hold that a surgeon must wait until he is able to secure the consent of the parents before giving the injured the benefit of his skill and learning, to the end that life may be preserved, would, we believe, result in the loss of many lives which might otherwise be saved. It is not to be presumed that competent surgeons will wantonly operate, nor that they will fail to obtain the consent of parents to operations where such consent may be reasonably obtained in view of the exigency. Their work, however, is highly humane and very largely charitable in character, and no rule should be announced which would tend in the slightest degree to deprive sufferers of the benefit of their services.

The judgment is affirmed.

o **Recap of the Case**. The plaintiff in this case was struck by a train. Shortly after his arrival at the hospital he lapsed into a coma. Since the patient was unable to consent to surgery, the practitioners treating him had to decide whether or not to amputate his foot. After consultations and following unsuccessful attempts to locate the patient's parents to get their consent, they amputated the injured foot. The patient sued, arguing that his foot should not have been amputated, at least not without his parents' consent. The court rejected the patient's argument primarily because expert testimony showed it was unlikely that either the patient or his parents would have refused to give consent if they had been able to do so.

FAILURE TO OBTAIN PARENTAL CONSENT FOR NONEMERGENCY SURGERY ON A MINOR RESULTS IN LIABILITY

In *Zoski v. Gaines* the court reached the exact opposite result of the *Luka* case. The defendant in this case operated to remove the tonsils of a minor child without notifying the child's parents and, therefore, without their prior consent to surgery.

The court determined that the patient's condition did not constitute an emergency, thereby relieving the defendant of the duty to get consent to treatment. The practical lesson for practitioners is clear: Careful determinations must be made regarding whether a situation actually constitutes an emergency before treatment is rendered without consent under the emergency exception to the requirement of obtaining informed consent before treatment is rendered.

Zoski v. Gaines, 271 Mich. 1, 260 N.W. 99 (1935)
Supreme Court of Michigan

In September, 1927, Tony Zoski was a 9 1/2 year old normal boy, in the fourth grade of his school. There being some suspicion of infected tonsils, he was taken by a visiting nurse to the city physician and later sent to the Shurly Hospital. At the same time there was delivered to the hospital a written memorandum from the city physician requesting the removal of the boy's tonsils and adenoids. The boy went to the hospital on Saturday, September 24, 1927, accompanied by his 15 year old brother, Theodore, where his tonsils were removed by Dr. Gaines, an associate of Dr. Shurly. Neither the city physician, Dr. Shurly, Dr. Gaines, nor any one acting for them, obtained the consent of either parent to operate. They did not know their son was in the hospital until Theodore, apparently frightened by Tony's appearance on his return from the operating room, reported the facts. The father who appears in his action as next friend, immediately went to the hospital and remained with the boy until about 9:30 p.m. On Sunday morning he returned, discovered blood on the floor near Tony's bed, dried blood on his face, and a bump on his forehead between the eyes. Tony claims he became frightened during the night because of bleeding from his throat, and when the nurse failed to respond to his cries, he tried to get out of bed, struck his head against another bed, and then lost consciousness. The father went home to dinner at 1 o'clock on Sunday when Tony said he was feeling better, returning about 3 o'clock, and remained until 9 o'clock. He came back early Monday morning, dressed Tony, who was still weak, and took him home in a taxi.

The record does not disclose any medical attention being required at home for the boy, although he was apparently slow in regaining his strength and suffered from headaches. On the morning of either the 2d or 10th of October (the father claiming the 2d and the hospital records showing the 10th), it was discovered that Tony had become blind. He was immediately again taken to the Shurly Hospital, where he was kept under observation for about six weeks and examined by members of the staff. Drs. Neff, Gaines, Bullock, Hewitt, Parker, and others were called in as consultants, in an attempt to ascertain the cause of the blindness. Dr. Walter Parker, according to the records, agreed with the diagnosis of others and noted on the medical chart, "that if vision does not recover in ten days following onset, recommend sub-temporal depression." The father, although requested by Dr. Shurly, refused to consent to the operation required to remove the intracranial pressure, which was thought to be the cause of the blindness, and the boy has since remained completely blind. Neither the headaches nor any other impairment of any bodily function afterwards appeared. . .

Except in the very extreme cases, a surgeon has no legal right to operate upon a child without the consent of his parents or guardian . . .

It seems to be reasonably established that a physician is liable for operating upon a patient unless he obtains the consent of the patient, if competent, and if not, of someone who, under the circumstances, would be legally authorized to give the requisite consent.

The trial court's judgment in favor of the plaintiff is affirmed.

o **Recap of the Case**. Practitioners in this case performed a tonsillectomy on a child without permission from the child's parents. A subsequent fall in the hospital resulted in the patient's blindness. The child's parents sued. The defendants argued that they were not liable because the situation was an emergency. The court rejected this argument and decided that surgery should not have been performed without the parents' consent.

GOOD SAMARITAN STATUTES DO NOT PROTECT PERSONNEL RESPONDING TO AN EMERGENCY IN A HOSPITAL

In many states, the health provider's right to render emergency treatment without incurring liability has been buttressed by statutes often called "Good Samaritan Statutes." While these statutes vary from state to state, they usually provide that physicians and other health professionals, including nurses, will not be liable for negligence when offering treatment at the scene of an emergency as long as the treatment is performed in good faith and without gross negligence or willful or wanton misconduct. Most of these statutes also require that treatment must be rendered without charge in order to claim the protection from liability provided by these statutes.

Some providers have attempted to extend the protection from liability given by Good Samaritan Statutes to include emergencies within healthcare institutions to further support their claims of lack of liability for emergency treatment rendered without first obtaining consent. An example of this type of case is *Hamburger v. Henry Ford Hospital.*

In this case, defendant Henry Ford Hospital attempted to avoid liability for treatment rendered without the patient's consent by its employees during an emergency. The court decided that the Good Samaritan Statute in Michigan does not include relief from liability for hospitals and their employees when treatment is provided within the institution.

Hamburger v. Henry Ford Hospital, 284 N.W.2d 155
(Mich. App. 1979)
Michigan Court of Appeals

Plaintiff Albert C. Hamburger, M.D., entered Henry Ford Hospital as a patient on December 31, 1975, having symptoms consistent with a mild stroke. He was sent to an x–ray room attended by Ms. Rita McKinney, who was a student trainee functioning as an x–ray technician but was not certified. The patient was placed on a stool with a low back during the x–ray procedure. Immediately after the procedure was completed the patient collapsed while still on the stool, became unconscious and started urinating. Ms. McKinney put a tongue depressor in his mouth and called to a passing fellow employee to call the "blue alert" team. This team consists of hospital personnel especially trained to respond to life–threatening emergencies. Before the alert team arrived, other hospital employees responded to her call for help. Five of them, including Ms. McKinney, lifted the patient onto a stretcher. The names and specific hospital functions of the other four hospital employees are not known. They failed to support the patient's head and it struck a metal guard rail, apparently resulting in the patient regaining consciousness. When the blue alert team arrived they did nothing further but send the patient back to his room. Plaintiffs claim the blow on the head caused the neurological deterioration thereafter experienced by Dr. Hamburger. Defendant claims the blow was not a cause of that deterioration. The jury returned a verdict of $192,500.00 in favor of Dr. Hamburger and $7,500.00 for his wife, Ruth Hamburger . . .

. . . Many states with the public welfare in mind have enacted "good samaritan" statutes to encourage prompt treatment of accident victims by excusing from civil liabilities those who render care in an emergency. Some states have extended this protection to nurses and some even to anyone assisting in an emergency . . .

Michigan originally enacted such a statute providing immunity for physicians for ordinary negligence at the scene of an emergency . . . [T]his immunity was extended to registered nurses . . .

We particularly emphasize that the statute excepted cases where a professional relationship had already been established with the patient.

1975 P.A. 123; M.C.L. §14.563(12) became effective on July 1, 1975, extending such protection to certain named persons in hospital settings *who were under no duty to respond.* It is this addition under which defendant claims that Ms. McKinney and the other four hospital employees who lifted Dr. Hamburger onto the stretcher were immune from liability for ordinary negligence. Defendant further claims that because they were immune the hospital is also immune. The 1975 addition to the statute (§2) reads as follows:

Sec. 2. (1) In instances where the actual hospital duty of that person did not require a response to that emergency situation, a physician, dentist, podiatrist, intern, resident, registered nurse, licensed practical nurse, registered physical therapist, clinical laboratory technologist, inhalation therapist, certified registered nurse anesthetist, x–ray technician, or paramedical person, who in good faith responds to a life threatening emergency or responds to a request for emergency assistance in a life threatening emergency within a hospital or other licensed medical care facility, shall not be liable for any civil damages as a result of an act or omission in the rendering of emergency care, except an act or omission amounting to gross negligence or willful and wanton mischief.

(2) The exemption from liability under subsection (1) shall not apply to a physician where a physician–patient relationship existed prior to the advent of the emergency nor to a licensed nurse where a nurse–patient relationship existed prior to the advent of the emergency.

(3) Nothing in this act shall diminish a hospital's responsibility to reasonably and adequately staff hospital emergency facilities when the hospital maintains or holds out to the general public that it maintains such emergency room facilities. (M.C.L. §691.1502; M.S.A. §14.563(12) . . .

The court must resolve the issue by construing the statute to determine the intent of the Legislature as to who is entitled to its protection . . .

At the outset we are aware that there is a dispute as to whether Ms. McKinney was an x–ray technician, within the meaning of the statute, and whether she had a duty to respond within the meaning of the statute. There is even greater doubt as to whether there was any evidence from which the jury could find that the other four employees who lifted Dr. Hamburger were within the protection of the statute, an issue on which we believe, and defendant admits, that defendant has the burden of proof. However, these are questions of fact, and are not necessary to a resolution of the issue. We therefore assume, for purposes of this opinion, that all five employees were entitled to the immunity of the statute at the time Dr. Hamburger was lifted and struck his head.

First it is of great significance that there was a hospital–patient relationship between defendant Henry Ford Hospital and Dr. Hamburger at the time of the injury. We note that in enacting the first section of the statute M.C.L. §691.1501; M.S.A. §14.563; the Legislature carefully excepted situations where a physician–patient relationship existed . . .

It is unreasonable to conclude, in the absence of express language, given: 1) the clear thrust of section one to <u>volunteers</u> only where no professional relationship was established; and 2) the exception of persons having a physician–patient relationship or having a duty to respond, in the 1975 addition; and 3) the history of good samaritan legislation applying to volunteers only, that the Legislature intended to protect hospitals in situations where a hospital–patient relationship existed at the time of the negligent act.

It is of course significant that no mention of a hospital's right to the protection was stated in the statute. It would have been easy to do so if the Legislature so intended.

Section 3 of the statute apparently confused the issue in the trial court. It is reasonable to assume that section 3 was included because people who are brought to an emergency room are not yet protected by a hospital–patient relationship. Therefore a hospital perhaps could, by the simple expedient of not assigning staff to the emergency room, make everyone who responds to an emergency there a volunteer for purposes of this statute. There is, of course, no question of the hospital's duty to adequately staff the hospital to care for its patients. Nonemergency admissions have careful, even exhaustive, admissions procedures, clearly establishing the hospital–patient relationship. We find no indication that the statute is to be applied to emergency rooms any differently than in the other hospital departments . . .

Affirmed.

o **Recap of the Case**. The patient in this case collapsed in radiology. Personnel came from all over the hospital in response to an emergency call. The patient was injured by those attempting to render treatment and sued. The defendants argued that they should not be liable to this patient based upon the Good Samaritan Statute in Michigan. They argued that they were not obligated to render emergency treatment and, therefore, should not be liable. The court rejected this argument on the basis that an established physician–patient relationship precludes immunity from liability based upon the Good Samaritan Statutes. Since hospitals already have a relationship with the patient, they cannot use Good Samaritan Statutes to avoid liability for emergency treatment.

2

Therapeutic Privilege

Consent from the patient is not required if the patient's physician decides to exercise the therapeutic privilege. The essence of this legal theory is that a practitioner may legally withhold information from a patient if disclosure may cause the patient's physical or mental condition to deteriorate. The basis of this theory is that their primary duty is to serve the interests of their patients.

Practitioners claiming this exemption to the requirement of obtaining informed consent must proceed with caution. There is a tendency to use this exception as a basis for repeated failures to obtain informed consent. Practitioners sometimes make general claims that providing information will be harmful to patients because it is upsetting, thereby hampering their recovery. Such blanket statements will not serve to trigger this exception. The intent of the law is not to allow this exception to swallow the disclosure requirement altogether. Rather, the intent is to provide for an exception to the duty to disclose in those rare situations when specific facts can be marshalled to show that the information conveyed would be harmful to the patient. As a practical matter, providers who utilize this exception must thoroughly document all of the facts which serve as bases for decisions to trigger this exception.

NO LIABILITY FOR ALLEGED DAMAGE TO PATIENT'S VOCAL CORDS DESPITE FAILURE TO DISCLOSE RISKS

Roberts v. Wood, is an example of a case in which the court recognized the practitioner's right to avoid liability for failure to give informed consent based upon this privilege. In the *Roberts* case, the plaintiff developed hoarseness following a second surgery for diffuse toxic goiter. Hoarseness is a potential risk of this type of surgery, but the surgeon had not informed the patient of this risk. However, the court decided that the surgeon had good reasons for invoking the privilege to withhold information. The specific relevant facts of this case were that the goiter itself caused the patient to be extremely nervous and anxious. The court also considered the fact that the patient was scheduled for a gynecological procedure at the same time which also made her extremely upset.

Roberts v. Wood, 206 F. Supp. 579 (S.D. Ala. 1962)
United States District Court

. . . Mrs. Roberts first visited Dr. Wood in 1953 at the suggestion of her family doctor in Mississippi. It was then determined that plaintiff had a diffuse toxic goiter and that an operation to remove a portion of her thyroid gland was necessary. As plaintiff was pregnant, this operation was not performed until sometime during the following year and after the birth of her child. The post–operative effect of the operation, in which 95% of the gland was removed, was a smooth, uneventful recovery and is not at issue here other than as background information relative to a second operation in 1959 which constitutes the subject matter of this suit.

Between 1954 and 1959 evidence of toxic goiter, extreme nervousness and anxiety, together with the recurrence of a nodule in the neck, prompted plaintiff to seek further medical attention. She consulted with her family physician who recommended that she see a local specialist. Plaintiff and her husband decided, however, to return to Dr. Wood inasmuch as he had performed the first operation and would be more familiar with her condition and medical history. The defendant determined a second operation was required and prescribed preoperative medication to prepare the patient for this. As it will be necessary to discuss in some detail the mechanics of the operation later in this opinion, that matter will not now be set out. Suffice it to say that the operation was performed in June of 1959 without any apparent complications; on the contrary, the operation appeared to be physiologically successful in all respects. Immediate post-operative examination revealed that the patient had full use of both vocal cords and had not suffered any incidental injury in the area where the surgery was accomplished.

Sometime thereafter the plaintiff experienced a hoarseness in her voice which interfered with her normal speech. The condition developed to the point where the plaintiff lost the use of her true vocal cords and unconsciously substituted the use of her false vocal cords. At the trial she spoke in what is best described as a loud stage whisper. It was the opinion of one of defendant's experts, a laryngologist, that the plaintiff is malingering, that the use of the false vocal cords is a deliberate and conscious effort on her part. Plaintiff's expert testified that in his opinion, if one has the use of his true vocal cords, he cannot use his false vocal cords. Neither of these views reflects those of a majority of the experts or of the Court. To begin with, this lady has been suffering from the condition for nearly three years, and she is obviously distressed and very much concerned over her lack of ability to phonate properly. In addition, the demonstration of the use of the false vocal cords by one of the doctors negates the testimony in that regard of plaintiff's expert. The Court also expresses its opinion that the institution of this suit was not, as suggested, by any reasons of malice or revenge on behalf of plaintiff or her husband. If the considerable amount of medical attention, with its attendant high costs, this family has been required to seek in the last few years has made them perhaps more anxious than some for satisfactory results and an end to the expense, it should not be taken to infer an opprobrious motive in bringing this suit. Although plaintiff's condition is subject to improvement, as will be noted later, it nevertheless exists now and is a very serious handicap to her.

It is difficult to determine when this condition was brought to the attention of Dr. Wood. According to the plaintiff's testimony, she told him of the trouble before being discharged from the hospital and again on numerous visits to his office and up to the time of her last visit to him on November 11, 1959. Mrs. Roberts stopped seeing the doctor then, although he told her to return in two weeks; but she continued visits to various doctors in and around Pascagoula, Mississippi. The defendant testified that while he was aware of a hoarseness which he thought would gradually improve, the first notice he had of any voice change was in a letter to him from the plaintiff's husband dated August 16, 1959. He further stated that on all visits subsequent to the operation the patient seemed to be using her true vocal cords.

Regardless of when this condition (the use of the false vocal cords) did develop, the proof is ample to support the conclusion that it was not while the patient was hospitalized. But the important question for purposes of determining the defendant's liability is not when the condition developed, but rather why.

Dr. Claude Warren, a court–appointed ear, nose and throat specialist, upon examining the plaintiff, determined that she is suffering from paralysis of abduction of the right vocal cord, which is due to failure of the recurrent laryngeal nerve to function properly. He further found that the right cord is affixed near the midline and that the left cord is unimpaired and capable of normal movement. Plaintiff contends that this condition is due to the negligent manner in which the operation was performed, resulting in injury to the recurrent laryngeal nerve.

The defendant does not deny that the nerve fails to function and that the failure may be due to the operation. He asserts, however, that risk of injury to this nerve is a normal and inherent hazard in the performance of thyroidectomies; that the hazard is increased with a second operation, particularly when, as here, the nodule to be removed is adhered to the nerve; and that paralysis of abduction of one vocal cord does not preclude the use of normal voice.

In passing on the issue of negligence, insofar as regards the operation itself, the Court is presented with two questions: Did the defendant select the correct surgical technique; and, did the defendant fail to perform the operation by the technique selected by him in accordance with that degree of care and skill which the law imposes upon him? An answer to these questions requires a consideration of the testimony of the various expert witnesses who appeared at the trial. That which now follows summarizes the most pertinent portions of that testimony.

The use of the vocal cords is controlled by impulses sent from the brain through the nervous system to the muscles attached to the vocal cords. There are two sets of nerves which serve as conduits of the impulse in this relay, the superior laryngeal nerves and the recurrent laryngeal nerves, with one of each affecting the use of each vocal cord. The superior laryngeal nerves control the motion of abduction, that is, the movement of the vocal cords towards each other. The recurrent laryngeal nerves control the motion of abduction, that is, the movement of the vocal cords away from each other. The recurrent laryngeal nerve which controls the movement of the right vocal cord now fails to function.

It is universal knowledge among surgeons that risk of injury to the recurrent laryngeal nerves presents one of several inherent hazards in performing a thyroidectomy. This is due primarily to the intimate relationship of these nerves to the thyroid gland because of variations in individuals of the course of those nerves around or, in some cases, through the thyroid gland. The hazard is increased because of the great sensitivity of these nerves to injury which may be produced by complete or partial severance, stretching, trauma, edema, or scar tissue. One of the main problems in thyroidectomy is, therefore, to perform the operations so as to avoid injury to these nerves. Surgeons are divided on two alternative techniques to accomplish this. Both techniques are acceptable, both are used in the Mobile area, and in some cases both are used by the same doctor in different instances.

The first technique is the so–called standard technique. In this operation the surgeon removes the greater portion of the thyroid gland leaving a residue in the area where the nerves would normally be located. He makes no attempt to expose or otherwise isolate the recurrent laryngeal nerves but relies on his knowledge of the area around the gland and by avoiding dissection of that area adjacent to the nerve attempts to protect it from injury.

The second technique is the Lahey method, a more modern procedure whereby the nerves are visualized, identified and put to one side. This is accomplished by turning the whole gland up and exposing the recurrent laryngeal nerve throughout its course as it passes behind the gland in intimate relationship with it at this point of entrance into the larynx. The gland may then be either partially or wholly removed.

While both of these techniques are correct, neither one entirely eliminates the possibility of damage to the nerve. The possibility exists in the standard technique because the nerve may not be in its normal location. It exists in the Lahey technique because the mere handling of the nerve produces trauma which may be sufficient to cause permanent damage. Moreover, regardless of which technique is used, there is an irreducible minimum percentage of cases in which this inherent hazard will materialize and in which the nerve will be injured, even in the most skilled hands.

The first operation performed on Mrs. Roberts by Dr. Wood was done according to the standard technique. As stated previously, this operation was successful in all respects. The operation performed in 1959 was done according to the Lahey technique. The reasons this technique was selected were that the nodule was adhered by dense scar tissue to the recurrent laryngeal nerve which controls the movement of the right vocal cord, and the doctor thought it necessary to remove the entire gland in order to prevent another recurrence of the nodule. The evidence establishes that this decision by the defendant was entirely correct and proper, necessary not only for the patient's future well–being but also to minimize risk of injury during the operation. It follows that liability does not lie on the ground that the defendant chose the wrong operative procedure . . .

First, plaintiff says she was not sufficiently advised as to the seriousness of the operation. In undertaking to perform the operation, Dr. Wood did not, absent express contractual agreement, thereby become a guarantor of a successful result. There is no evidence that he misrepresented the serious nature of the operation or failed to inform the patient of its attendant dangers. I do not mean to suggest that defendant should have told plaintiff of all the hazards involved, including risk of injury to the recurrent laryngeal nerve. Doctors frequently tailor the extent of their pre–operative warnings to the particular patient, and with this I can find no fault. Not only is much of the risk of a technical nature beyond the patient's understanding, but the anxiety, apprehension, and fear generated by a full disclosure thereof may have a very detrimental effect on some patients. In this case the defendant told the patient, among other things, that the operation would be similar to the one she had undergone in 1954. In view of the patient's emotional state and her concern over this condition as well as a gynecological operation to be performed at the same time, in addition to having previously experienced a thyroidectomy, I am of the opinion the patient was properly advised of the seriousness of the operation.

Second, plaintiff alleges that improper administration of anesthesia at the time of operating, and failure of defendant to remain advised as to the condition of the recurrent laryngeal nerve during the operation constitute negligence. There being a total lack of proof as to the existence or effect of these matters, it is unnecessary to consider them further.

The only evidence which remotely suggests negligence on the part of the defendant is the fact that plaintiff's right vocal cord is paralyzed, and the fact that she does not use her normal speaking voice. But these facts alone are not sufficient to prove negligence during the operation. Plaintiff's doctors would not say what caused the paralysis, although they did recognize the same possible causes of injury heretofore mentioned. It was the consensus among defendant's experts that the probable cause of the paralysis is that the nerve is bound up in scar tissue and has lost its power to transmit the nerve impulse. The defendant believes that it is perhaps due to trauma normally incidental to the surgery. This uncertainty among the doctors as to the cause of the nerve's disfunction points out the difficulty of plaintiff's proving her case as to negligence . . . The determination as to the existence of negligence is one of fact, which in this case must be resolved in favor of the defendant. Although all but one of the doctors recognize plaintiff's condition is attributable to the operation, none has attempted to indict the defendant for the manner in which he performed it. Considering that this was the second operation in the same area, that the nodule was affixed to the recurrent laryngeal nerve, that the operation in and of itself is trauma, the Court must conclude that plaintiff has simply failed to prove wherein the doctor is guilty of negligence. The proof of negligence lacking, I am of the opinion that the operation was performed according to the standards of skill and care exercised by surgeons generally in performing thyroidectomies in the Mobile area . . .

Plaintiff also seeks in the complaint to charge defendant with abandonment of the case in that he is guilty of an unwarranted lack of diligence in attending the patient after the operation. This charge really involves two separate principles of law, which principles will not be separately discussed.

. . . To constitute an abandonment, the termination of the relationship between physician and patient must have been brought about by the *unilateral act of the physician*. There can be no abandonment if the relationship is terminated by mutual consent, or by the dismissal of the physician by the patient . . .

It is clear that as applied to the instant case, this test has not been met. Although instructed by Dr. Wood to return in two weeks, Mrs. Roberts decided that the November 11, 1959 visit was to be her last. Having thus decided and acted accordingly, plaintiff cannot now be heard to complain that the defendant abandoned her as a patient.

With regard to the charge that defendant failed to exercise due diligence in the post-operative period, plaintiff seems to rely on some inexorable duty on the part of the defendant to employ therapy or corrective surgery to remedy the worsening speech impediment. The facts of the case and the expert opinions expressed at the trial indicate that such treatment or surgery was neither necessary nor proper.

All of the doctors except one expressed the view that unilateral paralysis of abduction should not result in an inability to use the true vocal cords. The medical literature introduced into evidence sustains this view. The following language is quoted from page 182 of the book, Practical Aspects of Thyroid Disease, written by Dr. George Crile, Jr., and is typical of other works: "When a vocal cord is paralyzed by injury to the recurrent nerve, it falls toward the mid–line and assumes that 'cadaveric' position . . . The voice may never be as strong as it was before the operation, but a speaking voice always returns. Persistent aphonia is a sign of hysteria, not of injury to the recurrent nerves."

One witness, Dr. James G. Donald, told of one instance in which he deliberately removed the recurrent nerve; and although one cord is completely immobile, that patient speaks with a normal voice. This example was related to reaffirm the belief among doctors that the voice always returns where the patient suffers unilateral abductive paralysis. The mystery lies in the fact that such has not been the result in Mrs. Roberts' case. A satisfactory explanation of this is wanting, although the inference of the testimony is that the patient needs speech therapy and/or psychiatric care to restore to her confidence in being able to use her true vocal cords. The fact that Dr. Wood did not initiate such therapy or recommend that she consult a specialist while under his care, cannot be the basis for liability unless such omission constitutes negligence.

Turning once again to the expert testimony and the medical literature to determine the surgeon's expected reaction to unilateral abductive paralysis, we approach a grey zone wherein the course to be followed is a decision left to the *expertise* of the particular surgeon faced with that patient and under the peculiar circumstances of that situation. The testimony shows that it is not unreasonable for the physician to hope for spontaneous recovery up to six months after the paralysis becomes manifest. Dr. Wood's diagnosis of the patient during the interim between June and November was that Mrs. Roberts had a hoarseness and was using her true vocal cords throughout this period. This diagnosis has not been impeached by the evidence. In fact the evidence shows that while paralysis usually occurs soon after the operation it may be delayed several months. In addition, the examination report of the plaintiff from Dr. Winstead, one of plaintiff's witnesses, dated September 23, 1959, addressed to Dr. Wood, fails to state that the nerve was at that time paralyzed, although again reference was made to the hoarseness of her voice and the fact that the cord did not move completely to the mid–line. Another of plaintiff's doctors, Dr. Robinson, testified that his examination at this same time revealed a sluggishness in the right cord in moving to the mid–line. It would not be unreasonable to assume that a progressive scar tissue was gradually choking off the nerve impulse. Be that as it may, however, not one of the doctors stated that he would have done something Dr. Wood did not do, or not have done anything Dr. Wood did during this five–month period. In response to a question from the Court, Dr. Donald did state that on September 24 he would have hoped for spontaneous recovery; but if the condition persisted for a few months beyond that time, he would have had the cords examined and probably recommended speech therapy. The fact is, however, the plaintiff stopped seeing him. Under these circumstances I fail to see wherein the defendant is guilty of a lack of diligence in treating the plaintiff. On the contrary, the record shows that he was fully cooperating with other doctors attending the patient and doing his best to help restore her normal voice.

The results of Mrs. Roberts' operation are, of course, most unfortunate, but I fail to see any negligence on the part of the defendant.

o **Recap of the Case**. The plaintiff had a goiter which was removed. Thereafter, she lost the ability to speak in a normal voice. She claimed that the surgery produced this condition and sued those individuals who operated on her. One of her claims was that the risks of surgery were not adequately explained to her. The court ruled against her on this point because the surgeon was able to explain to the court why the patient did not receive adequate information, namely, the nervousness and anxiety that accompanied her condition and her concern about another unrelated surgical procedure. The practical implication of this case is that providers should not claim therapeutic privilege and, therefore, fail to inform the patient unless there are specific facts upon which to base their decisions.

Part II

SUBSTITUTE CONSENT

Consent to treatment by competent adults (direct consent) is, at best, a complicated matter. The situation is even more complex when substitute consent or concurrent consent is required. Substitute consent is required when the patient lacks capacity to give consent, thereby resulting in the need for consent by a third party. Lack of capacity may, for example, result from mental retardation, mental illness, coma, senility, or extremely young age. Substitute consent may be given by a parent, guardian, attorney-in-fact, or a court. Concurrent consent means that consent is given by the patient *and* a third party. The two most important issues in the area of substitute and concurrent consent are: 1) When should substitute or concurrent consent as opposed to direct consent be given? and 2) Who may give substitute or concurrent consent?

3

Minors

In most states a minor is defined by statute as an individual under eighteen years of age. Minors generally lack the capacity to consent to medical treatment, thus requiring consent by a third party or substitute consent. Generally speaking, parents are authorized to consent to medical treatment on behalf of their minor children. Other family members are generally not authorized to consent to treatment on behalf of minors. Parents have this right primarily because they may be damaged financially as the result of treatment performed on their children. This basic parental right and the rationale for this right were established in cases like *Lacey v. Laird.*

PROVIDER ONLY TECHNICALLY LIABLE FOR SURGERY ON MINOR WITHOUT PARENTAL CONSENT

In *Lacey v. Laird*, an eighteen year old girl went to a plastic surgeon and asked him to perform surgery on her nose. She was unhappy with the results, and her parents sued the physician. First, the reader should not be misled by the age of the plaintiff. She was, indeed, a minor because the law in Ohio at that time was that an adult was anyone twenty-one years of age or older. In addition, special note should be taken of the fact that the court agreed that "technically" an assault and battery occurred when the practitioner operated on a minor without consent. However, the court also recognized that the plaintiff understood what she consented to even though she was technically a minor. Consequently, only a very small amount of money or nominal damages were awarded to the plaintiff.

Lacey v. Laird, 166 Ohio St. 12, 139 N.E. 2d.25
(1956) Supreme Court of Ohio

This is an action for damages originating in the Common Pleas Court of Cuyahoga County, wherein the plaintiff, Martha Lacey, a minor past 18 years of age, seeks damages against the defendant, Arthur W. Laird, through her amended petition setting up two causes of action, one for assault and battery and the other for malpractice . . .

Plaintiff, who was 18 years of age on October 5, 1951, testified that approximately a week before the operation, after seeing the advertisement of Laird in the telephone directory, in form, "Reshape Your Nose, Plastic Surgery," with face profiles before and after treatment, she went to Laird's office and was there interviewed by [office secretary Katherine] Cunningham, in which interview she, the plaintiff, advised Cunningham that she was 18 years of age, and that she did not have funds with which to pay for an operation, whereupon Cunningham advised her that a loan of money would be secured for her for that purpose; that after her conference with Cunningham a date was set for a plastic operation on plaintiff's nose, the date being October 5, 1951; and that on that date Laird performed a plastic operation on her nose without her consent and over her active protests.

The plaintiff on trial testified further:

"A. I was scared, I made an attempt to jump off the chair.

"Well, at first, when he was sticking the needles in my nose, he was hurting me and I told him to stop it. He was hurting me. He says, 'No, you sit back. You will be all right.' And after that he stuck another needle in it and I was crying. He told me it wasn't hurting me but it was."

The testimony of Laird was to the effect that plaintiff called at his office and made an appointment for treatment; that at that time she specifically stated she was 21 years of age; and that later she called at his office on several occasions for followup treatments.

The plaintiff claims that, as a result of this assault and violation of her bodily integrity, permanent changes in the tissues and structure of her nose were made with a detrimental effect upon her physical appearance, and that she was caused to suffer severe mental shock, humiliation, depression and a general personality and nervous breakdown, as a result of which she was unable to return to her employment . . .

The major issue presented in this case is whether, in the absence of an emergency, an operation performed upon a minor without the consent of the parents or persons standing in *loco parentis* is a legal wrong or a technical assault? . . .

The general rule seems to be that, unless there exists an emergency, which prevents any delay, or other exceptional circumstances, a surgeon who performs an operation upon a minor without the consent of his parents or guardian is guilty of a trespass and battery. This rule is not based upon the capacity of a minor to consent, so far as he is personally concerned, within the field of the law of torts or law of crimes, but is based upon the right of parents whose liability for support and maintenance of their child may be greatly increased by an unfavorable result from the operational procedures upon the part of a surgeon.

. . . And, since the parents of such a child are responsible for his nurture and training and are liable for his maintenance and support, others will not be permitted to interfere with such relationships or with matters touching the child's personal welfare . . .

The plaintiff's third claim of error is that the trial court erred in charging that there was a technical battery committed by Laird. The record shows that the plaintiff contacted Laird's office on September 28, 1951; and that a loan was negotiated for the plaintiff by Laird with which to finance the fee for the operation on plaintiff's nose, which operation took place on October 5, 1951. During this interim no effort was made to secure the consent of the parents of the plaintiff for such operation and none was secured. The physical contact made by Laird with the person of the plaintiff is best described by Laird himself in his testimony. He testified in part as follows:

"And then we injected the anesthetic, and then I proceeded to make an incision on each side at the lower part of the nasal bone, over the nasal bone, underneath the skin. That was loosened up, and I used a periosteal elevator on the periosteum over the bone, and then I used a nasal rasp to smooth down the bone.

"My incision was then carried down on the inside towards the tip of the nose and the end of the septum, and then at a right angle down toward the lip.

"A small portion of the end of the septum was cut off. The columella, that is, the bottom of the nose, was then sutured back to the septum. Then that which often happens when the nose is shortened, there is a more heavy tip, and I made an incision on each side of the inside of the nose through the cartilage, and a small portion of the cartilage was removed from each side."

In view of this undisputed testimony and under the law as hereinabove stated, there can be no question as to the commission of a technical battery on the plaintiff by Laird, and the trial court was justified in charging as to a technical battery . . .

The judgment of the Court of Appeals should be affirmed.

o **Recap of the Case**. The general rule governing treatment of minors is that surgery should never be performed without parental consent unless an emergency exists. However, the court in this case recognized that some minors are capable of understanding information about treatment. In these cases, only a nominal amount of money will be awarded to the patient even though, technically speaking, an assault and battery was committed.

Exceptions:
Emancipated Minors, Mature Minors, and Minors Seeking Certain Types of Treatment

A. EMANCIPATED MINORS: NO LIABILITY FOR VASECTOMY PERFORMED ON AN EMANCIPATED MINOR

In many states, legislatures have created statutory exceptions to the need for parental consent on behalf of minor children. For example, emancipated minors, i.e. minors who are no longer under the care or control of their parents, may consent to medical treatment on their own behalf. Emancipated minors often include minors who are married or the parent of a child. In some states, minors who no longer receive financial support from their parents are also emancipated and able to consent to medical treatment on their own behalf. This point is illustrated by *Smith v. Seibly*.

In *Smith*, the plaintiff who was eighteen years of age and a minor according to the statutes in effect in Washington at that time, asked the defendant to perform a vasectomy on him. Plaintiff made this request because he had myasthenia gravis and did not want any more children than he had already. The vasectomy was performed. However, when plaintiff became an adult he sued the surgeon who performed the vasectomy on the grounds that the defendant negligently performed surgery upon him as a minor. Instead of relying on the technical requirements of the statute, the court looked at all of the circumstances of this case and decided that the plaintiff was an emancipated minor at the time surgery was performed and could, therefore, give valid consent to the vasectomy. Specifically, the court considered the plaintiff's age, intelligence, maturity, training, experience, economic independence or lack thereof, general conduct as an adult and freedom from the control of parents. In this case the plaintiff was married, independent of parental control and financially independent.

Applying these principles to practice, nurses should be aware that there are statutes which emancipate minors for the purpose of giving consent prior to the age of maturity. These statutes vary from state to state. Even if there is no such statute, however, minors may still consent to treatment on the basis that they are emancipated if, utilizing the factors listed in *Smith*, the minor actually functions in society more like an adult than a child.

Smith v. Seibly, 72 Wash.2d 16, 431 P.2d 719 (1967)
Supreme Court of Washington

This litigation results from a vasectomy operation performed upon the person of Albert G. Smith, the appellant by the respondent, Walter W. Seibly, a practicing physician at Clarkston. At the time of the operation the appellant was 18 years old, married and the father of a child. He was gainfully employed, supported his family and maintained a home for himself, his wife and child. He was afflicted with a progressive muscular disease, myasthenia gravis, which is chronic and incurable and would possibly affect his future earning capacity and ability to support his family. Under these circumstances he and his wife decided to limit their family by having appellant sterilized.

The family doctor refused to perform the operation because of appellant's youth and the doctor's knowledge of the instability of marriage. Whereupon, appellant and his wife sought another doctor on March 9, 1961, visited the respondent's offices requesting that respondent perform the vasectomy. The appellant represented that the sterilization was desired because of his affliction with myasthenia gravis. Respondent illustrated the operation with a diagram and explained that it would result in permanent sterilization. There is a dispute as to whether the appellant represented that he was of legal age. The respondent read aloud and presented the following statement to appellant and his wife:

TO WHOM IT MAY CONCERN:
We, the undersigned, hereby consent to the sterilization operation to be performed on the husband, having been told that the operation is a permanent thing, that there is no chance for a reestablishment of a viable sperm in the semen.

The doctor then told appellant and his wife to go home, think about the operation and if they still wished it performed, sign the paper and return to his office.

Twelve days later appellant returned, presented the consent signed by himself and his wife, and the operation was performed.

After appellant reached his majority, he brought this action alleging that the respondent was negligent in performing the vasectomy upon an infant of 18 years, was negligent in failing to explain to appellant the permanent consequences of the surgery, and that such surgery was performed without valid permission. The appellant asked damages in the amount of $52,000. The respondent's answer denied the allegations of negligence and liability and alleged that the appellant was barred from recovery because he had signed a consent to the operation.

Although the complaint contained allegations based on a theory of negligence, all parties agree that the trial court properly submitted the case to the jury on an assault theory. One of the instructions read: ". . . The vasectomy is an assault and battery if surgery was performed without valid consent." Appellant's theory was that a minor could not give valid consent to such surgery. The respondent's view, adopted by the trial court, was that under some conditions a minor may be emancipated for the purpose of giving consent to surgery. The jury returned a verdict for respondent and judgment having been entered thereon, this appeal followed. . .

The exceptions taken to the trial court's action . . . were . . . , namely, that appellant, being a minor, could not give consent to the operation, that his consent was void, and that parental consent was necessary to insulate respondent from liability. It has long been recognized in this state that for certain purposes, emancipation of minors may occur even in the absence of statute . . .

Respondent contends that appellant was emancipated for the purpose of giving consent to the operation, or, at least that a jury question was presented on this issue . . .

'Emancipation' of a child is the relinquishment by the parent of control and authority over the child, conferring on him the right to his earnings and terminating the parent's legal duty to support the child. It may be express, as by voluntary agreement of parent and child, or implied from such acts and conduct as import consent; it may be conditional or absolute, complete or partial . . .

. . . A married minor, 18 years of age, who has successfully completed high school and is the head of his own family, who earns his own living and maintains his own home, is emancipated for the purpose of giving a valid consent to surgery if a full disclosure of the ramifications, implications and probable consequences of the surgery has been made by the doctor in terms which are fully comprehensible to the minor. Thus, age, intelligence, maturity, training, experience, economic independence or lack thereof, general conduct as an adult and freedom from the control of parents are all factors to be considered in such a case.

Appellant was married, independent of parental control and financial support and it was for the jury to decide if he was sufficiently intelligent, educated and knowledgeable to make a legally binding decision . . .

o **Recap of the Case**. In this case a vasectomy was performed on a minor who already had children and, due to his chronic illness, did not want any more children. After the patient became an adult, he sued on the basis that the permanent nature of the surgery was never explained to him and adequate permission was not obtained. The court rejected this argument because, even though the patient was technically a minor when the surgery was performed, he functioned more like an adult who was, therefore, able to give informed consent.

B. MATURE MINORS: MINOR'S CONSENT FOUND ADEQUATE

In addition, so-called "mature" minors may consent to treatment on their own behalf in many states. "Mature" minors are often allowed to consent to treatment if they are mature enough to understand the nature and outcome of proposed treatment. In *Younts v. St. Francis Hospital* the court allowed a seventeen year old to consent to treatment on her own behalf.

In this case, the plaintiff was the mother of a seventeen year old girl. While the plaintiff was in the hospital recovering from surgery, her daughter came to visit her. During the daughter's visit, a nurse accidentally closed a door on her finger. The daughter was treated in the emergency room. After the mother recovered, she sued the hospital on the grounds that treatment was rendered negligently to her daughter because the hospital did not obtain the mother's consent first.

The court decided against the plaintiff primarily because her daughter understood the nature and outcome of the proposed treatment, even though she was technically a minor. The court also based its decision on other criteria which will assist providers as they make decisions about whether minors should be considered "mature minors" and thus able to consent on their own to medical treatment. In *Younts*, the criteria considered by the court included the unavailability of either parent to give consent, age, maturity, intellect, the minor nature of the treatment, the results obtained, and the agreement of the daughter's family physician that treatment should be rendered. These same factors should be applied by nurses when they must decide if a minor is mature enough to consent to medical treatment.

Younts v. St. Francis Hospital,
205 Kan.292, 469 P.2d 330 (1970)
Supreme Court of Kansas

The claim was presented to the court on two theories. First, on the theory that one of the nurses employed by the hospital negligently caused the injury by closing a door on the daughter's finger, and second, on the theory that a resident surgeon employed by the hospital performed an unauthorized surgical procedure on the daughter to repair the finger without obtaining the consent of the daughter and her mother.

We will treat the contentions with respect to each separate theory in the order listed above.

The facts as to the accident are in dispute . . .

The mother had undergone major surgery on the day of the daughter's injury. The daughter was in the hospital and was concerned about her mother's condition. The mother was brought to her room on a surgical cart while the daughter waited outside her mother's room. The daughter followed the nurses into her mother's room. The nurses were preparing to transfer the mother from the surgical cart to the bed. The daughter was asked to step into the hall. When the daughter was in the hall one of the nurses (Wanda) closed the door to the room. She heard the daughter scream in pain. In a partial closing of the door the nurse's view of the daughter had been obscured by the door. The nurse could not anticipate and did not see the daughter's move toward the door. It may be inferred the daughter stepped forward after the door was partially closed and unconsciously placed her finger in the scissor–like action of the door hinge. A piece of flesh from the daughter's finger was found on the floor below the hinges of the door. The door was opened immediately for the nurse had not yet released the door handle. The daughter was suffering and her finger was bleeding. One of the nurses (Joyce) asked the daughter if she would like to go see about getting her finger fixed. The daughter said that she would. The nurse obtained permission at the nurses' station to take the daughter to the emergency room of the hospital. The resident surgeon in the hospital treated and repaired her finger.

The court made the following findings with regard to negligence of the hospital employees:

1. The injury sustained by the plaintiff, Nancy D. Younts, was not due to any wrongful or negligent act on the part of St. Francis Hospital and School of Nursing, Inc., its agents, servants or employees.

2. The injury sustained by the plaintiff, Nancy D. Younts, to her finger was not due to the failure of any care due plaintiff by defendant, its agents, servants or employees.

The judgment of the court denied plaintiff relief. . .

Plaintiff's claim based on the theory that one of the nurses employed by the hospital negligently caused the injury by closing a door on the daughter's finger is disposed of by the findings of the trial court. The findings are supported by substantial competent evidence and will not be overturned on appeal.

We turn now to plaintiff's second theory, that Dr. Winsky performed an unauthorized surgical procedure on the daughter without obtaining the consent of the daughter and her mother. In addition, the plaintiff contends the consent of the daughter cannot be sufficient because the doctor failed to adequately inform the daughter as to the consequences of this surgical procedure.

It will be helpful to examine some additional facts bearing upon the question. The injury occurred in the hospital at a time when the mother was semi–conscious by reason of a general anaesthetic. She was being returned to her room after major surgery. The injured daughter's parents were divorced. The father was living two hundred miles away. His address was unknown and not immediately available. The daughter was seventeen years old, intelligent and capable for her age. The injury resulted in loss of the fleshy tip of her right ring finger. The fingernail was left intact and the end of the bone was slightly fractured. The surgical repair, accomplished in the emergency room of the hospital, was of a minor nature. The plaintiff remained conscious throughout the treatment and was fully aware of what was being done. She raised no objection to the surgical procedure. The testimony of both the family doctor and the treating physician indicates the medical procedure utilized in the repair was necessary and customary for that particular injury. The functional and cosmetic results attained were good. The family doctor, who was consulted before the repair was undertaken, gave his consent. He indicated to the treating physician that the surgical procedure suggested was proper, necessary and should be undertaken.

The family physician, Dr. Thompson, testified in part as follows:

On the date of the incident, January 27, 1965, *Dr. Winsky called me.* I do not remember what time of day. I was in my office when he called. *He described the injury and outlined the plan of treatment which sounded good to me, so I instructed him to proceed and do it.* I leave a standing order at St. Francis Hospital with respect to treatment of patients of mine who present themselves for emergency care, at least those that are there for minor injuries. My orders are for them to go ahead and repair them if it is minor such as a laceration or such as this which would be a minor procedure. And Dr. Winsky consulted me.

I have been Nancy Younts' physician for several years prior to this occurrence . . .

I think the operation was well done. I think the graft took well . . .

"Miss Younts was in my office five days ago. There was no complaint at that time about the finger. She wasn't in for that anyway. I don't believe that I have an opinion to a reasonable degree of medical certainty as to whether *in* [sic] the injury or damage was occasioned or suffered by Miss Younts as a result of the alleged lack of parental consent or any other consent. The reason I say that is that she has a good functional result of the finger. I think almost perfect as a matter of fact. I don't believe the lack of consent had anything to do with the end result, if there was such a lack of consent. If this procedure had not been undertaken to stitch on a small piece of skin onto the finger tip, I think this would have healed over a period of time. I think these can be left out in the open and will heal. They'll heal faster this way and will probably heal with a scar on the end rather than probably the good result she has here now. I have not performed sensitivity tests on the finger tip; that's all subjective actually that we have as far as the sensitivity is concerned. By subjective, I mean what she says. I think the function of the finger now should be good. I have no knowledge of the portion of the finger tip which was torn off. In order for me to form an opinion as to whether or not it was usuable [sic] I would have had to have an opportunity to examine it. The reason a graft is ordinarily taken from the forearm on injuries of this kind is primarily because the skin there will have about the same type pigment as you have in the hand. If you take it off some place else that is covered and you put it out here, it'll turn dark. If you take it off the hip and put it on the finger, you will have a finger with a brown end on it. The skin from this area will have about the same pigment as the skin out here. One purpose is for aesthetic qualities . . .

. . . I don't know if there are any other places than the forearm to take the skin for this type of operation. I know this is the customary place to take it. I suppose there are other places. I have operated and taken it off the skin for [sic] the forearm, but that was a bigger area.

Dr. Winsky, the treating physician, testified as follows:

Later on the same day, I saw her in the emergency room. This was after lunch some time, probably between two and three o'clock. This is as close as I can recall. I was called down to the emergency room. I was the surgery resident on call that day. I was called down there to examine and repair this finger tip. I examined the finger at the time I arrived. There was also an x–ray there that had been taken of her finger before I arrived which demonstrated a small fracture in the tip of the bone of this last phalanx of the distal phalanx. The fracture was just on a small edge of the tuft. The tuft is the flared portion on the very end of the phalanx. It is real friable, somewhat fragile piece of bone. It's not a solid structure like the rest of it. There was a crack through this that was visualized on x–ray. A crack is a fracture. As I recall, the tip of her finger was missing. I didn't see any bone exposed. There was soft tissue there, but the entire skin was missing. The finger nail was still there. This was below the finger nail or the actual distal or past the finger nail. The finger nail was not affected. I don't recall the specific conversation, but I know vaguely what conversation went on. *I recall having told her what she already knew, that her finger tip was missing and that we would have to take a piece of skin, best from the arm, to put over this to cover it. She did not have any objection to this procedure as far as I recall. Before I commenced treatment of the finger, I talked to Dr. Dan Thompson. I called him at his office. I described what I have just described about her finger, told him what had happened or what I knew about it and told him what I thought ought to be done, and he said do it. So I did.* I took a small elliptical piece of skin from her forearm, and after I had taken it off, I reapproximated the edges where I had taken the skin from. I closed this, and then I took the little piece of skin very carefully with the scissors, took the fat off the back side so it has a better chance of growing, and cut it to the proper shape and sutured it to the tip of her finger. During the time I was stitching the skin on, I am sure I had conversation with Nancy concerning what I was doing. I don't remember specifically, but I talk a lot and I usually talk to people while I am working, and I almost invariably tell them, before you stick them with the needle, before you deaden the finger, 'This will hurt.' These are rather nonspecifics, but this has always been my policy. I don't have a clue as to how many stitches it took to sew the tip of the finger on. *The purpose in taking the skin from the wrist and putting it on the finger tip is that you have to have some kind of covering on the finger tip or else you get infection or you get granulation.* It piles up and forms an excessive amount of scar tissue which is extremely sensitive. It doesn't heal well unless you get a covering on it. *The reason for taking it from the wrist, it more nearly matches the finger than any other place. This is pretty standard procedure concerning the place to get grafts for the finger. . .*

Mrs. Johnson, the mother, testified on cross–examination as follows:

Dr. Thompson is our family doctor. Nancy has gone to Dr. Thompson. I have confidence in him. Had I known at the time that Dr. Thompson and Dr. Winsky had conferred and decided that this was the best procedure, I doubt if I would have consented for the graft to come from her arm. If Dr. Thompson and Dr. Winsky had indicated that they felt that that was the best procedure, *I would have taken some time with Dr. Thompson to talk and find out if it was the best. If he had then told me it was the best, I would have consented if he said so and she was agreeable* . . .

It is the settled general rule that in the absence of an emergency or unanticipated conditions arising during surgery a physician or surgeon before treating or operating must obtain the consent of the patient, or if the patient is incompetent the consent must be obtained from someone legally authorized to give it for him. A surgical operation on the body of a person is a technical battery or trespass, regardless of its result, unless the person or some authorized person consents to it. Generally the surgeon is liable for damages if the operation is unauthorized . . .

The consent of a patient to be sufficient for the purpose of authorizing a particular surgical procedure must be an informed consent. The patient must have reasonable knowledge of the nature of the surgery and some understanding of the risks involved and the possible results to be anticipated . . .

In the present case we are confronted with an additional question of whether a seventeen year old girl can give her consent to a minor surgical procedure without the knowledge or consent of her parents . . .

. . .[Generally] the consent of a parent to a surgical operation on a child is necessary. Certain exceptions are recognized . . . and those exceptions generally recognized by the courts are: 1) when an emergency exists; 2) when the child has been emancipated; 3) when the parents are so remote as to make it impracticable to obtain consent in time to accomplish proper results; and 4) when the child is close to maturity and knowingly gives an informed consent . . . [O]ne of the basic considerations to be taken into account is whether the proposed operation is for the benefit of the child and performed with a purpose of saving his life or limb . . .

Applying those rules of law to the facts and circumstances of the present case it appears that the father's consent was not available or necessary. The mother's consent was not obtained but her physical condition at the time would have necessitated delaying necessary treatment of a painful injury. The mother's testimony at the trial indicates that if she had been asked for her consent she would have relied largely upon the judgment of her family doctor. This doctor was consulted by the treating physician in advance and he approved the surgical procedure adopted, including the "pinch graft" taken from the girl's forearm. The plaintiff was conscious throughout the treatment and indicated her consent both verbally and by submitting herself to the treatment. She was of sufficient age and maturity to know and understand the nature and consequences of the "pinch graft" utilized in the repair of her finger. It is uncontradicted that the method of repair utilized was the approved surgical treatment and in the best interests of the patient. The desired results were accomplished and permanent damage resulting from the injury after the treatment was minimal from both a functional and cosmetic standpoint.

We hold that the facts and circumstances attending the injury and repair of the plaintiff's finger bring this case within an exception to the general rule requiring the consent of the parent to a surgical operation on the child. The exception applicable is that under the circumstances the daughter was mature enough to understand the nature and consequences and to knowingly consent to the beneficial surgical procedure made necessary by the accident.

The findings of the trial court in this regard are supported by substantial competent evidence and include a finding that the plaintiff suffers no disability or damage to her finger as a result of the treatment.

The judgment is affirmed.

o **Recap of the Case**. The *Younts* case provides nurses with criteria to use to decide if a minor is mature enough to consent to surgery without parental consent. If some or all of the following facts are present, treatment may be provided without fear of liability: 1) The minor patient's parents are unavailable to give consent; 2) The minor is close in age to adulthood; 3) The minor appears to be mature and intelligent; the minor generally seems to understand the injury or illness and the proposed treatment; 4) The treatment provided is minor in nature; 5) Treatment will be successful for the most part; and 6) There is general agreement among the professionals who treat the patient that the particular care at issue should be provided.

C. MINORS SEEKING CERTAIN TYPES OF TREATMENT: NO LIABILITY FOR ABORTION PERFORMED ON A MINOR

Finally, minors may consent when seeking certain kinds of treatment. For example, when minors seek contraception, abortion, or treatment for substance abuse, parental consent is not required in many jurisdictions. In *State of Washington v. Koome*, the court determined that an unmarried minor may obtain an abortion without her parents' consent.

At the time the events of this case occurred, a statute was in effect in the State of Washington which required minors to obtain the consent of their parents before they were permitted to have an abortion. The defendant, Koome, performed an abortion on a minor without her parents' permission. As a result, criminal charges were brought against him for violation of the statute.

The court decided that the Washington statute which required minors to have parental approval for an abortion was unconstitutional. Since this case was decided, many states have passed statutes which authorize performance of abortions on minors with only the minor's consent. Because these statutes vary considerably from state to state, nurses should check on the existence of such statutes in their states. It is helpful for nurses to be familiar with them and to be able to recognize the exceptions they establish within their own practice settings.

State of Washington v. Koome
84 Wash.2d 901, 530 P.2d 260 (1975)
Supreme Court of Washington

Appellant Dr. A. Frans Koome, was charged with performing an abortion on an unmarried minor woman without first obtaining the consent of her parents . . . His sole defense at trial was that the statute, insofar as it gives parents or guardians the unlimited power to overrule their daughter's decision to have a legal abortion, is unconstitutional. The trial court rejected that claim. We reverse.

In July, 1972, a young woman, 16 years old, unmarried, pregnant, and for some 18 months a ward of the King County Juvenile Court, petitioned that court for an order allowing her to have an abortion. Her parents and her temporary guardian, Catholic Children's Services, who had refused to consent to the operation, opposed the petition. A hearing was held at which considerable testimony and argument was presented, and after which the court entered the requested order authorizing the abortion.

The parents then petitioned this court for a writ of certiorari reviewing the order, and an immediate stay pending that review. The stay was granted, in effect suspending the consent to the abortion that the Juvenile Court had given, and Dr. Koome was advised of that fact. In spite of the stay, however, he performed the operation on August 15, 1972. For so contravening the court's order, he was subsequently held in contempt. In re Koome, 82 Wash.2d 816, 514 P.2d 520 (1973).

Dr. Koome's later criminal conviction for the same act, which is before us in this case . . .

Subjection of a minor woman's decision to terminate an unwanted pregnancy to absolute and potentially arbitrary parental veto clearly constitutes a substantial burden on her rights . . .

. . . Thus, the restrictions . . . before us here can only be sustained if some additional state interest is present in the case of unmarried minor women which will justify them. The State argues that two such purposes are furthered by the requirement of parental consent: the assurance of an adequately reflective and informed decision on the part of the minor woman, and the "support of the family unit and parental authority."

The contention that the statute can be justified as supportive of parental authority as an end in itself is not urged strongly by the State, and cannot be sustained. Although the family structure is a fundamental institution of our society, and parental prerogatives are entitled to considerable legal deference, . . . they are not absolute and must yield to fundamental rights of the child or important interests of the state . . .

In the circumstances envisioned by this statute, there seems to be little parental control left for the State to help salvage: An unmarried minor has become pregnant, and her determination to get an abortion is unalterably opposed by her parents. Reestablishment of parental control by resort to the pure force of the criminal law seems both futile and manifestly unwise in such a situation. Moreover, it should be recognized that considerations of the rights of the parents in raising children do not argue solely for the implementation of the pregnant minor woman's parents' will. She herself is on the verge of becoming a mother, and if she bears the child she will be entitled to its custody and control . . . The decision to continue or terminate her pregnancy is, in effect, her first "parental" decision. It should not arbitrarily be subordinated to her parents' last.

Nor does the asserted state interest in ensuring that the decision to complete or terminate a pregnancy be informed justify the decisive impact of this statute on the minor woman's rights. It is true that the gravity of the abortion decision is such that information and reflection are vital to its making. The need for such qualities or decision making may even be considered "compelling." Intelligence, however, is not what the statute here requires. The statute requires parental consent, and allows parents to refuse to consent not only where their judgment is better informed and considered than that of their daughter, but also where it is colored by personal religious belief, whim, or even hostility to her best interests.

This case graphically demonstrates that the reasons for refusing consent may be ill-advised or otherwise improper. The father of the minor woman testified that his opposition to the abortion stemmed from his belief that continuing her pregnancy to term would deter her from becoming pregnant in the future . . . Her guardian, Catholic Children's Services, opposed the abortion on religious grounds. That the legal imposition of such religious mores on a child is constitutionally impermissible is beyond question.

. . . The "conclusive presumption" that the parents' judgment is better than the pregnant woman's cannot withstand constitutional scrutiny . . .

State restrictions on fundamental freedoms must be narrowly drawn to conform to the legitimate state interests to be furthered, and must not sweep too broadly over the exercise of privacy rights . . .

State restrictions on fundamental freedoms must be narrowly drawn to conform to the legitimate state interests to be furthered, and must not sweep too broadly over the exercise of privacy rights . . . The statute here provides a parental veto power where less restrictive means are available which can as well insure adequacy of reflection and consideration in a minor's abortion decision. The physician–patient consultation which should precede *any* abortion . . . provides information, advice as to alternatives, and time for deliberation. If professional responsibility is not safeguard enough, the common law requires that physicians determine that a minor's decision to consent to any form of medical care, including abortion, is adequately informed and considered, and civil liability is available to enforce this injunction . . . Whatever additional guarantee of the "quality" of the abortion decision is necessary may be provided by other less drastic state requirements. If parental supervision is considered valuable in itself, perhaps the state could make a certificate of parental *consultation* prerequisite to a minor's abortion. A demand for parental *consent*, backed by the power of the criminal law of the state, is not necessary and cannot be constitutionally justified . . .

For these reasons we find that the parental consent requirement . . . violates the [Constitution] . . . By so holding, however, we do not rule that the State cannot in any way regulate the performance of abortions on minors. The interests put forth by the State for doing so are not without weight. A statutory scheme which protected them without sacrificing the privacy rights of pregnant minor women could pass constitutional muster. A requirement of consultation with parents or others able to advise would seem arguably permissible, as we have noted. Even a law allowing parents to stop an abortion where they can show that their daughter is not acting or capable of acting in her own best interests might be sustainable. But the present statute, which forces a woman who may have made her decision maturely and intelligently to resort to trying and possibly prolonged court action at best, or submit to an arbitrary and absolute veto at worst, cannot be upheld.

The decision of the trial court is reversed.

o **Recap of the Case**. In this case, a minor, who was sixteen years old, had an abortion without consent by a parent or guardian. The court decided that the patient could consent to an abortion and that no parental consent was necessary. After a number of courts reached this conclusion, state legislatures passed statutes which allow minors seeking certain types of treatment to consent on their own. These statutes often cover birth control information, treatment for use of drugs, and counseling for emotional disturbances. However, these statutes vary from state to state, so nurses should familiarize themselves with statutes of this type in their states.

5

Adults

Adults are presumed competent to consent unless their lack of capacity is proven. Generally, family members and spouses as such have no legal right to provide substitute or concurrent consent to medical treatment. Attempts to obtain their consent can only be to enhance the relationship between the patient's physician and family members and must be presented to the family in this vain. If "next of kin" had the right to consent to treatment, the family member would also have the right to refuse treatment on the patient's behalf. While the consent of family members is often sought and treatment withheld on the alleged authority of a family member, neither practice represents sound risk management.

Unfortunately, most nurses do not realize that "next of kin," including spouses, have no automatic authority to consent to medical treatment on behalf of their relatives. Discussions regarding diagnosis and treatment are routinely held with family members instead of the patient, especially if the patient is elderly, mentally impaired or has cancer. Consent forms are routinely given to "next of kin" for signature. These practices will result in liability for hospitals and individual healthcare providers.

FAILURE TO OBTAIN HUSBAND'S CONSENT TO SURGERY DOES NOT RESULT IN LIABILITY

In *Jeffcoat v. Phillips*, for example, the defendant performed an operation for removal of the plaintiff's varicose veins. Plaintiff later claimed that this surgery was unauthorized because she consented to the removal of an ulcer on her right leg only. Plaintiff's husband also claimed that the surgery was unauthorized because he had not given his consent. The court clearly rejected this argument and stated that the consent of spouses to medical treatment is unnecessary.

Jeffcoat v. Phillips, 417 S.W. 2d 903 (Tex.Civ.App. 1967)
Texas Court of Appeals

C. E. Jeffcoat and wife, Mary Jeffcoat, sued Dr. John R. Phillips for alleged ordinary and gross negligence in the performance of surgery upon Mrs. Jeffcoat and for alleged unauthorized surgery on Mrs. Jeffcoat. A jury trial resulted in the submission of no negligence or gross negligence issues on Dr. Phillips and in a verdict in favor of defendant on answers to issues inquiring about unauthorized surgery. The damages issue was answered "none". Judgment was entered that plaintiffs take nothing. Plaintiffs have appealed.

. . . "The testimony of defendant Doctor Phillips constitutes some evidence of probative force. According to his testimony he fully explained to Mrs. Jeffcoat about the operation which was eventually performed, that this information was discussed with her several days before surgery, that he told Mrs. Jeffcoat specifically about the necessity for making incisions in large troublesome veins; that Mrs. Jeffcoat checked into the hospital after being previously given full information of the intended operations by Dr. Phillips, that she had been reasonably warned and adequately by the discussion in question about the likelihood of the scarring of her legs, and Dr. Phillips further testified to the effect that the operations which were performed had been fully explained to Mrs. Jeffcoat by him.

There was also written evidence of the consent of Mrs. Jeffcoat to the surgery in question consisting of an authorization signed by Mrs. Jeffcoat specifically authorizing a bilateral vein ligation, together with such necessary and closely connected surgical procedures as would be caused in the course of the operation.

If appellee's testimony is to be believed, he proved both oral and written consent on the part of Mrs. Jeffcoat to the operations in question, as well as full informed consent by his oral testimony . . .

Mrs. Jeffcoat testified to the effect that she did not orally consent to the operations in question performed by Dr. Phillips, and that she signed the written authorization form in blank. Mrs. Jeffcoat testified to the effect that she had consented to an operation for the sole purpose of removal of an ulcer caused by a burn. She had been a patient of Dr. Phillips and had had previous surgery by Dr. Phillips as shown by the record, for conditions other than the operations complained of and sued upon. She also testified to the effect that Dr. Phillips on other occasions had recommended to her to allow him to operate on her legs for varicose veins, but that she in each instance refused to permit such surgery. Mrs. Jeffcoat also contradicted Dr. Phillips' testimony with reference to "informed consent", and warnings from Dr. Phillips that she might reasonably expect scarring on her legs from such operation, and in short Mrs. Jeffcoat contradicted Dr. Phillips' testimony on most of the material matters, thus leaving issues for the jury to determine. It appeared from Dr. Phillips' testimony and other medical testimony in the case that Mrs. Jeffcoat had severe varicose veins on one leg and somewhat less severe on the other leg. It was Dr. Phillips' testimony that both legs needed the operation, and that it was necessary to excise as well as strip the veins and that the operation was not a "routine operation" and was one that required excising and that scarring of the legs would result therefrom. Other doctors corroborated Dr. Phillips to the effect that the operation was not a "routine operation". Photographic exhibits show the scarring on Mrs. Jeffcoat's legs . . .

Appellants also contend to the effect that because there was no proof that Mr. Jeffcoat gave his consent to the operations in question performed on his wife, that coverture was a bar to a valid legal agreement on the part of the wife to consent to the operations in question. In other words, appellants contend to the effect that the failure of Dr. Phillips to obtain Mr. Jeffcoat's permission is reason for reversal of the judgment of the trial court. Appellants cite no authority in support of such proposition, and we have found no authority to support such a proposition. The record shows Mrs. Jeffcoat was an adult married woman and no question appears or is raised as to her mental capacity. As we view the matter, appellants' contention in this regard is without merit. A person does not fall within the classification of "property", and Mrs. Jeffcoat, a person, had the right to consent to the operations in question if she chose to do so, and her husband's consent was not necessary. . .

Expert testimony is essential in medical malpractice cases based on negligence except where the injury is so plain as to be within the common knowledge of laymen . . . Such expert testimony must come from a doctor of the same school of medicine as that of the defendant . . . However, this rule has been qualified to the extent that doctors of different schools may testify in malpractice cases: 1) where the particular subject of inquiry is common to and equally recognized in both schools of practice; and 2) where the subject of inquiry relates to the manner of use of electrical or mechanical appliances which are of common use in both schools of practice . . .

The medical experts who testified in the case confirmed the fact that the operation in question performed by Dr. Phillips was not a "routine" operation and that excision in some cases was proper. As we view the evidence, there was no evidence of probative force from any of the medical experts to the effect that they could say that the operation as actually performed by Dr. Phillips was improper. As we view it, there was no medical evidence of probative force to show "negligence" on the part of Dr. Phillips in performing the operation in question . . .

Finding no reversible error in the record, the judgment of the trial courts is affirmed.

o **Recap of the Case**. The patient said she consented to the removal of an ulcer. The surgeon removed varicose veins. The surgery permanently scarred the patient's legs, and the patient sued. Among other things, the patient claimed that the surgeon was liable because he did not get her husband's consent to the surgery. The court completely rejected this argument on the basis that any competent, married adult may consent to surgery. The practitioner has no obligation to get consent from the patient's spouse, too.

HUSBAND'S CONSENT TO SURGERY INADEQUATE TO PREVENT SURGERY

The court goes one step further in *Gravis v. Physicians' and Surgeons' Hospital of Alice*. In this case, plaintiff was admitted to the emergency room of defendant's hospital complaining of abdominal tenderness. A decision was made that surgery was necessary. The surgeon discussed the surgery with plaintiff's husband, Mr. Gravis, and Mr. Gravis signed the consent form. Mrs. Gravis later sued the surgeon for failure to obtain her consent. Despite the defendant's claims that the situation was an emergency so that no consent was necessary and that Mrs. Gravis lacked capacity because of the pain she was suffering, the court decided in plaintiff's favor. The spouse's consent was meaningless.

Gravis v. Physicians' and Surgeons' Hospital of Alice
427 S.W.2d 310 (Tex. 1968), Supreme Court of Texas

. . . On the evening of October 22, 1963, Mrs. Gravis complained of pain in her abdomen. Her husband telephoned Dr. Joseph, who agreed to and did meet them at the Physicians and Surgeons Hospital of Alice, a corporation, hereinafter referred to as the hospital. Dr. Joseph examined Mrs. Gravis in the emergency room of the hospital. This initial examination revealed generalized tenderness in the abdominal area but did not enable the doctor to reach any conclusion as to the probable cause of the patient's complaints. Mrs. Gravis was given medicine for pain and placed in a room in the hospital for observation. The following day she was given other examinations and tests. According to Dr. Joseph, the X-rays taken at that time showed a normal abdomen with no pathology indicated.

The situation had changed by the morning of October 24th. Mrs. Gravis' blood count was up, and X-rays taken that morning showed some dilation of the small intestine. Dr. Joseph then concluded for the first time that an exploratory operation was necessary. He performed the operation at about 12:30 o'clock p.m. the same day. Dr. Turnham was the assisting physician, and Mrs. Grose, who was employed by the hospital as anesthetist and supervisor of nurses, administered the spinal anesthetic and the pentothal sodium which Mrs. Gravis was given during the operation. An intestinal obstruction was found and corrected, but Mrs. Gravis has since suffered from a number of physical disabilities, including bladder trouble, phlebitis of the left leg, and partial paralysis.

Petitioners seek to establish liability upon a number of different theories, including: (1) assault and battery, (2) fraud, (3) breach of duty to warn, (4) breach of contract, and (5) negligence. We consider only the first of these theories. Before the operation was performed, Dr. Joseph discussed Mrs. Gravis' condition with her husband. Mr. Gravis consented in writing to the performing of whatever treatment or operation, and the administering of whatever anesthetics, the physician believed to be necessary or desirable. There is no contention, however, that Mr. Gravis was authorized by his wife to consent in her behalf, and the relationship of husband and wife does not in itself make one spouse the agent of the other.

Mrs. Gravis did not give her consent in writing, and the summary judgment proofs show a dispute as to whether she consented orally. According to the affidavits and deposition testimony of Dr. Joseph and Mrs. Grose, the operation and the anesthetics to be used were fully explained to Mrs. Gravis at about 11:00 o'clock a.m. on October 24th, and the patient then gave her consent to the operation and the anesthetic. This is categorically denied by Mrs. Gravis in her affidavit. She there states that Dr. Joseph never advised her that an operation was necessary and never discussed the anesthetic with her; that she did not consent to the operation or to the use of a spinal anesthetic; that she had refused to take a spinal anesthetic; that she had refused to take a spinal anesthetic in connection with another operation performed in 1956, because two previous spinals had caused her to suffer severe headaches for several weeks, and that if spinal anesthetic had ever been mentioned by Dr. Joseph, she would have refused to take it.

The Court of Civil Appeals reasoned that Mrs. Gravis' consent was not necessary because an emergency existed and she was under the influence of drugs to such an extent that she was incapable of giving consent. We recognize the rule that consent will be implied where the patient is unconscious or otherwise unable to give express consent and an immediate operation is necessary to preserve life or health. In the absence of exceptional circumstances, however, a surgeon is subject to liability for assault and battery where he operates without the consent of the patient or the person legally authorized to give such consent . . . Our problem then is to determine whether the summary judgment proofs establish a case of implied consent as a matter of law.

Certain parts of the affidavit and deposition testimony of Mrs. Garvis tend to support the conclusion that she was unable to give her consent after Dr. Joseph decided that an operation was necessary. When the deposition was taken, she did not remember anything that occurred the morning of October 24th. She stated in her affidavit that she was under pain relieving medicine to such an extent that she did not know what was happening about 80 per cent of the time prior to the operation; that if Dr. Joseph and Mrs. Grose were in her room together the morning of the operation, she was so heavily sedated that she did not know they were there; and that if Dr. Turnham was present, she was under sedation to the extent that she did not know him and could not have talked to him. Evidence of this nature, if offered at the trial, would also serve to discredit any testimony by Mrs. Gravis that Dr. Joseph never discussed the operation with her and that she did not give her consent. The statements referred to cannot be given conclusive effect, however, because the other summary judgment proofs indicate that Mrs. Gravis was in full possession of her mental faculties and quite capable of giving or withholding consent for some time before she was taken to the operating room.

If we accept as true the portions of the affidavits and depositions of Dr. Joseph, Dr. Turnham and Mrs. Grose that are favorable to petitioners, it appears that Dr. Joseph visited Mrs. Gravis in her room on at least two occasions after he decided that an operation was necessary. Dr. Turnham was present during one of these visits. The second visit was at about 10:30 or 11:00 o'clock in the morning, and Mrs. Grose was present at that time. On this occasion "Mrs. Gravis was calm and in full possession of her mental faculties and she was not under any sedation that did or could have affected her mental faculties." "She was perfectly normal and lucid at the time." In the opinion of Dr. Turnham, "she was lucid" when he saw her. The affidavit of Mrs. Grose states that the hospital chart showed the patient had had no sedation or tranquilizer since 11:00 o'clock p.m. In the meantime Dr. Joseph made his two visits to her room and performed at least one other operation. Dr. Turnham states that although he and Dr. Joseph agreed when they saw Mrs. Gravis that it was now time to operate, "there was no dire emergency, and she was operated as soon as the operating room was available." He explained that by the word "dire" he meant "immediate." It thus appears that there was ample time to discuss the operation with Mrs. Gravis and give her an opportunity to consent to or refuse the same.

In our opinion the record does not conclusively establish circumstances that would justify an operation without the patient's consent . . .

o **Recap of the Case**. The patient in this case was admitted to the hospital through the emergency room complaining of severe abdominal pain. Two days later she had surgery to correct an intestinal obstruction. Only the patient's husband consented to surgery. Following surgery, the patient sued. The defendants claimed that they did not get the patient's consent to surgery because an emergency existed which made it unnecessary to get consent at all and the patient was unable to consent because she received pain medication and was not lucid. The court rejected both of these arguments. The conclusion reached in this case serves as a reminder that providers must make careful determinations about the existence of an emergency and the competence of patients.

Since spouses and other family members may not provide substitute or concurrent consent on behalf of adults, who may provide consent if the adult patient is unable to consent because of mental retardation, mental illness, coma, senility, etc.? Under these circumstances, consent must be obtained from: 1) the patient's guardian, conservator, or "committee"; 2) the patient's attorney-in-fact, or 3) a court.

Adult patients have a guardian, conservator or "committee" only if they have been adjudicated incompetent in a court proceeding. The guardian may be an individual, or in more recent cases, a public agency. A guardianship may be temporary or for specific purposes. For example, a guardian *ad litem* is appointed only to protect the ward's interests in litigation. A guardianship may also be permanent. Permanent guardianships are revocable by the courts if incompetent persons or wards are able to show that they no longer lack capacity. A ward's relationshp to his or her guardian is roughly equivalent to the relationship between parent and child; the guardian has the right to consent to treatment on behalf of the ward as parents consent on behalf of their children. Note, however, that in some states there are two types of guardianship: guardianship may be "of the person" or "of the property" or both. In these states, a guardian of the property has a right to manage property only. Consent to medical treatment may be given by a guardian of the person only.

GUARDIAN OF THE PERSON CONSENTS TO TREATMENT ON PATIENT'S BEHALF

As a practical matter, healthcare providers cannot accept the word of an individual or agency representative that they hold guardianship over the patient with the right to consent to treatment because there are different types of guardianship. The alleged guardian must provide a copy of the guardianship decree which must be thoroughly reviewed to make certain that the guardian has the authority claimed. *In Re Estate of Brooks*, is an example of a case in which a guardian of the person only was appointed to consent to treatment.

In this case, plaintiff was a Jehovah's Witness who would not accept blood transfusions in order to save her life. Even though she signed a release absolving her physician of liability, the practitioner asked the court to appoint a guardian for her to consent to the transfusions. The court appointed a guardian of the person for plaintiff. The plaintiff's guardian of the person consented to the transfusions, and they were administered to the plaintiff. The plaintiff later sued on the grounds that her United States Constitutional right to freedom of religion should have precluded the appointment of a guardian in the first place. The court agreed with the plaintiff. For the purposes of a discussion of types of guardianship, the important point is that the court appointed a guardian of the person only, not a guardian of the property, because only a guardianship of the person is necessary to consent to medical treatment.

In Re Estate of Brooks, 32 Ill.2d 361, 205 N.E.2d 435 (1965)
Supreme Court of Illinois

. . . On and sometime before May 7, 1964, Bernice Brooks was in the McNeal General Hospital, Chicago, suffering from a peptic ulcer. She was being attended by Dr. Gilbert Demange, and had informed him repeatedly during a two-year period prior thereto that her religious and medical convictions precluded her from receiving blood transfusions. Mrs. Brooks, her husband and two adult children are all members of the religious sect commonly known as Jehovah's Witnesses. Among the religious beliefs adhered to by members of this group is the principle that blood transfusions are a violation of the law of God, and that transgressors will be punished by God. This organization's publication, "Blood, Medicine and the Law of God", which had been filed by Mrs. Brooks with her physician, states the principle: "The matter was not to be taken lightly. Any violation of the law on blood was a serious sin against God, and God himself would call the law violator to account. 'As for any man of the house of Israel or some alien resident who is residing as an alien in your midst who eats any sort of blood, I shall certainly set my face against the soul that is eating the blood, and I shall indeed cut him off from among his people'—Leviticus 17:10". Also a part of the foundation for this belief is the admonition found in the book of the Acts of the Apostles, 15:28–29: "For it seemed good to the Holy Ghost, and to us, to lay upon you no greater burden than these necessary things; that ye abstain from meats offered to idols, and from blood, and from things strangled, and from fornication; from which if ye keep yourselves, ye shall do

well." Various other Biblical texts are quoted as authority for
the belief, including Genesis 9:3-4: "Every moving animal that
is alive may serve as food for you. As in the case of green
vegetation, I do give it all to you. Only flesh with its soul—its
blood—you must not eat". Premised upon the belief that "The
blood is the soul" (Deuteronomy 12:33) and that "We cannot
drain from our body part of that blood, which represents our
life, and still love God with our whole soul, because we have
taken away part of 'our soul—our blood—' and given it to
someone else" (Blood, Medicine and the Law of God, p. 8),
members of Jehovah's Witnesses regard themselves commanded
by God to neither give nor receive transfusions of blood.

Mrs. Brooks and her husband had signed a document releasing
Dr. Demange and the hospital from all civil liability that might
result from the failure to administer blood transfusions to Mrs.
Brooks. The patient was assured that there would thereafter be
no further effort to persuade her to accept blood.

Notwithstanding these assurances, however, Dr. Demange,
together with several assistant State's attorneys, and the
attorney for the public guardian of Cook County, Illinois,
appeared before the probate division of the circuit court with a
petition by the public guardian requesting appointment of that
officer as conservator of the person of Bernice Brooks and
further requesting an order authorizing such conservator to
consent to the administration of whole blood to the patient. No
notice of this proceeding was given any member of the Brooks
family. Thereafter, the conservator of the person was
appointed, consented to the administration of a blood
transfusion, it was accomplished and apparently successfully so,
although appellants now argue that much distress resulted from
transfusions due to a "circulatory overload".

We are met at the outset with appellee's contention that
since the blood transfusions have been given, the conservator
has been discharged, and the estate has been closed, this cause
is now moot . . .

"Before we reach the merits, we meet the State's contention
that the case is now moot and should be dismissed because the
blood transfusion has been administered, the guardian
discharged, and the proceeding dismissed. Because the function
of court is to decide controverted issues in adversary
proceedings, moot cases which do not present live issues are not
ordinarily entertained. 'The general rule is that when a
reviewing court has notice of facts which show that only moot
questions or mere abstract propositions are involved or where

the substantial questions involved in the trial court no longer exist, it will dismiss the appeal or writ of error' . . .

"But when the issue presented is of substantial public interest, a well-recognized exception exists to the general rule that a case which has become moot will be dismissed upon appeal . . . Among the criteria considered in determining the existence of the requisite degree of public interest are the public or private nature of the question presented, the desirability of an authoritative determination for the future guidance of public officers, and the likelihood of future recurrence of the question.

Applying these criteria, we find that the present case falls within that highly sensitive area in which governmental action comes into contact with the religious beliefs of individual citizens . . . In situations like this one, public authorities must act promptly if their action is to be effective, and although the precise limits of authorized conduct cannot be fixed in advance, no greater uncertainty should exist than the nature of the problems makes inevitable. In addition, the very urgency which presses for prompt action by public officials makes it probable that any similar case arising in the future will likewise become moot by ordinary standards before it can be determined by this court. For these reasons the case should not be dismissed as moot.

We accordingly proceed to a consideration of the issues.

It is argued by appellants that the absence of notice in any form to Mrs. Brooks or her husband, who were readily available at the hospital, constituted a denial of due process vitiating the entire proceedings; that insufficient proof was presented to establish the patient's incompetency (the doctor testified Mrs. Brooks was "semidisoriented" and not "fully capable" but also stated "I think she would consent to surgery. It is the fact this is a transfusion of blood she objects to"); and that acceptance of medical treatment previously refused because of religious and medical reasons (blood transfusions are not entirely free from hazard) cannot be judicially compelled under the circumstances here present.

While, under the particular circumstances here, some merit is to be found in all of these contentions, we believe we should predicate our decision upon the fundamental issue posed by these facts, i.e.: When approaching death has so weakened the mental and physical faculties of a theretofore competent adult without minor children that she may properly be said to be incompetent, may she be judicially compelled to accept treatment of a nature which will probably preserve her life, but which is forbidden by her religious convictions, and which she has previously steadfastly refused to accept, knowing death would result from such refusal? . . .

. . . It seems to be clearly established that the First Amendment of the United States Constitution as extended to the individual States by the Fourteenth Amendment to that constitution, protects the absolute right of every individual to freedom in his religious belief and the exercise thereof, subject only to the qualification that the exercise thereof may properly be limited by governmental action where such exercise endangers, clearly and presently, the public health, welfare or morals. Those cases which have sustained governmental action as against the challenge that it violated the religious guarantees of the First Amendment have found the proscribed practice to be immediately deleterious to some phase of public welfare, health or morality. The decisions which have held the conduct complained of immune from proscription involve no such public injury and no danger thereof.

Applying the constitutional guarantees and the interpretations thereof heretofore enunciated to the facts before us we find a competent adult who has steadfastly maintained her belief that acceptance of a blood transfusion is a violation of the law of God. Knowing full well the hazards involved, she has firmly opposed acceptance of such transfusions, notifying the doctor and hospital of her convictions and desires, and executing documents releasing both the doctor and the hospital from any civil liability which might be thought to result from a failure on the part of either to administer such transfusions. No minor children are involved. No overt or affirmative act of appellants offers any clear and present danger to society—we have only a governmental agency compelling conduct offensive to appellant's religious principles. Even though we may consider appellant's beliefs unwise, foolish or ridiculous, in the absence of an overriding danger to society we may not permit interference therewith in the form of a conservative established in the waning hours of her life for the sole purpose of compelling her to accept medical treatment forbidden by her religious principles, and previously refused by her with full knowledge of the probable consequences. In the final analysis, what has happened here involves a judicial attempt to decide what course of action is best for a particular individual, notwithstanding that individual's contrary views based upon religious convictions. Such action cannot be constitutionally countenanced . . .

o **Recap of the Case**. After the patient refused to consent to blood transfusions, the court appointed a guardian of the person to consent to treatment on behalf of the patient. The guardian of the patient's person consented, and blood transfusions were administered to the patient. The important point is that only a guardian of the person can authorize medical treatment. A guardian of the property can make decisions about property matters only and cannot consent to medical treatment.

Healthcare providers have often resisted the suggestion that a guardianship should be sought if the patient lacks capacity to consent. The primary objection has been that the proceedings cannot be accomplished in a reasonable amount of time. The first space on the court docket is often several months away. However, many state statutes provide for emergency or at least expedited guardianship proceedings depending upon the circumstances. It is not uncommon for a judge to hold a "hearing" in his chambers or at the patient's bedside at 2:00 a.m., if necessary. Lack of time is rarely, if ever, an excuse to avoid obtaining a guardian for a patient who lacks capacity in a non-emergency situation.

In some instances, consent may be obtained from an attorney-in-fact. Attorneys-in-fact are individuals authorized to act on behalf of other individuals who have executed a power of attorney authorizing certain actions on their behalf. Great caution must be exercised if consent is sought from an attorney-in-fact. A power of attorney is invalid unless executed while the incompetent individual was still competent—a matter which is often difficult to determine. Even if the patient was competent when the power of attorney was executed, the powers granted to the attorney-in-fact may or may not continue after the patient becomes disabled. The law differs from state to state on this point. Finally, a power of attorney is a highly individualized legal instrument which, depending upon its purpose, may or may not grant the right to an attorney-in-fact to consent to medical treatment. Like decrees of guardianship, powers of attorney must be carefully reviewed to determine what the patient has authorized.

NEITHER GUARDIAN NOR COURT CAN CONSENT TO PSYCHOSURGERY

In some instances, a court itself may make decisions regarding healthcare. There is no general rule; whether or not the court provides substitute consent depends upon circumstances in particular cases. One example of such circumstances is found in *Kaimowitz v. Michigan Department of Mental Health*.

This suit was brought by Plaintiff Kaimowitz on behalf of John Doe, an inmate at the Ionia State Prison, who was transferred to the Lafayette Clinic for the purpose of conducting experimental psychosurgery. John Doe was committed to the Ionia State Hospital as a criminal sexual psychopath after he was charged with the murder and subsequent rape of a student nurse at the Kalamazoo Hospital while confined there as a psychiatric patient.

John Doe was identified as a suitable subject to participate in a research project funded by the Michigan Legislature. The purpose of the study was to compare the effects of surgery and medication on uncontrollable aggression. John Doe was selected as a subject for psychosurgery.

The court first examined the "state of the art" with regard to psychosurgery. Based upon this examination, the court concluded that a great deal remains unknown about techniques and the effects of psychosurgery. Consequently, the proposed psychosurgery could be characterized as a high-risk, low-benefit procedure. That is, because of all of the uncertainties surrounding psychosurgery, the procedure was associated with many potential risks and unlikely to produce benefits for John Doe.

The court also attempted to determine if John Doe was able to consent to the psychosurgery. The court examined institutional environments and decided that they are inherently coercive. After an individual has been in an institution for a long period of time, like John Doe, the individual is unable to make a voluntary decision concerning his affairs.

The court concluded that an individual who is involuntarily detained for a long period of time cannot make a decision regarding a high-risk low-benefit procedure like psychosurgery. The court then considered the possibility that a guardian might be able to give consent on John Doe's behalf, but concluded that a guardian cannot consent to something the ward cannot consent to himself. Since neither guardian nor ward can consent under these circumstances, the decision must be made by the court itself. Based upon current knowledge in the field of psychosurgery, the court declined to consent on John Doe's behalf.

Kaimowitz v. Michigan Department of Mental Health,
Slip op.
(Circuit Court of Wayne County, Mich. July 10, 1973)
Circuit Court of Wayne County, Michigan

This case came to this Court originally on a complaint for a Writ of Habeas Corpus brought by Plaintiff Kaimowitz on behalf of John Doe and the Medical Committee for Human Rights, alleging that John Doe was being illegally detained in the Lafayette Clinic for the purpose of experimental psychotherapy.

John Doe had been committed by the Kalamazoo County Circuit Court on January 11, 1955, to the Ionia State Hospital as a Criminal Sexual Psychopath, without a trial of criminal charges, under the terms of the then existing Criminal Sexual Psychopathic law. He had been charged with the murder and subsequent rape of a student nurse at the Kalamazoo State Hospital while he was confined there as a mental patient.

In 1972, Drs. Ernst Rodin and Jacques Gottlieb of the Lafayette Clinic, a facility of the Michigan Department of Mental Health, had filed a proposal "For the Study of Treatment of Uncontrollable Aggression."

This was funded by the Legislature of the State of Michigan for the fiscal year 1972. After more than 17 years at the Ionia State Hospital, John Doe was transferred to the Lafayette Clinic in November of 1972 as a suitable research subject for the Clinic's study of uncontrollable aggression.

Under the terms of the study, 24 criminal sexual psychopaths in the State's mental health system were to be subjects of experiment. The experiment was to compare the effects of surgery on the amygdaloid portion of the limbic system of the brain with the effects of the drug cyproterone acetate on the male hormone flow. The comparison was intended to show which, if either, could be used in controlling aggression of males in an institutional setting, and to afford lasting permanent relief from such aggression to the patient.

Substantial difficulties were encountered in locating a suitable patient population for the surgical procedures and a matched controlled group for the treatment by the anti-androgen drug. As a matter of fact, it was concluded that John Doe was the only known appropriate candidate available within the state mental health system for the surgical experiment.

John Doe signed an "informed consent" form to become an experimental subject prior to his transfer from the Ionia State

Hospital. He had obtained signatures from his parents giving consent for the experimental and innovative surgical procedures to be performed on his brain, and two separate three-man review committees were established by Dr. Rodin to review the scientific worthiness of the study and the validity of the consent obtained from Doe.

The Scientific Review Committee, headed by Dr. Elliot Luby, approved of the procedure, and the Human Rights Review Committee, consisting of Ralph Slovenko, a Professor of Law and Psychiatry at Wayne State University, Monsignor Clifford Sawher, and Frank Moran, a Certified Public Accountant, gave their approval to the procedure.

Even though no experimental subjects were found to be available in the state mental health system other than John Doe, Dr. Rodin prepared to proceed with the equipment on Doe, and depth electrodes were to be inserted into his brain, on or about January 15, 1973.

Early in January, 1973, Plaintiff Kaimowitz became aware of the work being contemplated on John Doe and made his concern known to the Detroit Free Press. Considerable newpaper publicity ensued and this action was filed shortly thereafter.

With the rush of publicity on the filing of the original suit, funds for the research project were stopped by Dr. Gordon Yudashkin, Director of the Department of Mental Health, and the investigators, Drs. Gottlieb and Rodin, dropped their plans to pursue the research set out in the proposal. They reaffirmed at trial, however, their belief in the scientific, medical and ethical soundness of the proposal . . .

The facts concerning the original experiment and the involvement of John Doe were to be considered by the Court as illustrative in determining whether legally adequate consent could be obtained from adults involuntarily confined in the state mental health system for experimental or innovative procedures on the brain to ameliorate behavior, and, if it could be, whether the State should allow such experimentation on human subjects to proceed.

The two issues framed for decision in this declaratory judgment action are as follows:

1. After failure of established therapies, may an adult or a legally appointed guardian, if the adult is voluntarily detained, at a facility within the jurisdiction of the State Department of Mental Health give legally adequate consent to an innovative or experimental surgical procedure on the brain, if there is demonstrable physical abnormality of the brain, and the

procedure is designed to ameliorate behavior, which is either personally tormenting to the patient, or so profoundly disruptive that the patient cannot safely live, or live with others?

2. If the answer to the above is yes, then is it legal in this State to undertake an innovative or experimental surgical procedure on the brain of an adult who is involuntarily detained at a facility within the jurisdiction of the State Department of Mental Health, if there is demonstrable physical abnormality of the brain, and the procedure is designed to ameliorate behavior, which is either personally tormenting to the patient, or so profoundly disruptive that the patient cannot safely live, or live with others?

Throughout this Opinion, the Court will use the term psychosurgery to describe the proposed innovative or experimental surgical procedure defined in the questions for consideration by the Court.

At least two definitions of psychosurgery have been furnished the Court. Dr. Bertram S. Brown, Director of the National Institute of Mental Health, defined the term as follows in his prepared statement before the United States Senate Subcommittee on health of the Committee on Labor and Public Welfare on February 23, 1973:

> Psychosurgery can best be defined as surgical removal or destruction of brain tissue or the cutting of brain tissue to disconnect one part of the brain from another, with the intent of altering the behavior, even though there may be no direct evidence or structural disease or damage to the brain.

Dr. Peter Breggin, a witness at the trial, defined psychosurgery as the destruction of normal brain tissue for the control of emotions or behavior; or the destruction of abnormal brain tissue for the control of emotions or behavior, where the abnormal tissue has not been shown to be the cause of the emotions or behavior in question.

The psychosurgery involved in this litigation is a sub-class, narrower than that defined by Dr. Brown. The proposed psychosurgery we are concerned with encompasses only experimental psychosurgery where there are demonstrable physical abnormalities in the brain. Therefore, temporal lobectomy, an established therapy for relief of clearly diagnosed epilepsy is not involved, nor are accepted neurological surgical procedures, for example, operations for

Parkinsonism, or operations for the removal of tumors or the relief of stroke.

We start with the indisputable medical fact that no significant activity in the brain occurs in isolation without correlated activity in other parts of the brain. As the level of complexity of human behavior increases, so does the degree of interaction and integration. Dr. Ayub Ommaya, a witness in the case, illustrated this through the phenomenon of vision. Pure visual sensation is one of the functions highly localized in the occipital lobe in the back of the brain. However, vision in its broader sense, such as the ability to recognize a face, does not depend upon this area of the brain alone. It requires the integration of that small part of the brain with the rest of the brain. Memory mechanisms interact with the visual sensation to permit the recognition of the face. Dr. Ommaya pointed out that the more we know about brain function, the more we realize with certainty that many functions are highly integrated, even for relatively simple activity.

It is clear from the record in this case that the understanding of the limbic system of the brain and its function is very limited. Practically every witness and exhibit established how little is known of the relationship of the limbic system to human behavior, in the absence of some clearly defined clinical disease such as epilepsy. Drs. Mark, Sweet and Ervin have noted repeatedly the primitive state of our understanding of the amygdala, for example, remarking that it is an area made up of nine to fourteen different nuclear structures, with many functions, some of which are competitive with others. They state that there are not even reliable guesses as to the functional location of some of the nuclei.

The testimony showed that any physical intervention in the brain must always be approached with extreme caution. Brain surgery is always irreversible in the sense that any intrusion into the brain destroys the brain cells and such cells do not regenerate. Dr. Ommaya testified that in the absence of well defined pathological signs, such as blood clots pressing on the brain due to trauma, or tumor in the brain, brain surgery is viewed as a treatment of last resort.

The record in this case demonstrates that animal experimentation and nonintrusive human experimentation have not been exhausted in determining and studying brain function. Any experimentation on the human brain, especially when it involves an intrusive, irreversible procedure in a non life-threatening situation, should be undertaken with extreme caution, and then only when answers cannot be obtained from animal experimentation and from non-intrusive human experimentation.

Psychosurgery should never be undertaken upon involuntarily committed populations, when there is a high-risk low-benefit ratio as demonstrated in this case. This is because of the impossibility of obtaining truly informed consent from such populations. The reasons such informed consent cannot be obtained are set forth in detail subsequently in this Opinion.

There is widespread concern about violence. Personal violence, whether in a domestic setting or reflected in street violence, tends to increase. Violence in group confrontations appears to have culminated in the late 60's but still invites study and suggested solutions. Violence, personal and group, has engaged the criminal law courts and the correctional systems, and has inspired the appointment of national commissions. The late President Lyndon B. Johnson convened a commission on violence under the chairmanship of Dr. Milton Eisenhower. It was a commission that had fifty consultants representing various fields of law, sociology, criminology, history, government, social psychiatry, and social psychology. Conspicuous by their absence were any professionals concerned with the human brain. It is not surprising, then, that of recent date, there has been theorizing as to violence and the brain, and just over two years ago, Frank Ervin, a psychiatrist, and Vernon H. Mark, a neurosurgeon, wrote *Violence and the Brain* detailing the application of brain surgery to problems of violent behavior.

Problems of violence are not strangers to this Court. Over many years we have studied personal and group violence in a court context. Nor are we unconcerned about the tragedies growing out of personal or group confrontations. Deep-seated public concern begets an impatient desire for miracle solutions. And necessarily, we deal here not only with legal and medical issues, but with ethical and social issues as well.

Is brain function related to abnormal aggressive behavior? This, fundamentally, is what the case is about. But, one cannot segment or simplify that which is inherently complex. As Vernon H. Mark has written, "Moral values are social concerns, not medical ones, in any presently recognized sense."

Violent behavior not associated with brain disease should not be dealt with surgically. At best, neurosurgery rightfully should concern itself with medical problems and not the behavior problems of a social etiology.

The Court does not in any way desire to impede medical progress. We are much concerned with violence and the possible effect of brain disease on violence. Much research on the brain is necessary and must be carried on, but when it takes the form of psychosurgery, it cannot be undertaken on involuntarily detained populations. Other avenues of research must be utilized and developed.

Although extensive psychosurgery has been performed in the United States and throughout the world in recent years to attempt change of objectionable behavior, there is no medically recognized syndrome for aggression and objectionable behavior associated with nonorganic brain abnormality.

The psychosurgery that has been done has in varying degrees blunted emotions and reduced spontaneous behavior. Dr. V. Balasubramaniam, a leading psychosurgeon, has characterized psychosurgery as "sedative neurosurgery," a procedure by which patients are made quiet and manageable. The amygdalotomy, for example, has been used to calm hyperactive children, to make retarded children more manageable in institutions, to blunt the emotions of people with depression, and to attempt to make schizophrenics more manageable.

As pointed out above, psychosurgery is clearly experimental, poses substantial danger to research subjects, and carries substantial unknown risks. There is no persuasive showing on this record that the type of psychosurgery we are concerned with would necessarily confer any substantial benefit on research subjects or significantly increase the body of scientific knowledge by providing answers to problems of deviant behavior.

The dangers of such surgery are undisputed. Though it may be urged, as did some of the witnesses in this case, that the incidents of morbidity and mortality are low from the procedures, all agree dangers are involved, and the benefits to the patient are uncertain.

Absent a clearly defined medical syndrome, nothing pinpoints the exact location in the brain of the cause of undesirable behavior so as to enable a surgeon to make a lesion, remove that portion of the brain, and thus affect undesirable behavior.

Psychosurgery flattens emotional responses, leads to lack of abstract reasoning ability, leads to a loss of capacity for new learning and causes general sedation and apathy. It can lead to impairment of memory, and in some instances unexpected responses to psychosurgery are observed. It has been found, for example, that heightened rage reaction can follow surgical intervention on the amygdala, just as placidity can.

It was unanimously agreed by all witnesses that psychosurgery does not, given the present state of the art, provide any assurance that a dangerously violent person can be restored to the community.

Simply stated, on this record there is no scientific basis for establishing that the removal or destruction of an area of the limbic brain would have any direct therapeutic effect in controlling aggressivity or improving tormenting personal behavior, absent the showing of a well defined clinical syndrome such as epilepsy.

To advance scientific knowledge, it is true that doctors may desire to experiment on human beings, but the need for scientific inquiry must be reconciled with the inviolability which our society provides for a person's mind and body. Under a free government, one of a person's greatest rights is the right to inviolability of his person, and it is axiomatic that this right necessarily forbids the physician or surgeon from violating, without permission, the bodily integrity of the patient.

Generally, individuals are allowed free choice about whether to undergo experimental medical procedures. But the State has the power to modify this free choice concerning experimental medical procedures when it cannot be freely given, or when the result would be contrary to public policy. For example, it is obvious that a person may not consent to acts that will constitute murder, manslaughter, or mayhem upon himself. In short, there are times when the State for good reason should withhold a person's ability to consent to certain medical procedures.

It is elementary tort law that consent is the mechanism by which the patient grants the physician the power to act, and which protects the patient against unauthorized invasions of his person. This requirement protects one of society's most fundamental values, the inviolability of the individual. An operation performed upon a patient without his informed consent is the tort of battery, and a doctor and a hospital have no right to impose compulsory medical treatment against the patient's will . . .

Jay Katz, in his outstanding book *Experimentation with Human Beings* (Russell Sage Foundation, N.Y. (1972) points out on page 523 that the concept of informed consent has been accepted as a cardinal principle for judging the propriety of research with human beings.

He points out that in the experimental setting, informed consent serves multiple purposes. He states (pages 523 and 524):

. . . Most clearly, requiring informed consent serves society's desire to respect each individual's autonomy, and his right to make choices concerning his own life.

Second, providing a subject with information about an experiment will encourage him to be an active partner and the process may also increase the rationality of the experimentation process.

Third, securing informed consent protects the experimentation process by encouraging the investigator to question the value of the proposed project and the adequacy of the measures he has taken to protect subjects, by reducing civil and criminal liability for nonnegligent injury to the subjects, and by diminishing adverse public reaction to an experiment.

Finally, informed consent may serve the function of increasing society's awareness about human research . . .

It is obvious that there must be close scrutiny of the adequacy of the consent when an experiment, as in this case, is dangerous, intrusive, irreversible, and of uncertain benefit to the patient and society.

Counsel for Drs. Rodin and Gottlieb argues that anyone who has ever been treated by a doctor for any relatively serious illness is likely to acknowledge that a competent doctor can get almost any patient to consent to almost anything. Counsel claims this is true because patients do not want to make decisions about complex medical matters and because there is the general problem of avoiding decision making in stress situations, characteristic of all human beings.

He further argues that a patient is always under duress when hospitalized and that in a hospital or institutional setting there is no such thing as a volunteer. Dr. Ingelfinger in Volume 287, page 466, of the *New England Journal of Medicine* (August 31, 1972) states:

. . . The process of obtaining "informed consent" with all its regulations and conditions, is no more than an elaborate ritual, a device that when the subject is uneducated and uncomprehending, confers no more than the semblance of propriety on human experimentation. The subject's only real protection, the public as well as the medical profession must recognize, depends on the conscience and compassion of the investigator and his peers.

Everything defendant's counsel argues militates against the obtaining of informed consent from involuntarily detained mental patients. If, as he argues, truly informed consent cannot be given for regular surgical procedures by noninstitutionalized persons, then certainly an adequate informed consent cannot be given by the involuntarily detained mental patient.

We do not agree that a truly informed consent cannot be given for a regular surgical procedure by a patient, institutionalized or not. The law has long recognized that such valid consent can be given. But we do hold that informed consent cannot be given by an involuntarily detained mental patient for experimental psychosurgery for the reasons set forth below . . .

. . . [The] physician cannot experiment without restraint or restriction. He must consider first of all the welfare of his patient. This concept is universally accepted by the medical profession, the legal profession, and responsible persons who have thought and written on the matter.

Furthermore, he must weigh the risk to the patient against the benefit to be obtained by trying something new. The risk–benefit ratio is an important ratio in considering any experimental surgery upon a human being. The risk must always be relatively low, in the non life–threatening situation to justify human experimentation.

Informed consent is a requirement of variable demands. Being certain that a patient has consented adequately to an operation, for example, is much more important when doctors are going to undertake an experimental, dangerous, and intrusive procedure than, for example, when they are going to remove an appendix. When a procedure is experimental, dangerous, and intrusive, special safeguards are necessary. The risk–benefit ratio must be carefully considered, and the question of consent thoroughly explored.

To be legally adequate, a subject's informed consent must be competent, knowing and voluntary.

In considering consent for experimentation, the ten principles known as the Nuremberg code give guidance . . .

. . . Certain basic principles must be observed in order to satisfy moral, ethical and legal concepts:

1. The voluntary consent of the human subject is absolutely essential.

This means that the person involved should have legal capacity to give consent; should be so situated as to be able to exercise free power of choice, without the intervention of any element of force, fraud, deceit, duress, overreaching, or other ulterior form of constraint or coercion; and should have sufficient knowledge and comprehension of the elements of the subject matter involved as to enable him to make an understanding and enlightened decision. This latter element requires that before the acceptance of an affirmative decision by the experimental subject, there should be made known to him the nature, duration and purpose of the experiment; the method and means by which it is to be conducted; all inconveniences and hazards reasonably to be expected; and the effects upon his health or person which may possibly come from his participation in the experiment.

The duty and responsibility for ascertaining the quality of the consent rests upon each individual who initiates, directs, or engages in the experiment. It is a personal duty and responsibility which may not be delegated to another with impunity.

2. The experiment should be such as to yield fruitful results for the good of society unprocurable by other methods or means of study and not random and unnecessary in nature.

3. The experiment should be so designed and based on the results of animal experimentation and a knowledge of the natural history of the disease or other problem under study that the anticipated results will justify the performance of the experiment.

4. The experiment should be so conducted as to avoid all unnecessary physical and mental suffering and injury.

5. No experiment should be conducted where there is an *a priori* reason to believe that death or disabling injury will occur; except, perhaps, in those experiments where the experimental physicians also serve as subjects.

6. The degree of risk to be taken should never exceed that determined by the humanitarian importance of the problem to be solved by the experiment.

7. Proper preparations should be made and adequate facilities to protect the experimental subject against even remote possibilities of injury, disability, or death.

8. The experiment should be conducted only by scientifically qualified persons. The highest degree of skill and care should be required through all stages of the experiment of those who conduct or engage in the experiment.

9. During the course of the experiment the human subject should be at liberty to bring the experiment to an end if he has reached the physical or mental state where continuation of the experiment seems to him to be impossible.

10. During the course of the experiment the scientist in charge must be prepared to terminate the experiment at any stage, if he has probable cause to believe, in the exercise of

good faith, superior skill, and careful judgment required of him that a continuation of the experiment is likely to result in injury, disability, or death to the experimental subject.

In the Nuremberg Judgment, the elements of what must guide us in decisions are found. The involuntarily detained mental patient must have legal capacity to give consent. He must be so situated as to be able to exercise free power of choice without any element of force, fraud, deceit, duress, overreaching, or other ulterior form of restraint or coercion. He must have sufficient knowledge and comprehension of the subject matter to enable him to make an understanding decision. The decision must be a totally voluntary one on his part.

We must first look to the competency of the involuntarily detained mental patient to consent. Competency requires the ability of the subject to understand rationally the nature of the procedure, its risks, and other relevant information. The standard governing required disclosure by a doctor is what a reasonable patient needs to know in order to make an intelligent decision . . .

Although an involuntarily detained mental patient may have a sufficient I.Q. to intellectually comprehend his circumstances (in Dr. Rodin's experiment, a person was required to have at least an I.Q. of 80), the very nature of his incarceration diminishes the capacity to consent to psychosurgery. He is particularly vulnerable as a result of his mental condition, the deprivation stemming from involuntary confinement and the effects of the phenomenon of "institutionalization."

The very moving testimony of John Doe in the instant case establishes this beyond any doubt. The fact of institutional confinement has special force in undermining the capacity of the mental patient to make a competent decision on this issue, even though he be intellectually competent to do so. In the routine of institutional life, most decisions are made for patients. For example, John Doe testified about the possible submission to psychosurgery, and how unusual it was to be considered by a physician about his preference.

Institutionalization tends to strip the individual of the support which permits him to maintain his sense of self-worth and the value of his own physical and mental integrity. An involuntarily confined mental patient clearly has diminished capacity for making a decision about irreversible experimental psychosurgery.

Equally great problems are found when the involuntarily detained mental patient is incompetent, and consent is sought from a guardian or parent. Although guardian or parental consent may be legally adequate when arising out of traditional circumstances, it is legally ineffective in the psychosurgery situation. The guardian or parent cannot do that which the patient, absent a guardian, would be legally unable to do.

The second element of an informed consent is knowledge of the risk involved and the procedures to be undertaken. It was obvious from the record made in this case that the facts surrounding experimental brain surgery are profoundly uncertain, and the lack of knowledge on the subject makes a knowledgeable consent to psychosurgery literally impossible.

We turn now to the third element of an informed consent, that of voluntariness. It is obvious that the most important thing to a large number of involuntarily detained mental patients incarcerated for an unknown length of time, is freedom.

The Nuremberg standards require that the experimental subjects be so situated as to exercise free power of choice without the intervention of any element of force, fraud, deceit, duress, overreaching, or other ulterior form of constraint or coercion. It is impossible for an involuntarily detained mental patient to be free of ulterior forms of restraint or coercion when his very release from the institution may depend upon his cooperating with the institutional authorities and giving consent to experimental surgery.

The privileges of an involuntarily detained patient and the rights he exercises in the institution are within the control of the institutional authorities. As was pointed out in the testimony of John Doe, such minor things as the right to have a lamp in his room, or the right to have ground privileges to go for a picnic with his family assumed major proportions. For 17 years he lived completely under the control of the hospital. Nearly every important aspect of his life was decided without any opportunity on his part to participate in the decision–making process.

The involuntarily detained mental patient is in an inherently coercive atmosphere even though no direct pressures may be placed upon him. He finds himself stripped of customary amenities and defenses. Free movement is restricted. He becomes a part of communal living subject to the control of the institutional authorities.

As pointed out in the testimony in this case, John Doe consented to this psychosurgery partly because of his effort to show the doctors in the hospital that he was a cooperative patient. Even Dr. Yudashkin, in his testimony, pointed out that involuntarily confined patients tend to tell their doctors what the patient thinks these people want to hear.

The inherently coercive atmosphere to which the involuntarily detained mental patient is subjected has bearing upon the voluntariness of his consent. This was pointed up graphically by Dr. Watson in his testimony . . . There he was asked if there was any significant difference between the kinds of coercion that exist in an open hospital setting and the kinds of coercion that exist on involuntarily detained patients in a state mental institution.

Dr. Watson answered in this way:

> There is an enormous difference. My perception of the patients at Ionia is that they are willing almost to try anything to somehow or other improve their lot, which is--you know--not bad. It is just plain normal--you know--that kind of desire. Again, that pressure-- again--I don't like to use the word "coercion" because it implies a kind of deliberateness and that is not what we are talking about--the pressure to accede is perhaps the more accurate way. I think--the pressure is perhaps so severe that it probably ought to cause us to not be willing to permit experimentation that has questionable gain and high risk from the standpoint of the patient's posture, which is, you see, the formula that I mentioned we hashed out in our Human Use Committee.

Involuntarily confined mental patients live in an inherently coercive institutional environment. Indirect and subtle psychological coercion has profound effect upon the patient population. Involuntarily confined patients cannot reason as equals with the doctors and administrators over whether they should undergo psychosurgery. They are not able to voluntarily give informed consent because of the inherent inequality in their position.

It has been argued by defendants that because 13 criminal sexual psychopaths in the Ionia State Hospital wrote a letter indicating they did not want to be subjects of psychosurgery, that consent can be obtained and that the arguments about coercive pressure are not valid.

The Court does not feel that this necessarily follows. There is no showing of the circumstances under which the refusal of these thirteen patients was obtained, and there is no showing whatever that any effort was made to obtain the consent of these patients for such experimentation.

The fact that thirteen patients unilaterally wrote a letter saying they did not want to be subjects of psychosurgery is irrelevant to the question of whether they can consent to that which they are legally precluded from doing.

The law has always been meticulous in scrutinizing inequality in bargaining power and the possibility of undue influence in commercial fields and in the law of wills. It also has been most careful in excluding from criminal cases confessions where there was no clear showing of their completely voluntary nature after full understanding of the consequences. No lesser standard can apply to involuntarily detained mental patients.

The keystone to any intrusion upon the body of a person must be full, adequate and informed consent. The integrity of the individual must be protected from invasion into his body and personality not voluntarily agreed to. Consent is not an idle or symbolic act; it is a fundamental requirement for the protection of the individual's integrity.

We therefore conclude that involuntarily detained mental patients cannot give informed and adequate consent to experimental psychosurgical procedures on the brain.

The three basic elements of informed consent— competency, knowledge, and voluntariness—cannot be ascertained with a degree of reliability warranting resort to use of such an invasive procedure.

To this point, the Court's central concern has primarily been the ability of an involuntarily detained mental patient to give a factually informed, legally adequate consent to psychosurgery. However, there are also compelling constitutional considerations that preclude the involuntarily detained mental patient from giving effective consent to this type of surgery . . .

Initially, we consider the application of the First Amendment to the problem before the Court, recognizing that when the State's interest is in conflict with the Federal Constitution, the State's interest, even though declared by statute or court rule, must give away . . .

A person's mental processes, the communication of ideas, and the generation of ideas, come within the ambit of the First Amendment. To the extent that the First Amendment protects the dissemination of ideas and expression of thoughts, it equally must protect the individual's right to generate ideas . . .

Freedom of speech and expression, and the right of all men to disseminate ideas, popular or unpopular, are fundamental to ordered liberty. Government has no power or right to control men's minds, thoughts, and expressions. This is the command of the First Amendment. And we adhere to it in holding that an involuntarily detained mental patient may not consent to experimental psychosurgery.

For, if the First Amendment protects the freedom to express ideas, it necessarily follows that it must protect the freedom to generate ideas. Without the latter protection, the former is meaningless.

Experimental psychosurgery, which is irreversible and intrusive, often leads to the blunting of emotions, the deadening of memory, the reduction of effect, and limits the ability to generate new ideas. Its potential for injury to the creativity of the individual is great, and can impinge upon the right of the individual to be free from interference with his mental processes.

The State's interest in performing psychosurgery and the legal ability of the involuntarily detained mental patient to give consent must bow to the First Amendment, which protects the generation and free flow of ideas from unwarranted interference with one's mental processes.

To allow an involuntarily detained mental patient to consent to the type of psychosurgery proposed in this case, and to permit the State to perform it, would be to condone the State action in violation of basic First Amendment rights of such patients, because impairing the power to generate ideas inhibits the full dissemination of ideas.

There is no showing in this case that the State has met its burden of demonstrating such a compelling State interest in the use of experimental psychosurgery on involuntarily detained mental patients to overcome its proscription by the First Amendment of the United States Constitution.

In recent years, the Supreme Court of the United States has developed a constitutional concept of right of privacy, relying upon the First, Fifth and Fourteenth Amendments . . .

There is no privacy more deserving of constitutional protection than that of one's mind . . .

Intrusion into one's intellect, when one is involuntarily detained and subject to the control of institutional authorities, is an intrusion into one's constitutionally protected right of privacy. If one is not protected in his thoughts, behavior, personality and identity, then the right of privacy becomes meaningless.

Before a State can violate one's constitutionally protected right of privacy and obtain a valid consent for experimental psychosurgery on involuntarily detained mental patients, a compelling State interest must be shown. None has been shown here . . .

Counsel for John Doe has argued persuasively that the use of the psychosurgery proposed in the instant case would constitute cruel and unusual punishment and should be barred under the Eighth Amendment. A determination of this issue is not necessary to decision, because of the many other legal and constitutional reasons for holding that the involuntarily detained mental patient may not give an informed and valid consent to experimental psychosurgery. We therefore do not pass on the issue of whether the psychosurgery proposed in this case constitutes cruel and unusual punishment within the meaning of the Eighth Amendment.

For the reasons given, we conclude that the answer to question number one posed for decision is no.

In reaching this conclusion, we emphasize two things.

First, the conclusion is based upon the state of the knowledge as of the time of the writing of this Opinion. When the state of medical knowledge develops to the extent that the type of psychosurgical intervention proposed here becomes an accepted neurosurgical procedure and is no longer experimental, it is possible, with appropriate review mechanisms, that involuntarily detained mental patients could consent to such an operation.

Second, we specifically hold that an involuntarily detained mental patient today can give adequate consent to accepted neurosurgical procedures.

In view of the fact we have answered the first question in the negative, it is not necessary to proceed to a consideration of the second question, although we cannot refrain from noting that had the answer to the first question been yes, serious constitutional problems would have arisen with reference to the second question.

o **Recap of the Case**. This case examines the question: Who may consent to high-risk, low-benefit medical procedures like psychosurgery. The court decided that patients who are in institutions for a long period of time are unable to give consent because of the inherent coerciveness of institutional environments. The court then examined the possibility of substitute consent by a guardian or the court itself and rejected both of these alternatives. Since consent cannot be obtained, the surgery cannot be performed. Providers should be aware that the same reasoning may apply to other high risk procedures which produce little benefit for the patient.

6

Special Situations:
Abortion and Sterilization

Some of the most difficult questions concerning substitute and concurrent consent are raised in regard to consent to sterilization and abortion by both competent and incompetent adults.

HUSBAND'S CONSENT TO STERILIZATION UNNECESSARY

A competent adult may consent to sterilization whether single or married. Concurrent consent of a spouse is not required.

This rule is illustrated by *Murray v. VanDevander*. In this case, the plaintiff was the husband of a competent, adult woman who was sterilized by the defendant. Prior to the surgery, plaintiff informed defendant that he strenuously objected to his wife's sterilization. Nonetheless, his wife elected to go ahead with the procedure. Following the operation, plaintiff sued defendant for loss of the right to reproduce another child. The court rejected all of plaintiff's arguments and affirmed that every adult woman may consent to surgery, including sterilization, without concurrent approval from anyone.

The situation described in *Murray* raises many concerns about honoring the desires of family members and "next of kin." Since nurses must often obtain signatures on consent forms, for example, they must confront irate husbands opposed to sterilization. Nurses undoubtedly experience great discomfort when patients' spouses oppose treatment. Nonetheless, nurses are required to "stick to their guns" in this type of situation. If nurses do not understand the law and their role in relation to it, competent adult women may be deprived of their right to receive certain types of medical treatment by interfering relatives.

However, restrictions on the process of consent to sterilization have been imposed by federal regulations. 42 C.F.R. §50.201 et seq. These regulations apply *only* to sterilization through programs or projects for health services which are supported in whole or in part by federal financial assistance programs administered by the Public Health Service. Such programs include the Medicaid program. The key requirements of these regulations include an absolute prohibition against performing sterilization procedures on anyone who is not at least twenty–one years of age. (Remember that in most states the age of majority is eighteen, not twenty–one, so that most eighteen year olds can consent to and undergo sterilization.) In addition, at least 30 days, but not more than 180 days, must have passed between the date of informed consent and the date of sterilization, except in cases of premature delivery or emergency abdominal surgery, in which case at least 72 hours must have passed after consent was given. This requirement also goes beyond the normal requirements of the law of informed consent. Except in cases to which these regulations apply, a competent adult may consent to sterilization and undergo the procedure immediately.

There are similarities between the requirements outlined in these regulations and the law of informed consent. The information practitioners are required to convey is the same. Neither the regulations nor court decisions involving informed consent will accept consent obtained while patients lack capacity for any reason. Spousal consent is not required by the regulations or the courts. Nurses whose practices include many Medicaid patients should pay special attention to these regulations.

COURTS MAY ORDER STERILIZATION WITHOUT INCURRING LIABILITY FOR INCORRECT DECISIONS

Additional difficulties are encountered, however, when the individual to be sterilized is an incompetent adult. Sterilization of incompetent adults is frequently sought for both males and females based on eugenic considerations, i.e. a desire to avoid perpetuation of mental impairments through heredity, and/or on the basis of convenience. As a practical matter, it may be difficult for some female adults lacking capacity to be responsible for their own hygiene during menstruation. Generally speaking, guardians may not consent to sterilization of their wards. In most cases, specific court authorization must be obtained. The definitive court case on this issue is *Stump v. Sparkman.*

The circumstances of this case are indeed tragic. Ora Spitler McFarlin, the mother of plaintiff Linda Kay Spitler Sparkman, filed a petition when Linda was fifteen years old asking the court to order that a tubal ligation should be performed on Linda. (That Linda's mother had to have the permission of the court represented a dramatic change in the law. Parents and even administrators of institutions for the mentally disabled previously caused mentally disabled persons, or those thought to be so disabled, to be sterilized by tubal ligation, vasectomy or hysterectomy without court approval.) The reasons for Mrs. McFarlin's request were that Linda was "somewhat retarded" and was staying out overnight with men. The petition was approved by Judge Stump, and Linda, who believed she was undergoing an appendectomy, was sterilized. Years later, after she was married and could not conceive, Linda learned that she had been sterilized. She then sued Judge Stump, attempting to hold him responsible for the approval of her mother's petition.

The Supreme Court of the United States decided this case. The court first stated that judges may approve requests that sterilization procedures be performed on the mentally disabled. The court then considered whether judges may be liable for improper decisions concerning sterilization. Recognizing the extreme importance of judicial immunity from liability in order to allow judges to perform their functions, the court refused to hold judges responsible for incorrect decisions concerning sterilization.

Murray v. VanDevander, 522 P.2d 302 (Okla.Ct.App. 1974)
Oklahoma Court of Appeals

. . . This action was commenced by appellant, hereafter called plaintiff, against appellees D. C. VanDevander, St. John's Hospital, and Hillcrest Medical Center . . . It is further alleged that VanDevander performed a hysterectomy on Artie V. Murray, wife of plaintiff, without her husband's consent. There was no allegation that the operation was unsuccessful or that

VanDevander was negligent. Plaintiff alleged that the actions of the defendants had interfered with the marital rights of the plaintiff and his wife. The petition further states that VanDevander "induced, and by the means of overreaching and unprofessional medical advice, prevailed upon the wife of plaintiff to submit to such surgery, . . ." The petition further states that "the plaintiff had warned and specifically notified said defendant that he did not approve, but in fact, strenuously objected to the performance of such surgery." As a result of the damage alleged to have been incurred by appellant to his right of consortium and "the right to reproduce another child", plaintiff sought recovery in the amount of $100,000.00.

The question presented on appeal is whether a husband can recover from a physician and hospitals for damage to a marital relationship resulting from an operation on the wife, consented to by her. It is the opinion of this court that such recovery was rightfully denied by the trial court . . .

We believe that the general rule in such cases is . . . as follows:

A married woman in full possession of her faculties has power, without consent of her husband, to submit to a surgical operation upon herself, and he has no inherent power to consent to a dangerous operation on her.

In his petition, plaintiff sought recovery for damage to his "right to reproduce another child." We have found no authority and plaintiff has cited none which holds that the husband has a right to a child–bearing wife as an incident to their marriage. We are neither prepared to create a right in a husband to have a fertile wife nor to allow recovery for damage to such a right. We find that the right of a person who is capable of competent consent to control his own body is paramount.

There is no allegation in the petition that plaintiff's wife was of diminished capacity or otherwise incapable of consent. There was no necessity for the physician in the instant case to obtain the consent of the plaintiff. No duty was breached by performance of the operation without consent of the husband of the patient.

It is argued by the plaintiff that VanDevander secured consent for the operation in question by means of "overreaching and unprofessional medical advice." Plaintiff contends that the use of his confidential and professional position by VanDevander to obtain the consent of plaintiff's wife renders such consent void. It is the opinion of this court that the plaintiff's wife rather than the plaintiff would be the proper party to complain of such behavior by the physician . . .

Affirmed.

Stump v. Sparkman, 435 U.S. 349 (1979)
Supreme Court of the United States

. . . On July 9, 1971, Ora Spitler McFarlin, the mother of respondent Linda Kay Spitler Sparkman, presented to Judge Harold D. Stump of the Circuit Court of DeKalb County, Ind., a document captioned "Petition To Have Tubal Ligation Performed on Minor and Indemnity Agreement." The document had been drafted by her attorney, a petitioner here. In this petition Mrs. McFarlin stated under oath that her daughter was 15 years of age and was "somewhat retarded," although she attended public school and had been promoted each year with her class. The petition further stated that Linda had been associating with "older youth or young men" and had stayed out overnight with them on several occasions. As a result of this behavior and Linda's mental capabilities, it was stated that it would be in the daughter's best interest if she underwent a tubal ligation in order "to prevent unfortunate circumstances . . ." In the same document Mrs. McFarlin also undertook to indemnify and hold harmless Dr. John Hines, who was to perform the operation, and the DeKalb Memorial Hospital, where the operation was to take place, against all causes of action that might arise as a result of the performance of the tubal ligation.

The petition was approved by Judge Stump on the same day. He affixed his signature as "Judge, DeKalb Circuit Court," to the statement that he did "hereby approve the above Petition by affidavit form on behalf of Ora Spitler McFarlin, to have Tubal Ligation performed upon her minor daughter, Linda Spitler, subject to said Ora Spitler McFarlin covenanting and agreeing to indemnify and keep indemnified Dr. John Hines and DeKalb Memorial Hospital from any matters or causes of action arising therefrom." On July 15, 1971, Linda Spitler entered the DeKalb Memorial Hospital, having been told that she was to have her appendix removed. The following day a tubal ligation was performed upon her. She was released several days later, unaware of the true nature of her surgery. Approximately two years after the operation, Linda Spitler was married to respondent Leo Sparkman. Her inability to become pregnant led her to discover that she had been sterilized during the 1971 operation. As a result of this revelation, the Sparkmans filed suit in the United States District Court for the Northern District of Indiana against Mrs. McFarlin, her attorney, Judge Stump, the doctors who had performed and assisted in the tubal ligation, and the DeKalb Memorial Hospital. Respondents sought damages for the alleged violation of Linda Sparkman's constitutional rights; also asserted were pendent state claims for assault and battery, medical malpractice, and loss of potential fatherhood . . .

The governing principle of law is well established and is not questioned by the parties. As early as 1872, the Court recognized that it was "a general principle of the highest importance to the proper administration of justice that a judicial officer, in exercising the authority vested in him, [should] be free to act upon his own convictions, without apprehension of personal consequences to himself . . . For that reason the Court held that "judges of courts of superior or general jurisdiction are not liable to civil actions for their judicial acts, even when such acts are in excess of their jurisdiction, and are alleged to have been done maliciously or corruptly" . . .

. . . [T]he necessary inquiry in determining whether a defendant judge is immune from suit is whether at the time he took the challenged action he had jurisdiction over the subject matter before him. Because "some of the most difficult and embarrassing questions which a judicial officer is called upon to consider and determine relate to his jurisdiction . . . ," . . . the scope of the judge's jurisdiction must be construed broadly where the issue is the immunity of the judge. A judge will not be deprived of immunity because the action he took was in error, was done maliciously, or was in excess of his authority; rather, he will be subject to liability only when he has acted in the "clear absence of all jurisdiction" . . .

We cannot agree that there was a "clear absence of all jurisdiction" in the DeKalb County Circuit Court to consider the petition presented by Mrs. McFarlin. As an Indiana Circuit Court Judge, Judge Stump had "original exclusive jurisdiction in all cases at law and in equity whatsoever . . . ," jurisdiction over the settlement of estates and over guardianships, appellate jurisdiction as conferred by law, and jurisdiction over "all other causes, matters and proceedings where exclusive jurisdiction thereof is not conferred by law upon some other court, board or officer . . ." It is true that the statutory grant of general jurisdiction to the Indiana circuit courts does not itemize types of cases those courts may hear and hence does not expressly mention sterilization petitions presented by the parents of a minor. But in our view, it is more significant that there was no Indiana statute and no case law in 1971 prohibiting a circuit court, a court of general jurisdiction, from considering a petition of the type presented to Judge Stump. The statutory authority for the sterilization of institutionalized persons in the custody of the State does not warrant the inference that a court of general jurisdiction has no power to act on a petition for sterilization of a minor in the custody of her parents, particularly where the parents have authority under the Indiana statutes to "consent to and contract for medical or hospital care or treatment of [the minor] including surgery." . . . [N]either by statute or case law has the broad jurisdiction granted to the circuit courts of Indiana been circumscribed to foreclose consideration of a petition for authorization of a minor's sterilization . . .

. . . Because the court over which Judge Stump presides is one of general jurisdiction, neither the procedural errors he may have committed nor the lack of a specific statute authorizing his approval of the petition in question rendered him liable in damages for the consequences of his actions.

The respondents argue that even if Judge Stump had jurisdiction to consider the petition presented to him by Mrs. McFarlin, he is still not entitled to judicial immunity because his approval of the petition did not constitute a "judicial" act. It is only for acts performed in his "judicial" capacity that a judge is absolutely immune, they say. We do not disagree with this statement of the law, but we cannot characterize the approval of the petition as a nonjudicial act.

Respondents themselves stated in their pleadings before the District Court that Judge Stump was "clothed with the authority of the state" at the time that he approved the petition and that "he was acting as a county circuit judge" . . . They nevertheless now argue that Judge Stump's approval of the petition was not a judicial act because the petition was not given a docket number, was not placed on file with the clerk's office, and was approved in an ex parte proceeding without notice to the minor, without a hearing, and without the appointment of a guardian ad litem.

This Court has not had occasion to consider, for purposes of the judicial immunity doctrine, the necessary attributes of a judicial act; but it has previously rejected the argument, somewhat similar to the one raised here, that the lack of formality involved in the Illinois Supreme Court's consideration of petitioner's application for admission to the state bar prevented it from being a "judicial proceeding" and from presenting a case or controversy that could be reviewed by this Court . . .

The relevant cases demonstrate that the factors determining whether an act by a judge is a "judicial" one relate to the nature of the act itself, i.e., whether it is a function normally performed by a judge, and to the expectations of the parties, i.e., whether they dealt with the judge in his judicial capacity. Here, both factors indicate that Judge Stump's approval of the sterilization petition was a judicial act. State judges with general jurisdiction not infrequently are called upon in their official capacity to approve petitions relating to the affairs of minors, as for example, a petition to settle a minor's claim. Furthermore, as even respondents have admitted, at the time he approved the petition presented to him by Mrs. McFarlin, Judge Stump was "acting as a county circuit judge" . . . We may infer from the record that it was only because Judge Stump served in that position that Mrs. McFarlin, on the advice of counsel, submitted the petition to him for his approval. Because Judge Stump performed the type of act normally performed only by judges and because he did so in his capacity as a Circuit Court Judge, we find no merit to respondents' argument that the informality with which he proceeded rendered his action nonjudicial and deprived him of his absolute immunity.

Both the Court of Appeals and the respondents seem to suggest that, because of the tragic consequences of Judge Stump's actions, he should not be immune. For example, the Court of Appeals noted that "[t]here are actions of purported judicial character that a judge, even when exercising general jurisdiction, is not empowered to take," . . . and respondents argue that Judge Stump's action was "so unfair" and "so totally devoid of judicial concern for the interests and well-being of the young girl involved" as to disqualify it as a judicial act . . . Disagreement with the action taken by the judge, however, does not justify depriving the judge of his immunity. Despite the unfairness to litigants that sometimes results, the doctrine of judicial immunity is thought to be in the best interests of "the proper administration of justice . . . [for it allows] a judicial officer, in exercising the authority vested in him [to] be free to act upon his own convictions, without apprehension of personal consequences to himself" . . . The fact that the issue before the judge is a controversial one is all the more reason that he should be able to act without fear of suit . . .

The Indiana law vested in Judge Stump the power to entertain and act upon the petition for sterilization. He is, therefore, under the controlling cases, immune from damages liability even if his approval of the petition was in error. Accordingly, the judgment of the Court of Appeals is reversed, and the case is remanded for further proceedings consistent with this opinion.

o **Recap of the Cases**. These two cases provide excellent guidance for nurses who must make decisions about adequate consent to sterilization. Clearly, competent adults may consent to sterilization without concurrent consent from anyone else. Competent adult women can consent to sterilization even if their husbands object. Guardians of the person usually cannot consent to sterilization. Apart from patients themselves, only courts may order patients sterilized. While these two cases happen to involve women, the principles stated above also apply to men.

ONLY COMPETENT WOMAN'S CONSENT NECESSARY TO UNDERGO ABORTION

A competent female adult may consent to an abortion. Spousal or concurrent consent may not constitutionally be required prior to an abortion. Generally speaking, a guardian may consent to abortion on behalf of an incompetent adult. The most important case addressing these issues is *Planned Parenthood of Central Missouri v. Danforth.*

The decision in this case was also made by the Supreme Court of the United States, which means that it applies throughout the country. The opinion of the court is divided into sections. Section C contains the court's discussion about the need for spousal consent before women can have abortions. According to the court, decisions concerning abortion should be made jointly. However, when partners cannot agree, the woman's wishes prevail because the woman must carry and bear the child. Primarily for this reason, the court decided that women can have abortions without their husbands' approval and even over their objections.

Planned Parenthood of Central Missouri v. Danforth
428 U.S. 52 (1976)
Supreme Court of the United States

. . . *The women's consent*. Under the Missouri Act [governing abortions] a woman, prior to submitting to an abortion during the first 12 weeks of pregnancy, must certify in writing her consent to the procedure and "that her consent is informed and freely given and is not the result of coercion." Appellants argue that this requirement . . . [imposes] an extra layer and burden of regulation on the abortion decision . . . Appellants also claim that the provision is overbroad and vague.

. . . [T]he decision to terminate a pregnancy, of course, "is often a stressful one," and . . . the consent requirement . . ." insures that the pregnant woman retains control over the discretions of her consulting physician." . . . [T]he consent requirement "does not single out the abortion procedure, but merely includes it within the category of medical operations for which consent is required" . . .

. . . Despite the fact that apparently no other Missouri statute . . . requires a patient's prior written consent to a surgical procedure, the imposition . . . of such a requirement for termination of pregnancy even during the first state, in our view, is not in itself an unconstitutional requirement. The decision to abort, indeed, is an important, and often a stressful one, and it is desirable and imperative that it be made with full knowledge of its nature and consequences. The woman is the one primarily concerned, and her awareness of the decision and its significance may be assured, constitutionally, by the State to the extent of requiring her prior written consent.

We could not say that a requirement imposed by the State that a prior written consent for any surgery would be unconstitutional. As a consequence, we see no constitutional defect in requiring it only for some types of surgery as, for example, an intracardiac procedure, or where the surgical risk is elevated above a specific mortality level, or, for that matter, for abortions.

The spouse's consent. [The Missouri statute] requires the prior written consent of the spouse of the woman seeking an abortion during the first 12 weeks of pregnancy, unless "the abortion is certified by a licensed physician to be necessary in order to preserve the life of the mother."

The appellees defend . . . on the ground that it was enacted in the light of the General Assembly's "perception of marriage as an institution" . . . and that any major change in family status is a decision to be made jointly by the marriage partners. Reference is made to an abortion's possible effect on the woman's childbearing potential . . . It is argued that "[r]ecognizing that the consent of both parties is generally necessary . . . to begin a family, the legislature has determined that a change in the family structure set in motion by mutual consent should be terminated only by mutual consent" . . . and that what the legislature did was to exercise its inherent policymaking power "for what was believed to be in the best interests of all the people of Missouri."

The appellants on the other hand, contend that [it] obviously is designed to afford the husband the right unilaterally to prevent or veto an abortion, whether or not he is the father of the fetus, and that this . . . is also in conflict with other decided cases . . . They also refer to the situation where the husband's consent cannot be obtained because he cannot be located . . .

. . . We now hold that the State may not constitutionally require the consent of the spouse, as is specified under . . . the Missouri Act, as a condition for abortion during the first 12 weeks of pregnancy . . . [T]he State cannot "delegate to a spouse a veto power which the state itself is absolutely and totally prohibited from exercising during the first trimester of pregnancy" . . . Since the State cannot regulate or proscribe abortion during the first stage, when the physician and his patient make that decision, the State cannot delegate authority to any particular person, even the spouse, to prevent abortion during that same period.

We are not unaware of the deep and proper concern and interest that a devoted and protective husband has in his wife's pregnancy and in the growth and development of the fetus she is carrying. Neither has this Court failed to appreciate the importance of the marital relationship in our society . . . Moreover, we recognize that the decision whether to undergo or to forego an abortion may have profound effects on the future of any marriage, effects that are both physical and mental, and possibly deleterious. Notwithstanding these factors, we cannot hold that the State has the constitutional authority to give the spouse unilaterally the ability to prohibit the wife from terminating her pregnancy, when the State itself lacks that right..

It seems manifest that, ideally, the decision to terminate a pregnancy should be one concurred in by both the wife and her husband. No marriage may be viewed as harmonious or successful if the marriage partners are fundamentally divided on so important and vital an issue. But it is difficult to believe that the goal of fostering mutuality and trust in a marriage, and of strengthening the marital relationship and the marriage institution, will be achieved by giving the husband a veto power exercisable for any reason whatsoever or for no reason at all. Even if the State had the ability to delegate to the husband a power it itself could not exercise, it is not at all likely that such action would further, as the District Court majority phrased it, the "interest of the state in protecting the mutuality of decisions vital to the marriage relationship." . . .

We recognize, of course, that when a woman, with the approval of her physician but without the approval of her husband, decides to terminate her pregnancy, it could be said that she is acting unilaterally. The obvious fact is that when the wife and the husband disagree on this decision, the view of only one of the two marriage partners can prevail. Inasmuch as it is the woman who physically bears the child and who is the more directly and immediately affected by the pregnancy, as between the two, the balance weighs in her favor.

Parental consent. [The statute] requires, with respect to the first 12 weeks of pregnancy, where the woman is unmarried and under the age of 18 years, the written consent of a parent or person *in loco parentis* unless, again, "the abortion is certified as necessary in order to preserve the life of the mother." It is to be observed that only one parent need consent.

The appellees defend the statute in several ways. They point out that the law properly may subject minors to more stringent limitations than are permissible with respect to adults . . . It is pointed out that the record contains testimony to the effect that children of tender years (even ages 10 and 11) have sought abortions. Thus, a State's permitting a child to obtain an abortion without the consent of an adult "who has responsibility or concern for the child would constitute an irresponsible abdication of the State's duty to protect the welfare of minors" . . . Finally, it is said that [this Section] imposes no additional burden on the physician because even prior to the passage of the Act the physician would require parental consent before performing an abortion on a minor.

The appellants, in their turn, emphasize that no other Missouri statute specifically requires the additional consent of a minor's parent for medical or surgical treatment, and that in Missouri a minor legally may consent to medical services for pregnancy (excluding abortion), venereal disease, and drug abuse . . . It is noted that in Missouri a woman under the age of 18 who marries with parental consent does not require parental consent to abort, and yet her contemporary who has chosen not to marry must obtain parental approval . . .

. . . [T]he State may not impose a blanket provision . . . requiring the consent of a parent or person *in loco parentis* as a condition for abortion of an unmarried minor during the first 12 weeks of her pregnancy. Just as with the requirement of consent from the spouse, so here, the State does not have the constitutional authority to give a third party an absolute, and possibly arbitrary, veto over the decision of the physician and his patient to terminate the patient's pregnancy, regardless of the reason for withholding the consent.

Constitutional rights do not mature and come into being magically only when one attains the state–defined age of majority. Minors, as well as adults, are protected by the Constitution and possess constitutional rights . . . The Court indeed, however, long has recognized that the State has somewhat broader authority to regulate the activities of children than of adults . . . It remains, then, to examine whether there is any significant state interest in conditioning an abortion on the consent of a parent or person *in loco parentis* that is not presently in the case of an adult.

One suggested interest is the safeguarding of the family unit and of parental authority . . . It is difficult, however, to conclude that providing a parent with absolute power to overrule a determination, made by the physician and his minor patient, to terminate the patient's pregnancy will serve to strengthen the family unit. Neither is it likely that such veto power will enhance parental authority or control where the minor and the nonconsenting parent are so fundamentally in conflict and the very existence of the pregnancy already has fractured the family structure. Any independent interest the parent may have in the termination of the minor daughter's pregnancy is no more weighty than the right of privacy of the competent minor mature enough to have become pregnant . . .

The judgment of the District Court is affirmed in part and reversed in part, and the case is remanded for further proceedings consistent with this opinion.

o **Recap of the Case**. Courts certainly recognize that, ideally speaking, a decision to undergo an abortion is a mutual one between husband and wife or parent and child, if the patient is a minor. However, the courts also recognize that mutual agreement about abortions is not always possible. In these situations, women, including minors, are free to make the decision alone, and these decisions must be honored.

Part III

WITHDRAWAL AND REFUSAL OF TREATMENT

7

Adults for Themselves

Once given, consent may be withdrawn at any time. It may be withdrawn by 1) a gesture, 2) verbally, or 3) in writing. Obviously, written withdrawal is most desirable in terms of risk management since it provides a record of the patient's decision.

As a practical matter, nurses are likely to hear of the patient's withdrawal of consent first. What should nurses do when patients change their minds and no longer wish to permit a particular procedure? First, nurses must be extremely careful not to put pressure on the patient so that the patient may later claim that consent was withdrawn but that the nursing staff resisted and refused to honor the patient's wishes. All the nurse has to do is acknowledge to the patient that she understands the patient's wishes and will communicate them to all personnel including physicians. After acknowledging the patient's decision, the nurse must immediately document in the patient's chart what happened. Her notes should include the date and time of withdrawal, a description of what the patient said or did to withdraw consent, the patient's emotional state, whether the patient appeared to be lucid and free from the influence of drugs, etc., as well as the names of any witnesses to the patient's withdrawal. She should then notify all appropriate personnel of the patient's decision and document that she has done so. Finally, a written document evidencing the patient's withdrawal of consent should be prepared and signed by the patient. Nurses should notify the proper person and assist them to prepare the form and to get it signed by the patient.

COMPETENT PATIENT'S DECISION TO REFUSE
TREATMENT UPHELD

Just as competent patients have the right to consent to treatment or withdraw consent, they also have the right to withhold consent or refuse to consent altogether. Competent adults may refuse treatment. *Lane v. Candura*, is an example of a case in which a competent adult's decision to refuse treatment was affirmed by the court.

Mrs. Candura had gangrene of her right leg and foot. Although she was somewhat confused, she refused to consent to amputation of her foot in order to save her life. Her daughter then asked the court to appoint her temporary guardian for her mother so that she could consent to surgery on her behalf. The court considered testimony from a number of sources and concluded that Mrs. Candura was a competent adult who was free to refuse treatment. The main reason for the judge's decision was that he was convinced that Mrs. Candura understood the consequences of her decision to refuse treatment, which included death. Thus, when patients refuse treatment, nurses should first assess whether the patient understands the consequences of refusal. If the patient seems to understand and is a competent adult, the patient's refusal must be honored. If the patient does not seem to understand the consequences of refusal, nurses should seek direction immediately from administration and legal counsel.

Lane v. Candura, 376 N.E.2d 1232 (Mass.App.1978)
Massachusetts Appeals Court

This case concerns a 77 year old widow, Mrs. Rosaria Candura, of Arlington, who is presently a patient at the Symmes Hospital in Arlington suffering from gangrene in the right foot and lower leg. Her attending physicians recommended in April that the leg be amputated without delay. After some vacillation, she refused to consent to the operation, and she persists in that refusal. Her daughter, Grace R. Lane of Medford, filed a petition in the Probate Court for Middlesex County seeking appointment of herself as temporary guardian with authority to consent to the operation on behalf of her mother. An order and a judgment were entered in the Probate Court to that effect, from which the guardian ad litem appointed to represent Mrs. Candura has appealed.

We hold that Mrs. Candura has the right under the law to refuse to submit either to medical treatment or a surgical operation, that on the evidence and findings in this case the decision is one that she may determine for herself, and that therefore her leg may not be amputated unless she consents to that course of action.

. . . "The constitutional right to privacy, as we conceive it, is an expression of the sanctity of individual free choice and self–determination as fundamental constituent of life. The value of life as so perceived is lessened not by a decision to refuse treatment, but by the failure to allow a competent human being the right of choice" . . . the case before us does not involve factors which would . . . warrant a court's overriding the will of a competent person.

The principal question arising on the record before us, therefore, is whether Mrs. Candura has the legally requisite competence of mind and will to make the choice for herself. We look first to the findings of fact made by the judge who heard the testimony, including that of Mrs. Candura herself. His decision does not include a clear–cut finding that Mrs. Candura lacks the requisite legal competence. The nearest approach to such a finding is contained in the following passage from his decision:

> It is fair to conclude––without necessarily finding that the ward is mentally ill for all purposes–-that she is incapable of making a rational and competent choice to undergo or reject the proposed surgery to her right leg. To this extent, at least, her behavior is irrational. She has closed her mind to the entire issue to the extent that the Court cannot conclude that her decision to reject further treatment is rational and informed . . . In the absence of substantial evidence that the ward has come to her current position as a result of a rational process after careful consideration of the medical alternatives, the Court finds that her confused mental condition resulting from her underlying senility and depression warrants the exercise of the jurisdiction of this Court and the application of a substitute choice for the ward.

In context, the quoted passage means only that, given some indications of a degree of senility and confusion on some subjects, the judge was not satisfied that Mrs. Candura arrived at her decision in a rational manner, i.e., "after careful consideration of the medical alternatives." We do not think that the passage can be construed as a finding of legal incompetence, and we do not think that the evidence in the case would have warranted such a finding.

The facts found by the judge or established by uncontradicted evidence are as follows. Mrs. Candura was born in Italy, emigrated to the United States in 1918, was married, and had a daughter and three sons. She lost her husband in 1976 and has been depressed and unhappy since that time. Her relationship with her children is marked by a considerable degree of conflict. She lived in her own home until her hospitalization in November, 1977. In 1974 she had an infection in a toe on her right foot which became gangrenous. It was discovered at that time that she was diabetic. The toe was amputated. In 1977 she bruised her right leg while getting into a bus. The bruise developed into gangrene which resulted in an operation in November, 1977, in which a portion of her right foot was amputated. At that time an arterial bypass was done to decrease the likelihood that gangrene would recur. She went from the hospital to a rehabilitation center, where she remained until April. She then returned to the hospital and was found to have gangrene in the remainder of the foot. She originally agreed to amputation of the leg, but she withdrew her consent on the morning scheduled for the operation, she was discharged on April 21 and went to her daughter's home but returned to the Symmes Hospital after a few days. Around May 9, responding to the persuasion of a doctor who has known Mrs. Candura for many years, she consented to the operation, but soon thereafter she reiterated her refusal. She has discussed with some persons the reason for her decision: that she has been unhappy since the death of her husband; that she does not wish to be a burden to her children; that she does not believe that the operation will cure her; that she does not wish to live as an invalid or in a nursing home; and that she does not fear death but welcomes it. She is discouraged by the failure of the earlier operations to arrest the advance of the gangrene. She tends to be stubborn and somewhat irascible. In her own testimony before the judge she expressed a desire to get well but indicated that she was resigned to death and was adamantly against the operation. Her testimony (corroborated by that of several of the witnesses) showed that she is lucid on some matters and confused on others. Her train of thought sometimes wanders. Her conception of time is distorted. She is hostile to certain doctors. She is on occasion defensive and sometimes combative in her responses to questioning. But she has exhibited a high degree of awareness and acuity. When responding to questions concerning the proposed operation, she has made it clear that she does not wish to have the operation even though that decision will in all likelihood lead shortly to her death. We find no indication in any of the testimony that that is not a choice with full appreciation of the consequences. The most that is shown is that the decision involves strong, emotional factors, that she does not choose to discuss the decision with certain persons, and that occasionally her resolve against giving consent weakens.

. . . Such evidence is lacking in this case. We recognize that Dr. Kelley, one of two psychiatrists who testified, did state that in his opinion Mrs. Candura was incompetent to make a rational choice whether to consent to the operation. His opinion appears to have been based upon (1) his inference from her unwillingness to discuss the problem with him that she was unable to face up to the problem or to understand that her refusal constituted a choice; (2) his characterization of "an unwilling[ness], for whatever reason, to consent to life saving treatment . . . as suicidal;" and (3) a possibility, not established by evidence as a reasonable probability, that her mind might be impaired by toxicity caused by the gangrenous condition. His testimony, read closely, and in the context of the question put to him, indicates that his opinion is not one of incompetency in the legal sense, but rather that her ability to make a rational choice (by which he means the *medically* rational choice) is impaired by the confusion existing in her mind by virtue of her consideration of irrational and emotional factors.

A careful analysis of the evidence in this case, including the superficially conflicting psychiatric testimony, indicates that there is no real conflict as to the underlying facts. Certainly, the evidence presents no issue of credibility. The principal question is whether the facts established by the evidence justify a conclusion of legal incompetence. The panel are unanimous in the opinion that they do not.

The decision of the judge, as well as the opinion of Dr. Kelley, predicates the necessity for the appointment of a guardian chiefly on the irrationality (in medical terms) of Mrs. Candura's decision to reject the amputation. Until she changed her original decision and withdrew her consent to the amputation, her competence was not questioned. But the irrationality of her decision does not justify a conclusion that Mrs. Candura is incompetent in the legal sense. The law protects her right to make her own decision to accept or reject treatment, whether that decision is wise or unwise . . .

Similarly, the fact that she has vicillated in her resolve not to submit to the operation does not justify a conclusion that her capacity to make the decison is impaired to the point of legal incompetence. Indeed, her reaction may be readily understandable in the light of her prior surgical experience and the prospect of living the remainder of her life nonambulatory. Senile symptoms, in the abstract, may, of course, justify a finding of incompetence, but the inquiry must be more particular. What is lacking in this case is evidence that Mrs. Candura's areas of forgetfulness and confusion cause, or relate in any way to, impairment of her ability to understand that in rejecting the amputation she is, in effect, choosing death over life . . .

Mrs. Candura's decision may be regarded by most as unfortunate, but on the record in this case it is not the uninformed decision of a person incapable of appreciating the nature and consequences of her act. We cannot anticipate whether she will reconsider and will consent to the operation, but we are all of the opinion that the operation may not be forced upon her against her will.

The order appointing a temporary guardian and the judgment authorizing the temporary guardian to consent to the operation are reversed, and a new judgment is to enter dismissing the petition.

o **Recap of the Case**. Throughout their careers, nurses must deal with patients who refuse treatment. Some of the patients who refuse treatment are competent adults. It is tempting to conclude that any adult who refuses treatment must be incompetent. Courts have rejected this conclusion. The key question is whether the patient understands the consequences of refusing treatment. If the patient understands the consequences of refusal, the court will not overrule the patient's decision.

GUARDIAN MAY REFUSE TREATMENT ON BEHALF OF WARD

The guardians of incompetent adults may refuse treatment on behalf of their wards. A set of circumstances warranting refusal to consent by guardians is described in *Superintendent of Belchertown v. Saikewicz*.

Mr. Saikewicz, who had an IQ of 10, was a resident of an institution for the mentally retarded. He was 67 years old when he developed leukemia. The superintendent of the Belchertown State School where Saikewicz resided asked the court to appoint a guardian to decide whether Saikewicz should receive chemotherapy. The court appointed a guardian *ad litem* who represented Saikewicz's interests before the court.

The judge identified six possible factors against administration of chemotherapy: 1) Saikewicz's advanced age; 2) the probable side effects of treatment; 3) the low chance of producing remission; 4) the certainty that treatment would cause immediate suffering; 5) Saikewicz's inability to cooperate with the treatment; and 6) the quality of life possible for Saikewicz even if the treatment resulted in remission. Weighed against these factors was the possibility of prolonging the patient's life.

The court decided that the factors against treatment outweighed the desirability of prolonging Saikewicz's life. The court also decided that guardians could make decisions to refuse or withhold treatment on behalf of their wards.

Note, however, that the court specifically rejected the sixth factor listed above. The court made it clear that treatment could never be withheld from a patient because a physical or mental disability diminished the quality of the patient's life.

Superintendent of Belchertown v. Saikewicz
370 N.E.2d 417 (Mass. 1977)
Supreme Judicial Court of Massachusetts

. . . Joseph Saikewicz, at the time the matter arose, was sixty–seven years old, with an I.Q. of ten and a mental age of approximately two years and eight months. He was profoundly mentally retarded. The record discloses that, apart from his leukemic condition, Saikewicz enjoyed generally good health. He was physically strong and well built, nutritionally nourished, and ambulatory. He was not, however, able to communicate verbally--resorting to gestures and grunts to make his wishes known to others and responding only to gestures or physical contacts. In the course of treatment for various medical conditions arising during Saikewicz's residency at the school, he had been unable to respond intelligibly to inquiries such as whether he was experiencing pain. It was the opinion of a consulting psychologist, not contested by the other experts relied on by the judge below, that Saikewicz was not aware of dangers and was disoriented outside his immediate environment. As a result of his condition, Saikewicz had lived in State institutions since 1923 and had resided at the Belchertown State School since 1928. Two of his sisters, the only members of his family who could be located, were notified of his condition and of the hearing, but they preferred not to attend or otherwise become involved.

On April 19, 1976, Saikewicz was diagnosed as suffering from acute myeloblastic monocytic leukemia. Leukemia is a disease of the blood. It arises when organs of the body produce an excessive number of white blood cells as well as other abnormal cellular structures, in particular undeveloped and immature white cells. Along with these symptoms in the composition of the blood the disease is accompanied by the enlargement of the organs which produce the cells, e.g., the spleen, lymph glands, and bone marrow. The disease tends to cause internal bleeding and weakness, and, in the acute form, severe anemia and high susceptibility to infection... The particular form of the disease present in this case, acute myeloblastic monocytic leukemia, is so defined because the particular cells which increase are the myeloblasts, the youngest form of a cell which at maturity is known as the granulocytes... The disease is invariably fatal.

Chemotherapy... involves the administration of drugs over several weeks, the purpose of which is to kill the leukemia cells. This treatment unfortunately affects normal cells as well. One expert testified that the end result, in effect, is to destroy the living vitality of the bone marrow. Because of this effect, the patient becomes very anemic and may bleed or suffer infections—a condition which requires a number of blood transfusions. In this sense, the patient immediately becomes much "sicker" with the commencement of chemotherapy, and there is a possibility that infections during the initial period of severe anemia may prove fatal. Moreover, while most patients survive chemotherapy, remission of the leukemia is achieved in only thirty to fifty percent of the cases. Remission is meant here as a temporary return to normal as measured by clinical and laboratory means. If remission does occur, it typically lasts for between two and thirteen months although longer periods of remission are possible. Estimates of the effectiveness of chemotherapy are complicated in cases, such as the one presented here, in which the patient's age becomes a factor. According to the medical testimony before the court below, persons over age sixty have more difficulty tolerating chemotherapy and the treatment is likely to be less successful than in younger patients. This prognosis may be compared with the doctors' estimates that, left untreated, a patient in Saikewicz's condition would live for a matter of weeks or, perhaps, several months. According to the testimony, a decision to allow the disease to run its natural course would not result in pain for the patient, and death would probably come without discomfort.

An important facet of the chemotherapy process . . . is the problem of serious adverse side effects caused by the treating drugs. Among these side effects are sever nausea, bladder irritation, numbness and tingling of the extremities, and loss of hair. The bladder irritation can be avoided, however, if the patient drinks fluids, and the nausea can be treated by drugs. It was the opinion of the guardian ad litem, as well as the doctors who testified before the probate judge, that most people elect to suffer the side effects of chemotherapy rather than to allow their leukemia to run its natural course.

5. That the majority of persons suffering from leukemia who are faced with a choice of receiving or foregoing such chemotherapy, and who are able to make an informed judgment thereon, choose to receive treatment in spite of its toxic side effects and risks of failure.

6. That such toxic side effects of chemotherapy include pain and discomfort, depressed bone marrow, pronounced anemia, increased chance of infection, possible bladder irritation, and possible loss of hair.

7. That administration of such chemotherapy requires cooperation from the patient over several weeks of time, which cooperation said JOSEPH SAIKEWICZ is unable to give due to his profound retardation.

8. That, considering the age and general state of health of said JOSEPH SAIKEWICZ, there is only a 30–40 percent chance that chemotherapy will produce a remission of said leukemia, which remission would probably be for a period of time of from 2 to 13 months, but that said chemotherapy will certainly not completely cure such leukemia.

9. That if such chemotherapy is to be administered at all it should be administered immediately, inasmuch as the risks involved will increase and the chances of successfully bringing about remission will decrease as time goes by.

10. That, at present, said JOSEPH SAIKEWICZ's leukemia condition is stable and is not deteriorating.

11. That said JOSEPH SAIKEWICZ is not now in pain and will probably die within a matter of weeks or months a relatively painless death due to the leukemia unless other factors should intervene to themselves cause death.

12. That it is impossible to predict how long said JOSEPH SAIKEWICZ will probably live without chemotherapy or how

long he will probably live with chemotherapy, but it is to a very high degree medically likely that he will die sooner, without treatment than with it.

Balancing these various factors, the judge concluded that the following considerations weighed *against* administering chemotherapy to Saikewicz: (1) his age, (2) his inability to cooperate with the treatment, (3) probable adverse side effects of treatment, (4) low chance of producing remission, (5) the certainty that treatment will cause immediate suffering, and (6) the quality of life possible for him even if the treatment does bring about remission.

The following considerations were determined to weigh in *favor* of chemotherapy: "(1) the chance that his life may be lengthened thereby, and (2) the fact that most people in his situation when given a chance to do so elect to take the gamble of treatment."

Concluding that, in this case, the negative factors of treatment exceeded the benefits, the probate judge ordered on May 13, 1976, that no treatment be administered to Saikewicz for his condition of acute myeloblastic monocytic leukemia except by further order of the court. The judge further ordered that all reasonable and necessary supportive measures be taken, medical or otherwise, to safeguard the well-being of Saikewicz in all other respects and to reduce as far as possible any suffering or discomfort which he might experience.

It is within this factual context that we issued our order of July 9, 1976.

Saikewicz died on September 4, 1976, at the Belchertown State School hospital. Death was due to bronchial pneumonia, a complication of the leukemia. Saikewicz died without pain or discomfort.

We recognize at the outset that this case presents novel issues of fundamental importance that should not be resolved by mechanical reliance on legal doctrine. Our task of establishing a framework in the law on which the activities of health care personnel and other persons can find support is furthered by seeking the collective guidance of those in health care, moral ethics, philosophy, and other disciplines . . . As thus illuminated, the principal areas of determination are:

A. The nature of the right of any person, competent or incompetent, to decline potentially life-prolonging treatment.

B. The legal standards that control the course of decision whether or not potentially life-prolonging, but not life-saving, treatment should be administered to a person who is not competent to make the choice.

C. The procedures that must be followed in arriving at that decision.

For reasons we develop in the body of this opinion, it becomes apparent that the questions to be discussed in the first two areas are closely interrelated. We take the view that the substantive rights of the competent and the incompetent person are the same in regard to the right to decline potentially life–prolonging treatment. The factors which distinguish the two types of persons are found only in the area of how the State should approach the preservation and implementation of the rights of an incompetent person and in the procedures necessary to that process of preservation and implementation. We treat the matter in the sequence above stated because we think it helpful to set forth our views on (A) what the rights of all persons in this area are and (B) the issue of how an incompetent person is to be afforded the status in law of a competent person with respect to such rights. Only then can we proceed to (C) the particular procedures to be followed to ensure the rights of the incompetent person.

A.

1. It has been said that "[t]he law always lags behind the most advanced thinking in every area. It must wait until the theologians and the moral leaders and events have created some common ground, some consensus" . . . We therefore think it advisable to consider the framework of medical ethics which influence a doctor's decision as to how to deal with the terminally ill patient. While these considerations are not controlling, they ought to be considered for the insights they give us.

Advances in medical science have given doctors greater control over the time and nature of death. Chemotherapy is, as evident from our previous discussion, one of these advances. Prior to the development of such new techniques the physician perceived his duty as that of making every conceivable effort to prolong life. On the other hand, the context in which such an ethos prevailed did not provide the range of options available to the physician today in terms of taking steps to postpone death irrespective of the effect on the patient. With the development of the new techniques, serious questions as to what may constitute acting in the best interests of the patient have arisen.

The nature of the choice has become more difficult because physicians have begun to realize that in many cases the effect of using extraordinary measures to prolong life is to "only prolong suffering, isolate the family from their loved one at a time when they may be close at hand or result in economic ruin for the family."

". . . [P]hysicians distinguish between curing the ill and comforting and easing the dying; that they refuse to treat the curable as if they were dying or ought to die, and that they have sometimes refused to treat the hopeless and dying as if they were curable" . . .

The essence of this distinction in defining the medical role is to draw the sometimes subtle distinction between those situations in which the withholding of extraordinary measures may be viewed as allowing the disease to take its natural course and those in which the same actions may be deemed to have been the cause of death . . . Recent literature suggests that health care institutions are drawing such a distinction, at least with regard to respecting the decision of competent patients to refuse such measures . . .

The current state of medical ethics in this area is expressed by one commentator who states that: "we should not use *extraordinary* means of prolonging life or its semblance when, after careful consideration, consultation and the application of the most well conceived therapy, it becomes apparent that there is no hope for the recovery of the patient. Recovery should not be defined simply as the ability to remain alive; it should mean life without intolerable suffering."

Our decision in this case is consistent with the current medical ethos in this area.

2. There is implicit recognition in the law of the Commonwealth, as elsewhere, that a person has a strong interest in being free from nonconsensual invasion of his bodily integrity . . . In short, the law recognizes the individual interest in preserving "the inviolability of his person" . . . One means by which the law has developed in a manner consistent with the protection of this interest is through the development of the doctrine of informed consent . . .

Of even broader import, but arising from the same regard for human dignity and self-determination, is the unwritten constitutional right of privacy found in the penumbra of specific guaranties of the Bill of Rights . . . As this constitutional guaranty reaches out to protest the freedom of a woman to terminate pregnancy under certain conditions . . . so it encompasses the right of a patient to preserve his or her right to privacy against unwanted infringements of bodily integrity in appropriate circumstances . . . In the case of a person incompetent to assert this constitutional right of privacy, it may be asserted by that person's guardian . . .

3. The question when the circumstances are appropriate for the exercise of this privacy depends on the proper identification of State interests. It is not surprising that courts have, in the course of investigating State interests in various medical contexts and under various formulations of the individual rights involved, reached differing views on the nature and the extent of State interests . . .

[T]hree State interests . . . [are] viewed as having greater import than the individual right: (1) the State interest in preventing suicide, (2) a parens patriae interest in protecting the patient's minor children from "abandonment" by their parent, and (3) the protection of the medical profession's desire to act affirmatively to save life without fear of civil liability . . .

. . . [T]he State has claimed interest in: (1) the preservation of life; (2) the protection of the interests of innocent third parties; (3) the prevention of suicide; and (4) maintaining the ethical integrity of the medical profession.

It is clear that the most significant of the asserted State interests is that of the preservation of human life. Recognition of such an interest, however, does not necessarily resolve the problem where the affliction or disease clearly indicates that life will soon, and inevitably, be extinguished. The interest of the State in prolonging a life must be reconciled with the interest of an individual to reject the traumatic cost of that prolongation. There is a substantial distinction in the State's insistence that human life be saved where the affliction is curable, as opposed to the State interest where, as here, the issue is not whether but when, for how long, and at what cost to the individual that life may be briefly extended. Even if we assume that the State has an additional interest in seeing to it that individual decisions on the prolongation of life do not in any way tend to "cheapen" the value which is placed in the concept of living . . . we believe it is not inconsistent to recognize a right to decline medical treatment in a situation of incurable illness. The constitutional right to privacy, as we conceive it, is an expression of the sanctity of individual free choice and self–determination as fundamental constituents of life. The value of life as so perceived is lessened not by a decision to refuse treatment, but by the failure to allow a competent human being the right of choice.

A second interest of considerable magnitude, which the State may have some interest in asserting, is that of protecting third parties, particularly minor children, from the emotional and financial damage which may occur as a result of the decision of a competent adult to refuse life–saving or life–prolonging treatment . . .

The last State interest requiring discussion is that of the maintenance of the ethical integrity of the medical profession as well as allowing hospitals the full opportunity to care for people under their control . . . Prevailing medical ethical practice does not, without exception, demand that all efforts toward life prolongation be made in all circumstances. Rather . . . the prevailing ethical practice seems to be to recognize that those dying are more often in need of comfort than treatment. Recognition of the right to refuse necessary treatment in appropriate circumstances is consistent with existing medical mores; such a doctrine does not threaten either the integrity of the medical profession, the proper role of hospitals in caring for such patients or the State's interest in the proper role of hospitals in caring for such patients or the State's interest in protecting the same. It is not necessary to deny a right of self–determination to a patient in order to recognize the interests of doctors, hospitals, and medical personnel in attendance on the patient. Also, if the doctrines of informed consent and right of privacy have as their foundations the right to bodily integrity . . . , and control of one's own fate, then those rights are superior to the institutional considerations.

Two of the four categories of State interests that we have identified, the protection of third parties and the prevention of suicide, are inapplicable to this case. The third, involving the protection of the ethical integrity of the medical profession was satisfied on two grounds. The probate judge's decision was in accord with the testimony of the attending physicians of the patient. The decision is in accord with the generally accepted views of the medical profession, as set forth in this opinion. The fourth State interest––the preservation of life––has been viewed with proper regard for the heavy physical and emotional burdens on the patient if a vigorous regimen of drug therapy were to be imposed to effect a brief and uncertain delay in the natural process of death. To be balanced against these State interests was the individual's interest in the freedom to choose to reject, or refuse to consent to, intrusions of his bodily integrity and privacy. We cannot say that the facts of this case required a result contrary to that reached by the probate judge with regard to the right of any person, competent or incompetent, to be spared the deleterious consequences of life–prolonging treatment. We therefore turn to consider the unique considerations arising in this case by virtue of the patient's inability to appreciate his predicament and articulate his desires.

B.

The question what legal standards govern the decision whether to administer potentially life–prolonging treatment to an incompetent person encompasses two distinct and important subissues. First, does a choice exist? That is, is it the unvarying responsibility of the State to order medical treatment in all circumstances involving the care of an incompetent person? Second, if a choice does exist under certain conditions, what considerations enter into the decision–making process?

We think that principles of equality and respect for all individuals require the conclusion that a choice exists . . . [W]e recognize a general right in all persons to refuse medical treatment in appropriate circumstances. The recognition of that right must extend to the case of an incompetent, as well as a competent, patient because the value of human dignity extends to both.

This is not to deny that the State has a traditional power and responsibility, under the doctrine of parens patriae, to care for and protect the "best interests" of the incompetent person. Indeed, the existence of this power and responsibility has impelled a number of courts to hold that the "best interests" of such a person mandate an unvarying responsibility by the courts to order necessary medical treatment for an incompetent person facing an immediate and severe danger to life . . . Whatever the merits of such a policy where life–saving treatment is available––a situation unfortunately not presented by this case––a more flexible view of the "best interests" of the incompetent patient is not precluded under other conditions. For example, other courts have refused to take it on themselves to order certain forms of treatment or therapy which are not immediately required although concededly beneficial to the innocent person . . . While some of these cases involved children who might eventually be competent to make the necessary decisions without judicial interference, it is also clear that the additional period of waiting might make the task of correction more difficult . . . These cases stand for the proposition that, even in the exercise of the parens patriae power, there must be respect for the bodily integrity of the child or respect for the rational decision of those parties, usually the parents, who for one reason or another are seeking to protect the bodily integrity or other personal interest of the child . . .

The "best interests" of an incompetent person are not necessarily served by imposing on such persons results not mandated as to competent persons similarly situated. It does not advance the interest of the State or the ward to treat the ward as a person of lesser status or dignity than others. To protect the incompetent person within its power, the State must recognize the dignity and worth of such a person and afford to that person the same panoply of rights and choices it recognizes in competent persons. If a competent person faced with death may choose to decline treatment which not only will not cure the person but which substantially may increase suffering in exchange for a possible yet brief prolongation of life, then it cannot be said that it is always in the "best interests" of the ward to require submission to such treatment. Nor do statistical factors indicating that a majority of competent persons similarly situated choose treatment resolve the issue. The significant decisions of life are more complex than statistical determinations. Individual choice is determined not by the vote of the majority but by the complexities of the singular situation viewed from the unique perspective of the person called on to make the decision. To presume that the incompetent person must always be subjected to what many rational and intelligent persons may decline is to downgrade the status of the incompetent person by placing a lesser value on his intrinsic human worth and vitality.

. . . Recognition of this principle of equality requires understanding that in certain circumstances it may be appropriate for a court to consent to the withholding of treatment from an incompetent individual. This leads us to the question of how the right of an incompetent person to decline treatment might best be exercised so as to give the fullest possible expression to the character and circumstances of that individual . . .

. . . [T]he primary test is subjective in nature—that is, the goal is to determine with as much accuracy as possible the wants and needs of the individual involved. This may or may not conform to what is thought wise or prudent by most people. The problems of arriving at an accurate substituted judgment in matters of life and death vary greatly in degree, if not in kind, in different circumstances . . .Joseph Saikewicz was profoundly retarded and noncommunicative his entire life, which was spent largely in the highly restrictive atmosphere of an institution. While it may thus be necessary to rely to a greater degree on objective criteria, such as the supposed inability of profoundly retarded persons to conceptualize or fear death, the effort to bring the substituted judgment into step with the values and desires of the affected individual must not, and need not, be abandoned . . .

. . . [W]e now reiterate the substituted judgment doctrine as we apply it in the instant case. We believe that both the guardian ad litem in his recommendation and the judge in his decision should have attempted (as they did) to ascertain the incompetent person's actual interests and preferences. In short, the decision in cases such as this should be that which would be made by the incompetent person, if that person were competent, but taking into account the present and future incompetency of the individual as one of the factors which would necessarily enter into the decision–making process of the competent person. Having recognized the right of a competent person to make for himself the same decision as the court made in this case, the question is, do the facts on the record support the proposition that Saikewicz himself would have made the decision under the standard set forth. We believe they do.

The two factors considered by the probate judge to weigh in favor of administering chemotherapy were: (1) the fact that most people elect chemotherapy and (2) the chance of a longer life. Both are appropriate indicators of what Saikewicz himself would have wanted, provided that due allowance is taken for this individual's present and future incompetency. We have already discussed the perspective this brings to the fact that most people choose to undergo chemotherapy. With regard to the second factor, the chance of a longer life carries the same weight for Saikewicz as for any other person, the value of life under the law having no relation to intelligence or social position. Intertwined with this consideration is the hope that a cure, temporary or permanent, will be discovered during the period of extra weeks or months potentially made available by chemotherapy. The guardian ad litem investigated this possibility and found no reason to hope for a dramatic breakthrough in the time frame relevant to the decision.

The probate judge identified six factors weighing against administration of chemotherapy. Four of these–– Saikewicz's age, the probable side effects of treatment, the low chance of producing remission, and the certainty that treatment will cause immediate suffering––were clearly established by the medical testimony to be considerations that any individual would weigh carefully. A fifth factor—Saikewicz's inability to cooperate with the treatment—introduces those considerations that are unique to this individual and which therefore are essential to the proper exercise of substituted judgment. The judge heard testimony that Saikewicz would have no comprehension of the reasons for the severe disruption of his formerly secure and stable environment occasioned by the chemotherapy. He therefore would experience fear without the understanding from which other patients draw strength. The inability to anticipate and prepare for the severe side effects of the drugs leaves room only for confusion and disorientation. The possibility that such a naturally uncooperative patient would have to be physically restrained to allow the slow intravenous administration of drugs could only compound his pain and fear, as well as possibly jeopardize the ability of his body to withstand the toxic effects of the drugs.

The sixth factor identified by the judge as weighing against chemotherapy was "the quality of life possible for him even if the treatment does bring about remission." To the extent that this formulation equates the value of life with any measure of the quality of life, we firmly reject it. A reading of the entire record clearly reveals, however, the judge's concern that special care be taken to respect the dignity and worth of Saikewicz's life precisely because of his vulnerable position. The judge, as well as all the parties, were keenly aware that the supposed ability of Saikewicz, by virtue of his mental retardation, to appreciate or experience life had no place in the decision before them. Rather than reading the judge's formulation in a manner that demeans the value of the life of one who is mentally retarded, the vague, and perhaps ill-chosen, term "quality of life" should be understood as a reference to the continuing state of pain and disorientation precipitated by the chemotherapy treatment. Viewing the term in this manner, together with the other factors properly considered by the judge, we are satisfied that the decision to withhold treatment from Saikewicz was based on a regard for his actual interests and preferences and that the facts supported this decision . . .

o **Recap of the Case**. The limitations on the lives of some handicapped individuals seem so severe that it is tempting to conclude that treatment prolonging life should not be rendered. Many courts specifically reject quality of life as a factor for making decisions regarding treatment for the disabled. Instead, courts consider the patient's age, possible side effects of treatment, the likelihood of a remission or cure, whether the treatment will cause pain, and the ability of the disabled person to cooperate during treatment. The court in *Saikewicz* also decided that guardians can utilize these criteria to make decisions on behalf of disabled persons to refuse consent. Approval by a court to refuse treatment on behalf of a disabled person is not usually necessary.

8

On Religious Grounds

Competent adults, primarily Jehovah's Witnesses, often refuse blood transfusions because of their religious beliefs. Refusal of blood transfusion sometimes means that physicians will not perform surgery because the doctor is unwilling to accept the risk of operating without transfusions. This situation raises the question of whether a court may override a competent adult's decision to refuse treatment.

Two cases are indicative of the case law in this area: *John F. Kennedy Hospital v. Heston*, 58 N.J. 576, 279 A.2d (1971) and *In Re Osborne*, 294 A.2d 372 (D.C. 1972). In *Heston* the court ordered transfusions, while the court did not order transfusions in *Osborne*. The answers to two critical questions seem to govern the Court's decisions: 1) Has the patient made a competent choice? and 2) Does the State have a compelling interest in overriding the decision of a competent adult?

COURT ORDERS BLOOD TRANSFUSIONS DESPITE PATIENT'S OBJECTIONS

In the *John F. Kennedy Memorial Hospital* case, Delores Heston, age 22, was severely injured in an automobile accident. Her spleen was ruptured and she required surgery and blood transfusions. Members of Heston's family resisted transfusions because they violate the religious tenets of Jehovah's Witnesses. After family members tried and failed to find a physician who would perform surgery without blood transfusions because Heston was in shock, the hospital asked the court to appoint a guardian to consent to treatment on Heston's behalf. The court appointed a guardian for Heston who consented to blood transfusions. Blood was administered, and surgery was performed. Heston survived.

Even though the specific dilemma posed by Heston was resolved, the court went on to consider whether or not it is proper and on what basis courts may overrule the wishes of patients who, like Jehovah's Witnesses, refuse transfusions. The court recognized the right of individuals to religious freedom and the duty of the State to respect religious beliefs. Nevertheless, the court also determined that the interest of the State in the preservation of life may override individual freedom. Consequently, the court concluded that courts may overrule the decisions of competent adults to refuse treatment.

Nurses should also take note of the court's discussion regarding the primary importance accorded nursing functions. The court recognized that nurses and other practitioners should not be required to choose between their professional standards which require action to preserve the lives of patients and respect for individuals' religious tenets. When choices are presented, the professional responsibilities of nurses and other providers must prevail.

As a practical matter, nurses cannot be expected to make decisions regarding whether to override the religious tenets of a patient to render treatment. As soon as nurses become aware of a dilemma in this area, they should notify and consult legal counsel.

John F. Kennedy Memorial Hospital v. Heston
58 N.J.576, 279 A.2d 670 (1970)
Supreme Court of New Jersey

Delores Heston, age 22 and unmarried, was severely injured in an automobile accident. She was taken to the plaintiff hospital where it was determined that she would expire unless operated upon for a ruptured spleen and that if operated upon she would expire unless whole blood was administered. Miss Heston and her parents are Jehovah's Witnesses and a tenet of their faith forbids blood transfusions. Miss Heston insists she expressed her refusal to accept blood, but the evidence indicates she was in shock on admittance to the hospital and in the judgment of the attending physicians and nurses was then or soon became disoriented and incoherent. Her mother remained adamant in her opposition to a transfusion, and signed a release of liability for the hospital and medical personnel. Miss Heston did not execute a release; presumably she could not. Her father could not be located.

Death being imminent, plaintiff on notice to the mother made application at 1:30 a.m. to a judge of the Superior Court for the appointment of a guardian for Miss Heston with directions to consent to transfusions as needed to save her life. At the hearing, the mother and her friends thought a certain doctor would pursue surgery without a transfusion, but the doctor, in response to the judge's telephone call, declined the case. The court appointed a guardian with authority to consent to blood transfusions "for the preservation of the life of Delores Heston." Surgery was performed at 4:00 a.m. the same morning. Blood was administered. Miss Heston survived . . .

The controversy is moot. Miss Heston is well and no longer in plaintiff's hospital. The prospect of her return at some future day in like circumstances is too remote to warrant a declaratory judgment as between the parties. Nonetheless, the public interest warrants a resolution of the cause, and for that reason we accept the issue . . .

It seems correct to say there is no constitutional right to choose to die. Attempted suicide was a crime at common law and was held to be a crime . . . It is now denounced as a disorderly persons offense . . . Ordinarily nothing would be gained by a prosecution, and hence the offense is rarely charged. Nonetheless the Constitution does not deny the State an interest in the subject. It is commonplace for the police and other citizens, often at great risk to themselves, to use force or stratagem to defeat efforts at suicide, and it could hardly be said that thus to save someone from himself violated a right of his under the Constitution subjecting the rescuer to civil or penal consequences.

Nor is constitutional right established by adding that one's religious faith ordains his death. Religious beliefs are absolute, but conduct in pursuance of religious beliefs is not wholly immune from governmental restraint . . .

Complicating the subject of suicide is the difficulty of knowing whether a decision to die is firmly held. Psychiatrists may find that beneath it all a person bent on self-destruction is hoping to be rescued, and most who are rescued do not repeat the attempt, at least not at once. Then, too, there is the question whether in any event the person was and continues to be competent (a difficult concept in this area) to choose to die. And of course there is no opportunity for a trial of these questions in advance of intervention by the State or citizen.

Appellant suggests there is a difference between passively submitting to death and actively seeking it. The distinction may be merely verbal, as it would be if an adult sought death by starvation instead of a drug. If the State may interrupt one mode of self-destruction, it may with equal authority interfere with the other. It is arguably different when an individual, overtaken by illness, decides to let it run a fatal course. But unless the medical option itself is laden with the risk of death or of serious infirmity, the State's interest in sustaining life in such circumstances is hardly distinguishable from its interest in the case of suicide.

Here we are not dealing with deadly options. The risk of death or permanent injury because of a transfusion is not a serious factor. Indeed, Miss Heston did not resist a transfusion on that basis. Nor did she wish to die. She wanted to live, but her faith demanded that she refuse blood even at the price of her life. The question is not whether the State could punish her for refusing a transfusion. It may be granted that it would serve no State interest to deal criminally with one who resisted a transfusion on the basis of religious faith. The question is whether the State may authorize force to prevent death or may tolerate the use of force by others to that end. Indeed, the issue is not solely between the State and Miss Heston, for the controversy is also between Miss Heston and a hospital and staff who did not seek her out and upon whom the dictates of her faith will fall as a burden.

Hospitals exist to aid the sick and the injured. The medical and nursing professions are consecrated to preserving life. That is their professional creed. To them, a failure to use a simple, established procedure in the circumstances of this case would be malpractice, however the law may characterize that failure because of the patient's private convictions. A surgeon should not be asked to operate under the strain of knowing that a transfusion may not be administered even though medically required to save his patient. The hospital and its staff should not be required to decide whether the patient is or continues to be competent to make a judgment upon the subject, or whether the release tendered by the patient or a member of his family will protect them from civil responsibility. The hospital could hardly avoid the problem by compelling the removal of a dying patient, and Miss Heston's family made no effort to take her elsewhere.

When the hospital and staff are thus involuntary hosts and their interests are pitted against the belief of the patient, we think it reasonable to resolve the problem by permitting the hospital and its staff to pursue their functions according to their professional standards. The solution sides with life, the conservation of which is, we think, a matter of State interest. A prior application to a court is appropriate if time permits it, although in the nature of the emergency the only question that can be explored satisfactorily is whether death will probably ensue if medical procedures are not followed. If a court finds, as the trial court did, that death will likely follow unless a transfusion is administered, the hospital and the physician should be permitted to follow the medical procedure.

. . . In any event, for the reasons already given, we find that the interest of the hospital and its staff, as well as the State's interest in life, warranted the transfusion of blood under the circumstances of this case . . .

COURT REFUSES TO OVERRULE PATIENT'S DECISION TO WITHHOLD CONSENT TO TRANSFUSIONS

In *In Re Osborne*, the court reached the exact opposite conclusion. Presented with similar facts, the court in this case refused to order blood transfusions for a Jehovah's Witness who faced almost certain death without them. The court reasoned that Mr. Osborne was a competent adult. He was not under the influence of drugs and his mental facilities were not impaired as a result of his injuries. He understood that the consequences of his decision included the possibility of death. In addition, this court found no compelling interest of the State strong enough to override the patient's desires. Initially, the court thought that the two minor children of the patient might be destitute if the patient died. If this were the case, the State would have an interest important enough to overrule the patient. However, testimony at several hearings showed that the patient was a member of a very close-knit family with a thriving business and that the needs of the patient's children would be met by other family members. Consequently, the court concluded that the patient's decision must be upheld.

The different results reached in these two cases further emphasize the suggestion that nurses cannot be expected to make decisions in this area. Again, any questions in this area should be referred to legal counsel for resolution.

Nurses should also take note of the speed with which the court acted in this case. The petition was first presented to Judge Bacon at her home the night of the accident. Judge Bacon conducted two hearings the very next day, one of which occurred at the patient's bedside. While lawyers and court systems do not always work as quickly as they should, this case is an example that claims of slow-moving court systems are no excuse for failure to confront and resolve legal issues.

In Re Osborne, 294 A.2d 372 (D.C. 1972)
District of Columbia Court of Appeals

This is an appeal, expedited of necessity, from an order of Judge Bacon of the Superior Court refusing to appoint a guardian to give consent for the administration of a blood transfusion to a patient, a member of the Jehovah's Witnesses faith, who was receiving emergency treatment at a hospital. The case originated by the hospital's petition which was accompanied by an affidavit. After two hasty hearings, ably conducted by Judge Bacon—one in her home the night of the accident and the other the following day on a request for reconsideration—the case came on for emergency consideration by this court. We directed a third hearing at the bedside of the patient. Judge Bacon asked Lawrence Speiser, Esquire, to attend and represent the patient and his family. In the meantime, we listened to a tape recording of the second hearing. Immediately upon completion of the bedside hearing, we had portions of the transcript read to us over the telephone from the hospital. Counsel then returned to the court house and we heard argument on behalf of the hospital and the patient. We then affirmed Judge Bacon's order and indicated an opinion would follow.

The 34–year–old patient was admitted to the hospital with injuries and internal bleeding caused when a tree fell on him. As the need for whole blood became apparent, the patient refused to give his consent for the necessary transfusion. The patient's wife also refused the required consent. Both gave as reasons their religious beliefs which forbid infusion of whole blood into the body.

When the petition was brought to Judge Bacon's home the night of the accident, the patient's wife, brother, and grandfather were present. They stated the views of the patient and agreed with them, explaining that those views are based on strong religious convictions. The grandfather explained that the patient "wants to live very much . . . He wants to live in the Bible's promised new world where life will never end. A few hours here would nowhere compare to everlasting life." His wife stated, "He told me he did not want blood—he did not care if he had to die."

Judge Bacon then correctly became concerned with the patient's capacity to make such a decision in light of his serious condition. She also recognized the possibility that the use of drugs might have impaired his judgment and ability for choice. Counsel for the hospital advised that the patient, though receiving fluid by vein, was conscious when spoken to by a staff physician, knew what the doctor was saying, understood the consequences of his decision, and had with full understanding executed a statement refusing the recommended transfusion and releasing the hospital from liability.

Judge Bacon took note of a possible overriding state interest based on the fact that the patient had two young children. It was concluded, however, that the maturity of this lucid patient, his long-standing beliefs and those of his family did not justify state intervention. At the hearing on the motion for reconsideration, it was revealed that a close family relationship existed which went beyond the immediate members, that the children would be well cared for, and that the family business would continue to supply material needs.

When the case was first presented to this court, we viewed it as unclear whether the patient would desire to continue his present physical life. We therefore directed the bedside hearing to develop that point without the exclusive use of what might be called hearsay statements. We also directed Judge Bacon to ask the patient whether he believed that he would be deprived of the opportunity for "everlasting life" if transfusion were ordered by the court. His response was, "Yes. In other words, it is between me and Jehovah; not the courts . . . I'm willing to take my chances. My faith is that strong." He also stated, "I wish to live, but with no blood transfusions. Now get that straight."

Judge Bacon was careful also to determine the extent, if any, of impairment of judgment or capacity for choice resulting from the use of drugs. She was informed that the patient was not then under the influence of any medication having such possible or usual side effects.

Further inquiry was then made of the patient's wife concerning the material and filial welfare of the two children. She responded:

> My husband has a business and it will be turned over to me. And his brothers work for him, so it will be carried on.

That is no problem. In fact, they are working on it right now. Business goes on.

As far as money—wise, everybody is all right. We have money saved up.

Everything will be all right. If anything ever happens, I have a big enough family and the family is prepared to care for the children.

In the past a few courts have considered whether to compel religiously rejected medical care ... The issue is always whether there is sufficient state interest to override individual desires based on religious beliefs. The degree of state interest justifying intrusion by court order has been viewed as "compelling" ... As is most often the case, factual situations vary with the result reached. In some cases the patient is comatose and his religious views must be expressed by family members or friends. In other cases, like this one, the patient is fully capable of making the choice. That is one reason why we directed the bedside hearing. Whenever possible it is better for the judge to make a first—hand appraisal of the patient's personal desires and ability for rational choice. In this way the court can always know, to the extent possible, that the judgment is that of the individual concerned and not that of those who believe, however, well—intentioned, that they speak for the person whose life is in the balance. Thus, where the patient is comatose, or suffering impairment of capacity for choice, it may be better to give weight to the known instinct for survival which can, in a critical situation, alter previously held convictions. In such cases it cannot be determined with certainty that a deliberate and intelligent choice has been made.

Another circumstance which is often present in cases like this is the existence of children, whose lives, if yet unborn, are also at stake, or whose welfare, as survivors, may be unclear. In those cases, it seems less difficult for courts to find sufficient state interest to intervene and circumvent religious convictions. But even then, it is important to note that courts may be more controlled by the interest of the surviving children when there is lack of clarity respecting first—hand knowledge that the patient's current choice is competently maintained.

An additional consideration which impelled us to order the bedside hearing was doubt on the initial record whether the patient, if forced to undergo the blood transfusion, would consider himself blameless to the extent that his religious life would be unaffected. We therefore obtained knowledge of the patient's beliefs respecting his view of accountability to God should he have no choice in the matter . . .

. . . However, he expressed the belief that he was accountable to God, in the sense of a loss of everlasting life, if he unwillingly received whole blood through transfusion.

Thus Judge Bacon and this court were faced with a man who did not wish to live if to do so required a blood transfusion, who viewed himself as deprived of life everlasting even if he involuntarily received the transfusion, and who had, through material provision and family and spiritual bonds, provided for the future well–being of his two children. In reaching her decision, Judge Bacon necessarily resolved the two critical questions presented––(1) has the patient validly and knowingly chosen this course for his life, and (2) is there compelling state interest which justifies overriding that decision? Based on this unique record, we have been unable to conclude that judicial intervention respecting the wishes and religious beliefs of the patient was warranted under our law. Judge Bacon's decision is supported by available evidence to the degree of certainty respecting the two basic questions.

A further point is worthy of mention since cases of this nature are very apt to arise in the future. Counsel for the hospital ably and commendably represented the hospital in insuring that it and the hospital staff did all they reasonably could do within their power to save the patient's life by acceptable medical procedures. Such was not only a duty, but a laudatory goal. Judge Bacon, however, appeared to recognize a need for experienced and able counsel to make independent inquiry of the patient and to represent his interests before the court. This procedure should, when possible, be followed in future cases of this nature. It is recognized that a proceeding like this lacks many of the characteristics of the usual adversary litigation. However, such counsel can, as is often done in criminal cases, make independent threshold observations respecting competence. He can also assist in determining facts respecting the welfare of survivors.

It was with commendable insight that Judge Bacon sought for the patient and his family the very able assistance of Mr. Speiser. We express to both counsel our appreciation for a most difficult and well–done job.

The judgment previously entered shall stand as our judgment on mandate.

o **Recap of the Cases**. In *Heston* the court overruled the patient and ordered transfusions. In *Osbourne*, the court upheld the patient's decision to refuse treatment. Why did the courts in these cases reach opposite conclusions? Both patients were competent. The courts then looked for overriding reasons to reject the patients' decisions. The court in *Osbourne* could not find a reason to overrule the patient. The court in *Heston* decided that the state's interest in protecting the health of its citizens and providers' interest in using their expertise to save lives were sufficient to override the patient's wishes.

9

Adults on Behalf of Minors

Generally

Minors who are "mature" or emancipated and otherwise competent may, of course, refuse to consent to treatment without concurrent consent from parents. Otherwise, parental prerogatives to refuse treatment are limited. If the parents' decision is likely to cause the child serious injury or death, the court will intervene to protect the child's interest as *In Re Clark*.

PARENTS' REFUSAL OF TREATMENT OVERRULED BY COURT

This case involved a three-year-old boy whose parents were Jehovah's Witnesses and thus opposed to blood transfusions. The child was admitted to the hospital with severe burns over 40% of his body. It soon became clear that blood transfusions were necessary in order to preserve his life. The treating practitioners correctly turned to the parents of the minor child for permission to administer transfusions. The child's parents refused to consent based solely on their religious beliefs. The attending staff and the hospital then asked the court to provide them with the authority to administer transfusions to the boy.

The court gave the hospital and staff the authorization requested. The child's parents promptly protested to the court, and a hearing was held immediately. After hearing testimony, the court decided that when a child's life is at stake, parents' religious beliefs are less important than the welfare of the child. The court affirmed its original decision to allow the physicians to administer transfusions.

In Re Clark, 185 N.E.2d 128 (Ohio, 1962)
Supreme Court of Ohio

On September 6, 1962, the Court received from officials of Mercy Hospital an application for authority to administer blood transfusions to one Kenneth Clark, aged 3 years. The original application was oral; later that day it was supported by a written statement.

It was made to appear that the child was suffering second and third degree burns over 40% of his body; that he had been received a few days before from a hospital in an adjoining county which did not feel itself so well equipped to handle this very exacting case; that the child's blood condition was deteriorating, and that it might become necessary at any time to administer blood transfusions; that the child's parents refused to authorize same because the religious sect to which they belong (Jehovah's Witnesses) forbids it as violating certain Biblical injunctions; that the hospital and attending surgeon could not adequately or safely treat the patient without the authority sought.

Ohio's Juvenile Code empowers the juvenile court to protect the rights of a child in this condition:

. . . Upon the certificate of one or more reputable practicing physicians, the court may summarily provide for emergency medical and surgical treatment which appears to be immediately necessary for any child concerning whom a complaint or an application for care has been filed, pending the service of a citation upon its parents, guardian, or custodian.

Even without this specific authorization we believe the court would have had ample power to act summarily under its broad equitable jurisdiction. We accordingly made the following docket entry:

9-6-62: It appearing to the Court that an emergency exists in that Kenneth Clark, a minor, aged 3 years, has been critically burned and in order to save his life a blood transfusion will become necessary, and it further appearing that the said Kenneth Clark is a child whose condition is such as to warrant the State in the interest of the child in assuming his guardianship, authorization is hereby given to Dr. James G. Sullivan or other competent member of the medical staff of Mercy Hospital, to administer any and all blood transfusions necessary in the premises, any objection to the contrary notwithstanding. It is further ordered that such child be not removed from said Mercy Hospital without the consent of Dr. James G. Sullivan.

Counsel for the parents promptly protested verbally to the Court, and demanded to be heard and to cross-examine the doctors. Accordingly, a hearing was scheduled at an early date and the parents, hospital authorities and attending surgeon were cited.

Now, we have long noted in the reported cases dealing with children's rights, a tendency to identify them with parental rights, i.e., to regard them as identical. This is quite understandable, but not always correct. One doesn't have to work in a family court very long to learn that in countless circumstances a juvenile's rights and interests at many points are at sharp variance with those of his parents. This case clearly promised to be one such, so we entered the following on the court docket:

9-10-62: It appearing that a conflict of interest may develop between parent and child, John M. Mahoney, Esq. is hereby assigned as legal counsel for the child, Kenneth Clark.

The parents attacked the order of 9-6 authorizing blood transfusions, moving to vacate it on these grounds:

1. No emergency existed in fact.

2. The order is void because made before the parents were cited to appear.

3. The statute under which it was made is unconstitutional and violates the due process clause of the 14th Amendment.

4. Blood transfusions are dangerous and contrary to good medical practice.

5. Blood transfusions are forbidden by Holy Scripture.

To take up these points in order:

1. The evidence showed that at the moment of the order the child was not at death's door, but that his blood condition had been steadily deteriorating, and if he were allowed to continue without a blood transfusion he might die. The witness James G. Sullivan, M.D., the attending surgeon, testified that he did not then know how long the child could live without a transfusion, but that he "did not propose to find out." Out of consideration for the parents' feelings he postponed giving one until a week after he received authorization, and from that time the deterioration ceased and the child's condition showed steady improvement.

The witness made it clear that whether or not the situation was emergent at the time he sought the court authorization, nevertheless it was pregnant with emergency in that the need for blood might become imperative at any moment, and for the child's sake the attending surgeon did not dare cast himself in the role of a foolish virgin.

This evidence was uncontroverted and therefrom the Court finds that an emergency did exist within the purview of the statute, and moreover one such as to warrant the court's intervention under its broad equitable powers.

2. True, the emergency order was issued before the parents were notified or hearing was had. Although conforming to statute, this was in contravention of the orderly processes of the law in litigation seeking ordinary remedies. But the law in litigation seeking ordinary remedies. But the law provides extraordinary remedies too; e.g., the temporary restraining order, whereby, for cause shown, the court may act first and inquire later.

Where a child's well-being, especially his life, is concerned, it would be precisely preposterous to withhold all measures in his behalf until a time for hearing had been found (or made) in the court's overflowing calendar; notices had been prepared; citations had been served; and hearing held--at best a week or two later. By that time the child might be cold in his grave.

The court had not only the right but the duty to act in the child's behalf first and give the parents their day in court later. Incidentally, the parents were in constant touch with the doctor and hospital, and had full knowledge of what was taking place.

None of counsel's numerous authorities on the necessity of notice, process, etc. strike us as being applicable to this set of facts, and we hold the order is not void for want of proper service.

3. The complaint that the parents were deprived of "due process" can only mean that they were deprived of life, liberty or property without due process. This imports an unpleasant consideration, to say the least.

There was no syllable of suggestion, much less evidence, that they were deprived of their life or of their liberty. This leaves only their property. What the parents were deprived of was their *claimed* right to deny their child certain treatment which medical science deemed necessary. Would this be a property right? Do the parents *own* their child's body? Is he their *chattel*?

It is true that parents exercise a dominion over their child so mighty and yet so minute as to be sometimes frightening. For example, they determine whether and whom the child may marry . . . ;whether and where he goes to school or college; which, if any, religious faith he may espouse; where he shall live; whether and where he may work, and his recreation, and so on; even whether he wears his rubbers, his pink tie, or she has her hair bobbed. Parents may, within bounds, deprive their child of his liberty and his property.

But there are well–defined limitations upon this appalling power of parent over child . . .

No longer can parents virtually exercise the power of life or death over their children. No longer can they put their child of tender years out to work and collect his earnings. They may not abuse their child or contribute to his dependency, neglect, or delinquency. Nor may they abandon him, deny him proper parental care, neglect or refuse to provide him with proper or necessary subsistence, education, medical or surgical care, or other care necessary for his health, morals or well–being; or neglect or refuse to provide the special care made necessary by his mental condition; or permit him to visit disreputable places or places prohibited by law, or associate with vagrant, vicious, criminal, notorious or immoral persons; or permit him to engage in an occupation prohibited by law or one dangerous to life or limb or injurious to his health or morals . . . And while they may, under certain circumstances, deprive him of his liberty or his property, under no circumstances, with or without due process, with or without religious sanction, may they deprive him of his *life*!

The evidence was undisputed that blood transfusion was necessary and the best available medical opinion held that to deprive the child of it would have been to risk his life. We hold the parents had no right to subject their child to such a risk, and there could have been no violation of the 14th Amendment . . .

4. The attack on the practice of giving blood transfusions was not supported by any evidence—only some medical references. The practice is so nearly universal and upheld by such an overwhelming array of medical scientists as to appear beyond lay attack. This point is not an issue.

5. The Biblical passages relied on to require vacation of the Court's emergency order were as follows:

Genesis	9:3,4
Leviticus	3:17; 17:14
Deuteronomy	12:23
Acts	15:28, 29

To a layman unversed in the seemingly esoteric art of theological interpretation of the 17th century version of ancient Hebrew and Greek Scriptures, these passages are, to say the least, somewhat obscure. They have to do with blood and the eating or taking thereof. Blood transfusion as administered by modern medicine was unknown to the authors of these cryptic dicta. Had its beneficent effects been known to them, it is likely some exception would have been made in its favor—especially by St. Luke who is said to have been a physician.

But in our humble civil court we must confine ourselves to the civil law of the State. Religious doctrines and dogmas, be they obviously sound or curiously dubious, may not control. The parents in this case have a perfect right to worship as they please and believe what they please. They enjoy complete freedom of religion. The parents also have the right to use all lawful means to vindicate this right (and in the present instance they appear to have done their full duty by their religion).

But this right of theirs ends where somebody else's right begins. Their child is a human being in his own right, with a soul and body of his own. He has rights of his own—the right to live and to grow up without disfigurement.

The child is a citizen of the State. While he "belongs" to his parents, he belongs also to his State. Their rights in him entail many duties. Likewise the fact the child belongs to the State imposes upon the State many duties. Chief among them is the duty to protect his right to live and to grow up with a sound mind in a sound body, and to brook no interference with that right by any person or organization.

When a religious doctrine espoused by the parents threatens to defend or curtail such a right of their child, the State's duty to step in and preserve the child's right is immediately operative.

To put it another way, when a child's right to live and his parents' religious belief collide, the former is paramount, and the religious doctrine must give way.

The motion to vacate is overruled; the subsisting order may stand until further order . . .

o **Recap of the Case**. The important point of this case for nurses is that parents may not refuse to consent to medical treatment for their children if their refusal may result in death or serious injury. Nurses should remember that when confronted with these situations, the parents' decision cannot be honored. Nurses should seek support immediately from administrators and legal counsel to resolve these matters.

FATHER'S DECISION TO REFUSE TREATMENT FOR SON UPHELD BY COURT

However, where the situation is not life–threatening, the refusal of a parent to give consent has not traditionally been overruled by the courts. *In Re Seiferth*, is an example of such a case. This case involved a fourteen–year–old boy with a cleft palate and a harelip. The boy's father had strong religious beliefs about mental healing. That is, he believed that the child would be healed through natural forces. The child shared the father's religious beliefs. Consequently, both father and son were opposed to surgical correction of the child's cleft palate and harelip. The court decided to honor the wishes of father and son, at least for the time being. This decision represents the traditional view that unless parental refusal is likely to result in severe bodily harm or death to the child, the parents' wishes must be respected. This traditional view is still applied by some judges.

In Re Seiferth, 309 N.Y.80, 127 N.E.2d 820 (1955)
New York Court of Appeals

This is a case involving a fourteen–year–old boy with cleft palate and harelip, whose father holds strong convictions with which the boy has become imbued against medicine and surgery. This proceeding has been instituted by the deputy commissioner of the Erie County Health Department on petition to the Children's Court to have Martin declared a neglected child, and to have his custody transferred from his parents to the Commissioner of Social Welfare of Erie County for the purpose of consenting to such medical, surgical and dental services as may be necessary to rectify his condition. The medical testimony is to the effect that such cases are almost always given surgical treatment at an earlier age, and the older the patient is the less favorable are likely to be the results according to experience. The surgery recommended by the plastic surgeon called for petitioner consists of three operations (1) repair of the harelip by bringing the split together, (2) closing the cleft or split in the rear of the palate, the boy being already too late in life to have the front part mended by surgery; and (3) repairing the front part of the palate by dental appliances. The only risk of mortality is the negligible one due to the use of anesthesia. These operations would be spaced a few months apart and six months would be expected to complete the work, two years at the outside in case of difficulty. Petitioner's plastic surgeon declined to be precise about how detrimental it would be to the prognosis to defer this work for several years. He said: "I do not think it is emergent, that it has to be done this month or next month, but every year that goes is important to this child, yes." A year and a half has already elapsed since this testimony was taken in December, 1953.

Even after the operation, Martin will not be able to talk normally, at least not without going to school for an extended period for concentrated speech therapy. There are certain phases of a child's life when the importance of these defects becomes of greater significance. The first is past when children enter grade school, the next is the period of adolescence, particularly toward the close of adolescence when social interests arise in secondary school. Concerning this last, petitioner's plastic surgeon stated: "That is an extremely important period of time. That child is approaching that age where it is very important that correction, that it is very significant that correction made at this time could probably put him in a great deal better position to enter that period of life than would otherwise. Another thing which is difficult is that we have very excellent speech facilities at the Buffalo Public Schools through grade level. At secondary school level and in higher age groups speech training facilities are less satisfactory, so that it is important that it be done at this age.

However, the most important thing of all is this gradually progressive with time. The earlier done, the better results. Normally the lip is repaired in early infancy, one to three years of age. Speech training would begin at school or earlier. Every year lost has been that much more lost to the boy. Each year lost continues to be lost. The time to repair is not too early." He testified that in twenty years of plastic surgery he had never encountered a child with this boy's defects who had not been operated upon at his age. Nevertheless, he testified that such an operation can be performed "from the time the child is born until he dies." In his doctor's view, the consideration bulked larger than the quality of postoperative results, that the boy's increasing social contacts required that he be made to look and to speak normally as he approached adolescence.

Everyone testified that the boy is likeable, he has a newspaper route, and his marks in school were all over 90 during the last year. However, his father did testify that recently the boy had withdrawn a little more from his fellows, although he said that "As soon as anyone contacts Martin, he is so likeable nobody is tempted to ridicule him . . . Through his pleasantness he overcomes it."

The father testified that "If the child decides on an operation, I shall not be opposed", and that "I want to say in a few years the child should decide for himself . . . whether to have the operation or not." The father believes in mental healing by letting "the forces of the universe work on the body", although he denied that this is an established religion of any kind stating that it is purely his own philosophy and that "it is not classified as religion." There is no doubt, however, that the father is strong minded about this, and has inculcated a distrust and dread of surgery in the boy since childhood.

The Erie County Children's Court Judge caused the various surgical procedures to be explained to Martin by competent and qualified practitioners in the field of plastic surgery and orthodontia. Photographs of other children who had undergone similar remedial surgery were exhibited to him showing their condition both before and after treatment. He was also taken to the speech correction school where he heard the reproduction of his own voice and speech, as well as records depicting various stages of progress of other children. He met other children of his own age, talked to them and attended class in speech correction. Both the boy and the father were given opportunity to ask questions, which they did freely not only of the professional staff but of the different children.

On February 11, 1954, Martin, his father and attorney met after these demonstrations in Judge Wylegala's chambers. Judge Wylegala wrote in his opinion that Martin "was very much pleased with what was shown him, but had come to the conclusion that he should try for some time longer to close the cleft palate and the split lip himself through 'natural forces.' " After stating that an order for surgery would have been granted without hesitation if this proceeding had been instituted before this child acquired convictions of his own, Judge Wylegala summed up his conclusions as follows: "After duly deliberating upon the psychological effect of surgery upon this mature, intelligent boy, schooled as he has been for all of his young years in the existence of 'forces of nature' and his fear of surgery upon the human body, I have come to the conclusion that no order should be made at this time compelling the child to submit to surgery. His condition is not emergent and there is no serious threat to his health or life. He has time until he becomes 21 years of age to apply for financial assistance under County and State aid to physically handicapped children to have the corrections made. This has also been explained to him after he made known his decision to me." The petition accordingly was dismissed.

The Appellate Division, Fourth Department, reversed by a divided court, and granted the petition requiring Martin Seiferth to submit to surgery.

As everyone agrees, there are important considerations both ways. The Children's Court has power in drastic situations to direct the operation over the objection of parents . . . Nevertheless, there is no present emergency, time is less of the essence than it was a few years ago insofar as concerns the physical prognosis, and we are impressed by the circumstance that in order to benefit from the operation upon the cleft palate, it will almost certainly be necessary to enlist Martin's cooperation in developing normal speech patterns through a lengthy course in concentrated speech therapy. It will be almost impossible to secure his cooperation if he continues to believe, as he does now, that it will be necessary "to remedy the surgeon's distortion first and then go back to the primary task of healing the body." This is an aspect of the problem with which petitioner's plastic surgeon did not especially concern himself, for he did not attempt to view the case from the psychological viewpoint of this misguided youth. Upon the other hand, the Children's Court Judge, who saw and heard the witnesses, and arranged the conferences for the boy and his father which have been mentioned, appears to have been keenly aware of this aspect of the situation, and to have concluded that less would be lost by permitting the lapse of several more years, when the boy may make his own decision to submit to plastic surgery, than might be sacrificed if he were compelled to undergo it now against this sincere and frightened antagonism. One cannot be certain of begin right under these circumstances, but this appears to be a situation where the discretion of the trier of the facts should be preferred to that of the Appellate Division.

The order of the Appellate Division should be reversed and that of the Children's Court reinstated dismissing the petition, without prejudice to renew the application if circumstances warrant.

o **Recap of the Case**. A father in *Seiferth* refused to consent to treatment of his son's harelip and cleft palate. The court upheld this decision because neither death nor serious harm would result. To determine whether death or serious harm may occur, nurses should consult with a wide range of practitioners, administrators and legal counsel in an attempt to reach a consensus on this point. If no consensus can be reached, suit may be filed in order to get the court's guidance.

MOTHER'S DECISION REGARDING
TREATMENT OVERRULED

However, there are indications that the some judges' attitudes are beginning to change in situations which are not life threatening; the courts are beginning to take a more protective role even where the proposed treatment does not threaten the child's life. For example, in *In Re Sampson*, the court authorized blood transfusions for the child of a Jehovah's Witness in order to permit surgeons to repair a gross disfigurement of the child's face. The disfigurement was caused by neurofibromatosis and was, according to the court, "grotesque and repulsive." The judge readily admitted that there was no threat of death or even serious bodily harm to the child from the deformity of his face. The court then determined that no serious emotional harm to the child had occurred as a result of his deformity. Nonetheless, the court decided that it posed an unusual but extremely serious threat to the life of the child in the form of an inevitable, extremely negative effect upon his personality development, his opportunity for education and later employment, and upon every aspect of his relationships with his peers. The court authorized blood transfusions so that the child could have surgery to repair his face.

In Re Sampson, 317 N.Y.S.2d 641 (1970)
New York Supreme Court, Appellate Division

The Commissioner of Health of Ulster County brings this neglect proceeding pursuant to Article 10 of the Family Court Act charging that Kevin Sampson, a male child under sixteen years of age is neglected by reason of the failure of his mother, Mildred Sampson, to provide him with proper medical and surgical care. The mother is not opposed to having the recommended surgery performed upon her son, but because she is a member of the religious sect known as Jehovah's Witnesses she has steadfastly refused to give her consent to the administration of any blood transfusions during the course of the surgery, without which the proposed surgery may not safely be performed. After extensive hearings the Court finds that the following facts are established by the evidence.

The boy, Kevin Sampson, who is now fifteen years of age, having been born on January 25, 1955, suffers from extensive neurofibromatosis or Von Recklinghausen's disease which has caused a massive deformity of the right side of his face and neck. The outward manifestation of the disease is a large fold or flap of an overgrowth of facial tissue which causes the whole cheek, the corner of his mouth and right ear to drop down giving him an appearance which can only be described as grotesque and repulsive. Fortunately, however, the disease has not yet progressed to a point where his vision has been affected or his hearing impaired. Dr. Robert C. Lonergan, an eye doctor appointed by the Court to examine Kevin reported that "I do not believe ocular condition related to systemic disease—in any event it does not alter or require any change in treatment—the eye condition requires no treatment." Dr. Elbert Loughran, an ear doctor appointed by the Court to examine Kevin reported that he found "normal drum heads bilateral. Effect on hearing limited to occlusion of external ear canal on right side by folds of skin. The left ear drum and canal are normal. Gross hearing normal on both sides."

Thus, insofar as the boy's sight and hearing are concerned, it appears from the doctor's reports that the neurofibromatosis poses no immediate threat to either and that there is, therefore, no need for treatment of either his eyes or his ears.

However, the massive deformity of the entire right side of his face and neck is patently so gross and so disfiguring that it must inevitably exert a most negative effect upon his personality development, his opportunity for education and later employment and upon every phase of his relationship with his peers and others. Although the staff psychiatrist of the County Mental Health Center reports that "there is no evidence of any thinking disorder" and that "in spite of marked facial disfigurement he failed to show any outstanding personality aberration", this finding hardly justifies a conclusion that he has been or will continue to be wholly unaffected by his misfortune. Although Kevin was found to be not psychotic, a psychologist found him to be a "boy (who) is extremely dependent and (who) sees himself as an inadequate personality." The staff psychiatrist reports that "Kevin demonstrates inferiority feeling and low self concept. Such inadequate personality is often noted in cases of mental retardation, facial disfigurement and emotional deprivation."

If the boy exhibited to the psychologist some mental retardation it is hardly surprising in view of the fact that he has been exempted from school since November 24, 1964 and is currently exempted from school by reason of his facial disfigurement. As a result, although various tests administered by school authorities show him to be intellectually capable of being educated and trained to a reasonable level of self-sufficiency, he is, at 15 years of age, a virtual illiterate.

From all the information available to the Court as the result of extended hearings and various reports, particularly those supplied by those educators who have become familiar with the pattern of Kevin's development, or more accurately, lack thereof, the conclusion is inescapable that the marked facial disfigurement from which this boy suffers constitutes such an overriding limiting factor militating against his future development that unless some constructive steps are taken to alleviate his condition, his chances for a normal, useful life are virtually nil.

The unanimous recommendation of all those who have dealt with the many problems posed by Kevin's affliction—educators, psychologists, psychiatrists, physicians and surgeons is that steps be taken to correct the condition through surgery. It is conceded, however, by the surgeons that, insofar as his health and his life is concerned, this is not a necessary operation. The disease poses no immediate threat to his life nor has it as yet seriously affected his general health. Moreover, the surgery will not cure him of the disease. In fact, for the condition from which he suffers there is no known cure. According to Dr. Brandon Maccomber, one of the highly qualified plastic surgeons who testified as to the need for surgery, "where (the disease) is interfering with function or appearance many times it can be excised partially, it never can be cured, but it can be excised, removed and by plastic procedures you may be able to improve not only the function but the appearance."

The surgery which the surgeons recommend for the alleviation of the diseased condition cannot, however, be performed without substantial risk. In the words of Dr. Ferdinand Stanley Hoffmeister, the other highly qualified surgeon who testified as to the need for corrective surgery and who had previously performed some limited surgery upon this boy, "I think it's a dangerous procedure. I think it involves considerable risk. It's a massive surgery of six to eight hours duration with great blood loss. This is a risky surgical procedure." When asked if the risk would be much above average he replied, "much, much, much." The surgeon repeatedly "emphasiz(ed) the surgery risk in operating on this patient even with blood."

Without the mother's permission to administer blood transfusions the risk becomes wholly unacceptable. According to Dr. Hoffmeister, "if this tumor had to be removed as extensively as it is desirable to improve his appearance, I think the loss of blood would be so extensive, that I personally would not dare to undertake such a procedure having only plasma expanders at my disposal". The surgeons are adamant in their refusal to operate upon Kevin unless they have permission to use blood and to administer during the surgery such blood transfusions as the patient's condition requires.

Mrs. Sampson, while not opposed to surgery as such, having already given her permission for surgery limited to the use of plasma, is equally adamant in her refusal to give her consent to the use of blood. As previously noted, Mrs. Sampson is an adherent to the religious sect known as Jehovah's Witnesses who according to the minister of the Kingston Congregation of Jehovah's Witnesses "feel that the Bible is explicit on the matter of taking any form of blood into our system either by eating, through mouth, food, through the body, through the veins. This is specifically prohibited in the Scriptures for Christians". Although not opposed to medicine or surgery on religious grounds, Jehovah's Witnesses hold as a cardinal principle of their faith that the eating or ingestion of blood into the body by any means whatever, including modern surgical procedures for the transfusion of blood are explicitly forbidden by the law of God. According to Jehovah's Witnesses' doctrine the divine proscription dates back to God's pronouncement to Noah immediately after the global flood over 4300 years ago, was reiterated and emphasized to the Jews and when the Nation of Israel was brought into the convenant relationship with Jehovah, applies to the eating of human blood as well as animal blood and was made applicable to Christians by the new covenant made over the blood of Jesus Christ. Jehovah's Witnesses regard the prohibition against the consumption of blood as more than a mere dietary law of the Jews—the eating of blood in any form is a sin against God and draws upon the soul of the transgressor the enmity of God . . .

While Jehovah's Witnesses emphasize that their refusal to submit to blood transfusions is based upon the law of God as recorded in their Bible, New World Translation of the Holy Scriptures, they find further support for their position in the substantial risk to health and even to life which medical science acknowledges to be inherent in the transfusion of human blood. In addition to the adverse reaction in a patient to be anticipated from the mismatching of incompatible blood types or the ofttime fatal consequence of a circulatory overload or an air embolism caused by inept procedures, the Court finds considerable support for the Witnesses' fear that the current widespread practice of using blood from commercial blood banks poses a serious risk to the patient's health through the transmission of such diseases as syphilis, malaria, hepatitis and a variety of allergic conditions.

Finally, the Court finds that the child's parent has been offered the financial means with which to have the recommended surgery performed, but that for the reasons heretofore expressed she adamantly refuses to give her consent . . .

The question is, however, whether the court should exercise the power which it undoubtedly has, to compel this boy to undergo a dangerous surgical procedure for the partial correction, but not a cure, of the facial deformity from which he suffers, over the sincerely held religious objection of his mother? The answer to this question requires a most careful balancing of the potential good to be attained against the risks of life necessarily involved in so dangerous a surgical procedure and consideration of the validity of the religious objections which have been raised to the administration of blood transfusions. These two facets of the question will be examined in inverse order.

The Religious Objections.

The free exercise of religion is, of course, one of our more precious freedoms and is guaranteed by both the United States and New York State Constitutions . . .

The courts have, however, drawn a distinction between the free exercise of religious belief which is constitutionally protected against any infringement and religious practices that are inimical or detrimental to public health or welfare which are not . . .

But the family itself is not beyond regulation in the public interest, as against a claim of religious liberty . . . And neither rights of religion nor rights of parenthood are beyond limitation . . . Its authority is not nullified merely because the parent grounds his claim to control the child's course of conduct on religion or conscience . . . The right to practice religion freely does not include liberty to expose the community or the child to communicable disease or the latter to ill health or death . . . The catalogue need not be lengthened. It is sufficient to show what indeed appellant hardly disputes, that the state has a wide range of power for limiting parental freedom and authority in things affecting the child's welfare; and that this includes, to some extent, matters of conscience and religious conviction . . .

Specifically, the same issue presented here—i.e. the power of the state through its courts to order a necessary blood transfusion for a minor over the religious objections of a parent has been frequently contested by Jehovah's Witnesses before. However, in every reported case courts have unequivocally upheld the power of the state to authorize the administration of a blood transfusion over the religious objections of the parent where the blood transfusion was shown to be necessary for the preservation of the minor's life or the success of needed surgery . . .

. . . I conclude that although the mother's religious objections to the administration of a blood transfusion to her son in the event surgery is to be performed upon his face is founded upon the scriptures and is sincerely held, it must give way before the state's paramount duty to insure his right to live and grow up without disfigurement—the right to live and grow up with a sound mind in a sound body. "Parents may be free to become martyrs themselves. But it does not follow they are free, in identical circumstances, to make martyrs of their children before they have reached the age of full and legal discretion when they can make that choice for themselves . . ."

The Potential Good vs. The Risk to Life.

In the opinion of the surgeons who are familiar with Kevin's condition the neurofibromatosis from which he suffers poses no immediate threat to his life or even to his general health and the proposed surgery for its excision would have no material effect upon his life expectancy. Fortunately, according to Dr. Maccomber, "To date there are no signs of any central nervous system, that is brain or spinal cord, involvement."

It is not necessary, however, that a child's life be in danger before this court may act to safeguard his health or general welfare . . .

. . . There is no requirement in the statute that there be an emergency or danger to the child's life before the Court may act--only a requirement that the child be within the jurisdiction of the Court and appear to the Court to be in need . . . I therefore conclude that this court's authority to deal with the abused, neglected or physically handicapped child is not limited to "drastic situations" or to those which constitute a "present emergency," but that the Court has a "wide discretion" to order medical or surgical care and treatment for an infant even over parental objection, if in the Court's judgment the health, safety or welfare of the child requires it.

The question still remains, however, whether this Court should, under the circumstances of this case, order this boy to undergo a risky surgical procedure, which the surgeons concede will not cure him of the disease. Dr. Hoffmeister, one of the plastic surgeons who testified in this case concedes, "we would certainly leave a tumor behind. This is a non-resectable lesion." Dr. Maccomber, the other surgeon also was frank in admitting the limitations upon the surgeon's skill when he said: "well, you can remove--you can't get it all, this is for sure." Although the results of the surgery would be to change his physical appearance, Dr. Maccomber conceded that "he can't be returned to a normal face, impossible."

Counsel for Mrs. Sampson stresses the surgical risk involved in the contemplated procedure which the surgeons candidly concede is a "dangerous procedure" and involves "considerable risk" even with the use of blood transfusions. Moreover, counsel points out with much persuasiveness that Dr. Hoffmeister expressed the opinion that, while the contemplated surgery would still be risky, it would be less risky if the operation were delayed for five or six years, because the boy's blood volume would then be larger and while the loss of blood would be about the same, relative blood loss would be smaller than now.

Because of the high surgical risk inherent in the operation and the minimization of the risk as the boy grows older by reason of the lower relative blood loss to total blood supply, counsel for Mrs. Sampson and the Law Guardian counsel delay until the boy is old enough to make the decision for himself. In fact, even Dr. Hoffmeister counsels delay. He said: "I would suggest to the Court wait until the child is 21 years old and have him make his own decision because I feel we are not losing by waiting five or six years.

"Q. In other words you feel it is not increasing the degree of risk to wait five or six years?

"A. I think it's decreasing the degree of risk.

"Q. It's decreasing?

"A. Because of the blood volume we alluded to."

From the surgeon's point of view the fact that the surgical risk may decrease as the boy grows older is certainly a most persuasive reason for postponing the surgery. However, to postpone the surgery merely to allow the boy to become of age so that he may make the decision himself as suggested by the surgeon and urged by both counsel for the mother and the Law Guardian . . . totally ignores the developmental and psychological factors stemming from his deformity which the Court deems to be of the utmost importance in any consideration of the boy's future welfare and begs the whole question.

This Court cannot evade the responsibility for a decision now by the simple expedient of foisting upon this boy the responsibility for making a decision at some later day, which by the time it is made, if at all, will be too late to undo the irreparable damage he will have suffered in the interim. This Court plainly has a duty to perform and though the responsibility for decision is awesome, the burden cannot be shared by transferring even a small part of it to another . . .

It is conceded that "there are important considerations both ways" . . . Nevertheless, a decision must be made, and so, after much deliberation, I am persuaded that if this court is to meet its responsibilities to this boy it can neither shift the responsibility for the ultimate decision onto his shoulders nor can it permit his mother's religious beliefs to stand in the way of attaining through corrective surgery whatever chance he may have for a normal, happy existence, which, to paraphrase Judge Fuld, is difficult to attainment under the most propitious circumstances, but will unquestionably be impossible if the disfigurement is not corrected.

If this boy has any chance at all for a normal, happy existence, without a disfigurement so gross as to overshadow all else in his life, some risk must be taken. The surgeons acknowledge that in every case of surgery performed under anesthesia there is always a risk of cardiac arrest, but as Dr. Maccomber said, "if we worried about that all the time we wouldn't do any good for anybody." He acknowledged: "we know there's a risk and they have to have surgery." But then he added: "Here the risk shouldn't be too great with blood. In other words, we're not working on vital organs that can go haywire, but with this, we surely, if we didn't have blood, no one should touch him."

Thus, while the surgeons concede that there are risks inherent in the contemplated surgery, in their opinion that risk should not be too great if they have permission to use blood. In any event, when one considers the bleak prospect for this boy's future of the alternative of doing nothing, it is a risk which I believe must be taken. However, this conclusion must be qualified by stating that if in the judgment of those surgeons who have been consulted concerning Kevin's condition and who have the responsibility for the actual performance of the surgery, the contemplated procedures pose an unacceptable risk to his life, they ought not to undertake such surgery. This is a judgment that only the surgeons are qualified to make and nothing in this decision should be so construed as to require any surgeon to perform any surgery upon this boy if, in their judgment, such surgery ought not to be undertaken. The court wishes to leave the surgeons completely free to exercise their own professional judgment as to the nature, extent and timing of any surgery that may be required for the correction of Kevin's deformity.

For the reasons heretofore expressed the court finds the mother's religious objections to the administration of blood transfusions untenable. It is both illogical and impractical for Mrs. Sampson to consent to surgery for her son and then for religious reasons attempt to limit or circumscribe the surgeons in the employment of their surgical skills. In passing it should be noted, however, that this is not a case in which the mother resists medical or surgical treatment for her son because of her sole reliance upon the power of God to heal, for it does not appear that either Jehovah's Witnesses or Mrs. Sampson individually make any pretext of reliance upon divine power to heal through prayer. Consequently, since that issue is not presented, it is unnecessary to pass upon it.

Because of the refusal of Mrs. Mildred Sampson to give her consent to the blood transfusions essential for the safety of the surgical procedures necessary to insure the physical, mental and emotional well being of her son, the Court adjudicates Kevin Sampson to be a neglected child . . .

This adjudication, however, in no way imports a finding that the mother failed in her duty to the child in any other respect . . .

The court therefore orders that the child, Kevin Sampson, be released to the custody of his mother and further orders that Mrs. Mildred Sampson be placed under the supervision of the Commissioner of Social Services of Ulster County for the maximum period of one year upon the following terms and conditions: (a) that Mrs. Mildred Sampson cooperate with the Department of Social Services to remedy her omission to provide her son with such surgical care and treatment as may be necessary to remedy or alleviate the facial disfigurement from which he suffers; (b) report to the Department of Social Services as directed by the court or the Department of Social Services; (c) permit authorized representatives of the Department of Social Services to visit the home or any other place where the boy may be; (d) notify the Department of Social Services of any change of address or employment.

In addition, the court specifically orders and directs that the mother, Mrs. Mildred Sampson permit Kevin to undergo such surgery as, in the judgment of the Commissioner of Health of Ulster County upon the advice and recommendation of duly qualified surgeons, shall be necessary or required to remedy or correct the facial condition of neurofibromatosis or Von Recklinghausen's disease from which he suffers. During the course of such surgery the surgeons are authorized to administer from time to time such blood transfusions as in their judgment may be necessary. The cost of such surgical treatment and hospital care as may be necessary shall be borne by the County of Ulster.

o **Recap of the Case**. The important point of this case for nurses is that even if refusal of treatment will not result in physical harm or death to a child, some courts may overrule parental decisions to refuse treatment. The "bottom line" is that any parental decision to refuse treatment which concerns nurses should be brought to the attention of proper personnel for careful resolution.

On Behalf of Impaired Newborns

When babies are born with severe deformities as well as a life-threatening but easily correctable defect, parents are sometimes tempted to forego correction of the defect, thereby insuring the death of the child. Historically, physicians and administrators have accepted the parents' decision without question or protest. However, parents rarely took their newborns home to die. Rather, these children were often left in the hospital nursery to starve to death, either because their correctable defects involved the digestive system and they were not able to take nourishment, or parents wished to deprive them of sustenance in order to hasten death. Nurses often suffered a great deal as a result of these decisions. Nurses, not parents and physicians, had to stand by watching the painful process of death by starvation in the nursery. They also suffered professionally since they were not allowed to do what was dictated by their professional standards, i.e. do everything possible to sustain the lives of their patients.

COURT ORDERS REPAIR OF HANDICAPPED INFANT'S LIFE-THREATENING DEFECT

Fortunately, attitudes toward these situations are changing. There is a much greater belief that the child's interest in life is more important than parental concerns about the quality of life and financial burdens. In *Maine Medical Center v. Houle*, the court appointed a guardian *ad litem* to consent to correction of a tracheal esophageal fistula which prevented the ingestion of nourishment. The court took this action because the repair was medically necessary and feasible.

Special note should be taken of the fact that the court specifically rejected testimony by the treating physicians about the child's so-called quality of life. The reasons courts are reluctant to consider this type of testimony is that it is often speculative at best. It is extremely difficult to determine the potential of a handicapped child at birth. In addition, courts reject the idea that handicapped persons may be denied the right to life or the right to the prolongation of life because they are disabled and, at least in the eyes of some people, experience a diminished quality of life compared to nonhandicapped persons.

Maine Medical Center v. Houle, No. 74–145, Slip op.
(Superior Ct; Cumberland, Maine, Feb. 14, 1974)
Superior Court of Cumberland, Maine

The complaint herein seeks the intervention of the court between the parents of a newborn child and the hospital and attending physician concerning parental decision as to the future course of treatment . . .

The testimony herein indicates that a male child was born to the defendants on February 9, 1974 at the Maine Medical Center. Medical examination by the hospital staff revealed the absence of a left eye, a rudimentary left ear with no ear canal, a malformed left thumb and a tracheal esophageal fistula. The latter condition prevented the ingestion of nourishment, necessitated intravenous feeding and allowed the entry of fluid into the infant's lungs, leading to the development of pneumonia and other complications. The recommended medical treatment was surgical repair of the tracheal esophageal fistula to allow normal feeding and respiration. Prior to February 11, 1974, the child's father directed the attending physician not to conduct surgical repair of the fistula and to cease intravenous feeding.

By Temporary Restraining Order issued *ex parte* on February 11, 1974, this court authorized the continuance of such measures as might be medically dictated to maintain said child in a stable and viable condition and restrained the defendants from issuing any orders, which, in the opinion of the attending physician, would be injurious to the current medical situation of said child.

In the interim the child's condition has deteriorated. Periods of apnea have necessitated the use of a bag breathing device to artificially sustain respiration. Several convulsive seizures of unknown cause have occurred. Medications administered include gentimycin for the treatment of pneumonia and phenobarbitol to control convulsive seizures. Further medical evaluation indicates the lack of response of the right eye to light stimuli, the existence of some non–fused vertebrae and the virtual certainty of some brain damage resulting from anoxia. The most recent developments have caused the attending physician to form the opinion that all life supporting measures should be withdrawn. The doctor is further of the opinion that without surgical correction of the tracheal esophageal fistula the child will certainly die and that with surgical correction the child can survive but with some degree of permanent brain damage.

The court heard further testimony concerning the present posture of the mother's emotional condition and attitude toward the future survival of the child. Without disparaging the seriousness of the emotional impact upon the parents and without ignoring the difficulties which this court's decision may cause in the future, it is the firm opinion of this court that questions of permanent custody, maintenance and further care of the child are for the moment legally irrelevant.

Quite literally the court must make a decision concerning the life or death of a newborn infant. Recent decisions concerning the right of the state to intervene with the medical and moral judgments of a prospective parent and attending physician may have cast doubts upon the legal rights of an unborn child, but at the moment of live birth there does exist a human being entitled to the fullest protection of the law. The most basic right enjoyed by every human being is the right to life itself.

Where the condition of a child does not involve serious risk of life and where treatment involves a considerable risk, parents as the natural guardians have a considerable degree of discretion and the courts ought not intervene. The measures proposed in this case are not in any sense heroic measures except for the doctor's opinion that probable brain damage has rendered life not worth preserving. Were it his opinion that life itself could not be preserved, heroic measures ought not be required. However, the doctor's qualitative evaluation of the value of the life to be preserved is not legally within the scope of his expertise.

In the court's opinion the issue before the court is not the prospective quality of the life to be preserved, but the medical feasibility of the proposed treatment compared with the almost certain risk of death should treatment be withheld. Being satisfied that corrective surgery is medically necessary and medically feasible, the court finds that the defendants herein have no right to withhold such treatment and that to do so constitutes neglect in the legal sense. Therefore, the court will authorize the guardian *ad litem* to consent to the surgical correction of the tracheal esophageal fistula and such other normal life supportive measures as may be medically required in the immediate future. It is further ordered that Respondents are hereby enjoined until further order of this court from issuing any orders to Petitioners or their employees which, in the opinion of the attending physicians or surgeons would be injurious to the medical condition of the child.

The court will retain jurisdiction for the purpose of determining any further measures that may be required to be taken and eventually for the purpose of determining the future custody of the child should the court determine that it is appropriate to do so.

o <u>**Recap of the Case**</u>. The court ordered repair of a handicapped infant's fistula even though the infant's parents refused to consent. The court took this action because the child's condition was life-threatening, which made repair medically necessary. Another reason for the court's action was that correction of the infant's condition was medically feasible. The surgery itself was relatively safe and, without surgery, the infant would certainly die. The factors considered certainly by the court in this case provide guidance for nurses who confront similar situations.

Part IV

SPECIAL SITUATIONS

10

Right To Terminate Life-Sustaining Treatment

COURT REFUSES TO PERMIT REMOVAL OF RESPIRATOR

The most well-known case in this area is *In Re Karen Quinlan*. In this case, the court balanced the patient's constitutional right of privacy, specifically her right to refuse treatment given her particular circumstances, versus the interest the state may have in protecting the patient's life. The court determined that the removal of life support systems is a medical determination which must be made by treating professionals.

The court considered a variety of circumstances and testimony prior to reaching this conclusion. The court carefully reviewed Quinlan's medical status and concluded that she was not legally or medically dead by any criteria recognized in New Jersey. She was in a persistent, vegetative state, prognosis unclear. Quinlan was a Catholic and cessation of so-called heroic measures was consistent with her religious beliefs. On several occasions prior to her illness, Quinlan expressed a desire not to be kept alive under circumstances similar to those in which she was now placed. The court discounted this testimony, however, because Quinlan was not actually confronted by the possibility of death when she made them. The court also defined its duty with regard to Quinlan which was to take action in her best interests and to protect her. Since the removal of the respirator meant that Karen would probably die, the court decided that removal of the respirator was not in her best interests and would not protect her. If, however, a medical determination was made that it was in her best interests, the court would affirm medical opinion.

In Re Karen Quinlan
137 N.J. Superior 227, 348 A.2d 801 (1975)
New Jersey Superior Court

In this initial pleading Joseph Quinlan, father of 21-year old Karen Ann Quinlan, seeks, on grounds of mental incompetency, to be appointed the guardian of the person and property of his daughter . . .

Karen Ann Quinlan, one of three children of Joseph and Julia Quinlan, was born April 24, 1954. She was baptized and raised a Roman Catholic. She attended Roman Catholic Church-affiliated elementary and secondary schools. She is a member of her parents' local Roman Catholic Church in Mount Arlington, New Jersey. The parish priest is Father Thomas A. Trapasso.

Sometime in late 1974 or early 1975 Karen Quinlan moved from her parents' home. Thereafter she had at least two subsequent residences, with the last being a lake cottage in Sussex County, New Jersey.

On the night of April 15, 1975 friends of Karen summoned the local police and emergency rescue squad, and she was taken to Newton Memorial Hospital. The precise events leading up to her admission to Newton Memorial Hospital are unclear. She apparently ceased breathing for at least two 15-minute periods. Mouth-to-mouth resuscitation was applied by her friends the first time and by a police respirator the second time. The exact amount of time she was without spontaneous respiration is unknown.

Upon her admission to Newton Memorial urine and blood tests were administered which indicated the presence of quinine, aspirin, barbiturates in normal range and traces of valium and librium. The drugs found present were indicated by Dr. Robert Morse, the neurologist in charge of her care at St. Clare's, to be in the therapeutic range, and the quinine consistent with mixing in drinks like soda water.

The cause of the unconsciousness and periodic cessations of respiration is undetermined. The interruption in respiration apparently caused anoxia—insufficient supply of oxygen in the blood—resulting in her present condition.

Hospital records at the time of admission reflected Karen's vital signs to be normal, a temperature of 100, pupils unreactive, unresponsivity to deep pain, legs rigid and curled up, with decorticate brain activity. Her blood oxygen level was low at the time. She was placed upon a respirator at Newton Hospital.

At 10 p.m. on April 16, 1975 Dr. Morse examined Karen at the request of her then attending physician. He found her in a state of coma, with evidence of decortication indicating altered level of consciousness. She required the respirator for assistance. She did not trigger the respirator, which means that she did not breathe spontaneously nor independently of it at any time during the examination. Due to her decorticate posturing, no reflexes could be elicited.

In the decorticate posturing the upper arms are drawn into the side of the body. The forearms are drawn in against the chest with the hands generally at right angles to the forearms, pointing towards the waist. The legs are drawn up against the body, knees are up, feet are in near the buttocks and extended in ballet–type pose.

He found her oculocephalic and oculovestibular reflexes normal. The oculocephalic reflex test consists of turning the head from side to side with the eyes open. In a positive response, when the head is rotated to the right, the eyes deviate to the left. As part of this test the head is also moved front and back, the neck is flexed in the back movement, causing the eyelids to open. This phenomenon is called "doll's––eyelid response." (Dr. Morse found that reflex intact on April 26, according to hospital records.) The oculovestibular reflex ascertained by a caloric stimulation test consists of the slow introduction of ice water into the ear canal. The eyes drift or move toward the irrigated ear. It is a lateral eye movement test.

He also found pupilary reaction to light in both eyes.

Her weight at the time was 115 pounds.

Dr. Morse could not obtain any initial history (*i.e.*, the circumstances and events occurring prior to Karen's becoming unconscious). There was no information available from her friends. He speculated at the outset on the possibility of an overdose of drugs, past history of lead poisoning, foul play, or head injury due to a fall. He indicated that the lack of an initial history seriously inhibits a diagnosis.

Karen was transferred to the Intensive Care Unit (I.C.U.) of St. Clare's Hospital, under the care of Dr. Morse. At the time of her transfer she was still unconscious, still on the respirator; a catheter was inserted into her bladder and a tracheostomy had been performed.

Upon entry into the St. Clare's I.C.U. she was placed on a MA-1 respirator, which provides air to her lungs on a controlled volume basis. It also has a "sigh volume," which is a periodic increase in the volume of air to purge the lungs of any accumulation of fluids or excretions. The machine takes over completely the breathing function when the patient does not breathe spontaneously.

Subsequently, the serial blood gas or arterial blood gas examinations were made. The tests indicate the degree of acidity (pH) in the blood, the level of oxygen (pO_2) in the blood and the level of carbon dioxide (pCO_2) in the blood. The latter is indicia of the extent carbon dioxide is charged from the lungs. The pH reflects whether there is an excess of acid (acidosis) or an insufficiency of acid (alkalosis) in the blood. I note, parenthetically, that the blood gas tests have been conducted continuously from the time of Karen's admission to St. Clare's up to the present. There are constant references through the hospital records of pH, pO_2 and pCO_2 measurements. Dr. Javed, the attending pulmonary internist, indicated some 300 tests were conducted.

Dr. Javed testified the blood tests were all normal while Karen was on the respirator.

In an effort to ascertain the cause of the coma, Dr. Morse conducted a brain scan, an angiogram, an electroencephalogram (EEG), a lumbar tap and several other tests. The first three are related to the brain and are conducted, according to the testimony, with the object of finding an injury or insult to the brain, such as a subdural hematoma or the like, or for ascertaining any abnormality in the brain activity patterns. The latter is particularly true of the EEG where electrodes are placed on the skull. The measurement is made of cortical neurons. The neuron is basically a conducting cell of nervous energy. The recordings are made on awake and sleep cycles. The awake recorded data, referred to in the testimony as alpha rhythm or activity, indicates a frequency of pattern which can be compared against normal frequencies or patterns to determine whether any abnormality exists. The EEG establishes the existence or nonexistence of normal patterns. It does not precisely locate the insult or lesion causing, in this case, the unconsciousness. Dr. Morse indicated that the EEG performed at the outset established nothing abnormal for a comatose person and did not establish the offending agent to her central nervous system which caused her unconsciousness. Subsequent EEGs provided no further information. All indicated brain rhythm or activity.

Subsequent tests and examinations did not further the establishment of the precise location and cause of Karen's comatose condition.

Dr. Morse testified concerning the treatment of Karen at St. Clare's. He averred she receives oral feedings since intravenous feeding is insufficient to sustain her. She is fed a high calorie nutrient called "Vivenex," which she receives through a small nasal gastro tube inserted in her gastro–intestinal system. He asserts this is necessary to keep her "viable." She has apparently lost considerable weight, being described as emaciated by most of the examining experts, who also indicate her weight condition to be good under the circumstances.

There is constant threat of infection, according to Dr. Morse. Antibiotics are administered to thwart potential infection, with tests constantly being made to keep a check on this threat. The hospital records indicate specialists consulted with respect to the cleaning, utilization and operation of the urethral catheter and with respect to the treatment and care of decubiti (lesions commonly known as bed sores) generated by her continous repose.

The day–by–day charts, entitled "Vital Signs," kept by nurses who give her 24–hour care, indicate, in part, the following:

1. Her color was generally pale, her skin warm, she was almost constantly suffering from diaphoresis (sweating), many times profusely but occasionally moderately or not at all;

2. There was always a reaction to painful stimuli; she responded decerebrately to pain, which would be followed by increased rigidity of her arms and legs;

3. There would be periodic contractions and spasms, periodic yawning, periodic movements of spastic nature;

4. Pupils were sometimes dilated, sometimes normal, but almost always sluggish to light;

5. Body waste disposal through the urethral catheter and the bowel was indicated to occur;

6. Feedings of Vivinex were given alternately with water on various nurses' shifts;

7. The nurses were constantly moving, positioning and bathing her;

8. Body rashes occurred at times; decubiti were treated with heat lamps on occasions;

9. Sometimes she would trigger and assist the respirator; other times she would go for periods without triggering it at all;

10. Her extremities remained rigid with contraction of them being described as severe at times;

11. On May 7 nurses indicated she blinked her eyes two times when asked to and appeared responsive by moving her eyes when talked to, but there is no further evidence of this type of reaction thereafter.

Dr. Javed indicated that efforts were made to wean or remove Karen from the respirator. The hospital records support this. Dr. Javed testified that for weaning to be successful, the patient must have a stable respiratory pattern. Karen was taken off the respirator for short periods of time. Each time, her respiratory rate, rate of breathing, went up and the volume of air intake would decrease. He indicated her breathing rate would more than double in intensity while her "tidal volume" or air intake would drop 50%. The longest period of time she was off the respirator was one-half hour. He further indicated that during removal from the respirator her pO_2 dropped. He stated that the respiratory problem is secondary to the neurological problem, and without improvement in the latter she cannot be removed from the respirator since she would be unable to maintain her vital processes without its assistance.

Dr. Morse's hospital notes indicate there is no neurological improvement from the time of her admission to St. Clare's to date. He testified that Karen changed from a sleeping comatose condition to a sleep–awake type comatose condition but described this as normal in comatose patients and not any indication of improvement. During the awake cycle she is still unconscious.

In Dr. Morse's opinion the cause of Karen's condition is a lesion on the cerebral hemispheres and a lesion in the brain stem. In response to various questions from respective counsel he described the cortex of the brain as being affected, with involvement of the brain stem. He indicated that the lesion involves the central hemisphere as far down as the thalamus, with patchy areas of the diencephalon and the respiratory centers located in the pons and medulla areas, and also noted there is evidence of possible cerebral hemorrhage, subcortical white matter involvement, and possible involvement of the diencephalon and certain portions of the brain stem. In Dorland's *Illustrated Medical Dictionary* (25 ed. 1965), 365, the cortex is defined as the outer layer or thin layer of gray matter on the surface of the cerebral hemisphere, and that it reaches its highest development in man, where it is responsible for the higher mental functions, for general movement, for visceral functions, perception, and behavioral reaction, and for the association and integration of these functions. The testimony indicated that white matter is located under the cortex. It also reflected a system of nerves commencing with the spine, leading through the brain stem and spreading out in network fashion through the cerebral hemisphere, encompassing the white matter and cortex.

The brain stem is described as consisting of essentially three parts: the pons, the medulla oblongata, and the midbrain, with some authorities including the diencephalon. It is the stemlike portion of the brain that connects the cerebral hemispheres with the spinal cord. The brain stem, apparently, including the diencephalon, is the control for the respiratory functioning of the body.

In the absence of a clear history, Dr. Morse relied basically upon the decorticate posturing of Karen Quinlan and the respiratory difficulty for reaching his conclusion as to the brain lesion locations. He contrasted the decorticate posture to decerebrate posture of a patient for drawing his conclusions.

He asserted with medical clarity that Karen Quinlan is not brain—dead. He identified the Ad Hoc Committee of Harvard Medical School Criteria as the ordinary medical standard for determining brain death, and that Karen satisfied none of the criteria. These criteria are set forth in a 1968 report entitled, "Report of the Ad Hoc Committee of Harvard Medical School to Examine the Definition of Brain Death: A Definition of 'Irreversible Coma,' " 205 *J.A.M.A.* 85 (1968).

The report reflects that it is concerned "only with those comatose individuals who have discernible central nervous system activity" and the problem of determining the characteristics of a permanently nonfunctioning brain. The criteria as established are:

1. Unreceptivity and Unresponsivity—There is a total unawareness to externally applied stimuli and inner need and complete unresponsiveness . . . Even the most intensely painful stimuli evoke no vocal or other response, not even a groan, withdrawal of a limb, or quickening of respiration.

2. No Movements or Breathing—Observations covering a period of at least one hour by physicians is adequate to satisfy the criteria of no spontaneous muscular movement or spontaneous respiration or response to stimuli such as a pain, touch, sound or light. After the patient is on a mechanical respirator, the total absence of spontaneous breathing may be

established by turning off the respirator for three minutes and observing whether there is any effect on the part of the subject to breathe spontaneously.

3. No Reflexes—Irreversible coma with abolition of central nervous system activity is evidenced in part by the absence of elicitable reflexes. The pupil will be fixed and dilated and will not respond to a direct source of bright light. Since the establishment of a fixed, dilated pupil is clear-cut in clinical practice, there would be no uncertainty as to its presence. Ocular movement (to head turning and to irrigation of ears with ice water) and blinking are absent. There is no evidence of postural activity (deliberate or other). Swallowing, yawning, vocalization are in abeyance. Corneal and pharyngeal reflexes are absent.

As a rule the stretch of tendon reflexes cannot be elicited; i.e., tapping the tendons of the biceps, triceps, and pronator muscles, quadriceps and gastrocnemius muscles with reflex hammer elicits no contraction of the respective muscles. Plantar or noxious stimulation gives no response.

4. Flat—Electroencephalogram—of great confirmatory value is that flat or isoelectric EEG . . .

All tests must be repeated at least 24 hours later with no change.

The validity of such data as indications of irreversible cerebral damage depends on the exclusion of two conditions; hypothermia (temperature below 90°F) or central nervous system depressants, such as barbiturates.

Dr. Morse reflected carefully in his testimony on Karen's prognosis. He described her condition as a chronic or "persistent vegetative state." Dr. Fred Plum, a creator of the phrase, describes its significance by indicating the brain as working in two ways:

We have an internal vegetative regulation which controls body temperature, which controls breathing, which controls to a considerable degree blood pressure, which controls to some degree heart rate, which controls chewing, swallowing and which controls sleeping and waking. We have a more highly developed brain, which is uniquely human, which controls our relation to the outside world, our capacity to talk, to see, to feel, to sing, to think . . . Brain death necessarily must mean the death of both of these functions of the brain, vegetative and the sapient. Therefore, the presence of any function which is regulated or governed or controlled by the deeper parts of the brain which in layman's terms might be considered purely vegetative would mean that the brain is not biologically dead.

Dr. Morse, in reflecting on the prognosis, notes Karen's absence of awareness of anything or anyone around her. In response to a direct question he noted she is not suffering from locked-in syndrome in which a patient is conscious but so totally paralyzed that communications can be made only through a complex system of eye or eyelid movements.

Dr. Morse states Karen Quinlan will not return to a level of cognitive function (*i.e.*, that she will be able to say "Mr. Coburn I'm glad you are my guardian.") What level or plateau she will reach is unknown. He does not know of any course of treatment that can be given and cannot see how her condition can be reversed, but is unwilling to say she is in an irreversible state or condition. He indicated there is a possibility of recovery but that level is unknown, particularly due to the absence of pre-hospital history.

Karen Ann Quinlan was examined by several experts for the various parties. All were neurologists with extensive experience and backgrounds. Some had done research in the area of brain injury, conscious and comatose behavior. The qualifications of all were admitted.

On October 2, 1975 Dr. Stuart Cook, Dr. Eugene Loesser and Dr. Fred Plum, in the presence of Doctors Morse, Javed and others, examined Karen. Each reviewed the medical and hospital records and talked with the attending physicians. The examination consisted in part of Karen's removal from the respirator for a 3-minute and 45-second interval and an EEG.

Their testimonies did not vary significantly. Some gave in greater detail than others. A general synopsis of their testimonies indicates they found Karen comatose, emaciated and in a posture of extreme flexion and rigidity of the arms, legs and related muscles which could not be overcome, with her joints severely rigid and deformed. During the examination she went through awake and asleep periods but mostly awake. The eyes moved spontaneously. She made stereotyped cries and sounds and her mouth opened wide when she did so. Cries were evoked when there was noxious stimulation. She reflexed to noxious stimuli. Her pupils reacted to light and her retinas were normal. Her reflex activity, deep tendon reflexes and plantar stimulation of soles of her feet could not be elicited because of the severe flexion contractures. She triggered the respirator during the entire examination except for the interval of removal. When she was removed from the respirator, with an oxygen catheter inserted through the tracheostomy, she breathed spontaneously and her blood gases were in a normal range. Her EEG showed normal electrical activity for a sedated person. (She was sedated for the EEG). She does not have the locked–in syndrome.

All agree she is in a persistent vegetative state. She is described as having irreversible brain damage; no cognitive or cerebral functioning; chances for useful sapient life or return of discriminative functioning are remote. The absence of knowledge on the events precipitating the condition, and the fact that other patients have been comatose for longer periods of time and recovered to function as a human, made Dr. Cook qualify his statement as to the return to discriminative functioning. All agree she is not brain–dead by present–known medical criteria and that her continued existence away from the respirator is a determination for a pulmonary internist.

Dr. Sidney Diamond examined Karen and testified on behalf of the State. There was no EEG or removal from the respirator during his examination. He reviewed her history and talked with the treating physicians. His physical observations of her conformed with those of the other examining neurologists. He states Karen is not brain–dead within the Harvard Criteria.

He considered "empirical data" which included Dr. Javed's weaning attempts and said he was convinced there is no evidence she can continue to exist physically without the respirator. His opinion is that no physician would interrupt the use of the respirator and that the continued use of the respirator does not deviate from standard medical practice.

Dr. Julius Korein testified as an expert on behalf of the plaintiff. There was no removal from the respirator when he examined Karen. He also reviewed medical and hospital records and talked to treating physicians. He made caloric stimulation and EEG tests.

His description of Karen's posturing, reflexes, eyes, body movements and other conditions did not vary significantly from other experts. His diagnosis of the extent and area of the brain injury or lesion—in the cerebral hemisphere with brain stem involvement—essentially agrees with that of Dr. Morse. He described the upper brain area injury as a severe bilateral cerebral involvement with anoxia as the probable cause. He found a palmomental reflex, evidencing interruption in the brain stem fibre. He indicates the extensiveness of the reflex, a dimpling of the chin generated by stimulation of the palm, is greater than usually found because any stimulation along the entire arm generated it.

He described her condition as a persistent vegetative state.

In response to questions concerning her dependency on the respirator, he acknowledged that the information of Dr. Javed showing respiratory difficulty and low oxygen in the blood while off the respirator establishes her need to continue on it if her life is to continue.

He described the responses to caloric stimulation as abnormal.

He is the only expert who testified on the concepts of "ordinary" and "extraordinary" medical treatment. Essentially, he considers use of a respirator at the admission of a patient an "ordinary" medical practice. He equates the usage of it with an "extraordinary" practice when it is used for a prolonged period of time in concert with other hospital resources, including extensive nursing care. He acknowledges the term "extraordinary" lacks precision in definition.

Testimony of other doctors reflects an inclination that the use of the respirator is an ordinary medical practice.

The decision to request removal of their daughter from the respirator, understandably came torturously, arduously to the Quinlans. At the outset they authorized Dr. Morse to do everything he could to keep her alive, believing she would recover. They participated in a constant vigil over her with other family members. They were in constant contact with the doctors, particularly Dr. Morse, receiving day–by–day reports concerning her prognosis which, as time passed, became more and more pessimistic and more and more discouraging to them.

Mrs. Quinlan and the children were the first to conclude Karen should be removed from the respirator. Mrs. Quinlan, working at the local parish church, had ongoing talks with Father Trapasso, who supported her conclusion and indicated that it was a permissible practice within the tenets of Roman Catholic teachings.

Mr. Quinlan was slower in making his decision. His hope for recovery continued despite the disheartening medical reports. Neither his wife nor Father Trapasso made any attempt to influence him. A conflict existed between letting her natural body function control her life and the hope for recovery. Precisely when he came to a decision is not clear. By his testimony he indicated early September, but he signed a release to the hospital dated July 31, 1975, hereafter referred to, which makes it reasonably inferrable that the decision was made in July. Once having made the decision, he sought Father Trapasso's encouragement, which he received.

Father Trapasso based his support of the position taken by the Quinlans on the traditional, moral precepts of the Roman Catholic faith and upon a declaration, designated an *allocutio*, by Pope Pius XII made on November 24, 1957. Speaking to a group of anesthesiologists the Pope was requested to respond to the question:

When the blood circulation and the life of a patient who is deeply unconscious because of a central paralysis are maintained only through artificial respiration, and no improvement is noted after a few days, at what time does the Catholic Church consider the patient "dead," or when must he be declared dead according to natural law?

The Papal response was:

Where the verification of the fact in particular cases is concerned, the answer cannot be deduced from any religious and moral principle and, under this aspect, does not fall within the competence of the Church. Until an answer can be given, the question must remain open. But considerations of a general nature allow us to believe that human life continues for as long as its vital functions,--distinguished from the simple life of organs--manifest themselves spontaneously or even with the help of artificial processes. A great number of these cases are the object of insoluble doubt, and must be dealt with according to the presumptions of law and of fact of which we have spoken.

Father Trapasso acknowledges it is not a sinful act under the church teachings or the Papal *allocutio* to either continue extraordinary treatment or discontinue it. It is acknowledged to be a matter left optional to a Roman Catholic believer. Mr. Quinlan indicates that had Roman Catholic traditions and morals considered it a sin, he would not be seeking termination of the respiratorial support. Mr. Quinlan avers Karen's natural bodily functions should be allowed to operate free of the respirator. He states that then, if it is God's will to take her, she can go on to life after death, and that is a belief of Roman Catholics. He asserts he does not believe or support the concept of euthanasia.

Once having made the determination, the Quinlans approached hospital officials to effectuate their decision. Father Paschal Caccavalle, chaplain of St. Clare's, at a meeting between hospital representatives and the Quinlans, read the Papal *allocutio* of November 1957.

The Quinlans on July 31, 1975 signed the following:

We authorize and direct Doctor Morse to discontinue all extraordinary measures, including the use of a respirator for our daugher Karen Quinlan.

We acknowledge that the above named physician has thoroughly discussed the above with us and that the consequences have been fully explained to us. Therefore, we hereby RELEASE from any and all liability the above named physician, associates and assistants of his choice, Saint Clare's Hospital and its agents and employees.

The Quinlans, upon signing the release, considered the matter decided. Dr. Morse, however, felt he could not and would not agree to the cessation of the respirator assistance. He testified—characterizing the issue of extraordinary treatment and the termination of it as something brought up suddenly in July—that he advised the Quinlans prior to the time of the release that he wanted to check into the matter further before giving his approval. After checking on other medical case histories he concluded that to terminate the respirator would be a substantial deviation from medical tradition, that it involved ascertaining "quality of life," and that he would not do so.

Karen Quinlan is quoted as saying she never wanted to be kept alive by extraordinary means. The statements attributed to her by her mother, sister and a friend are indicated to have been made essentially in relation to instances where close friends or relatives were terminally ill. In one instance an aunt, in great pain, was terminally ill from cancer. In another instance the father of a girl friend was dying under like circumstances. In a third circumstance a close family friend was dying of a brain tumor. Mrs. Quinlan testified that her daughter was very full of life, that she loved life and did not want to be kept alive in any way she would not enjoy life to the fullest.

No testimony was elicited concerning the nature and extent of the assets of Karen Quinlan. By affidavit in support of the application Joseph Quinlan indicates she receives $157.70 a month from a federal Supplemental Security Income program and has a personal estate valued at approximately $300, consisting primarily of personal possessions . . .

Plaintiff urges that the court may resolve the matter in his favor through declaratory judgment and its inherent equitable powers. He urges there is a sufficient controversy to justify declaratory relief. He asserts that an injunction should issue to prevent the risk of arrest and prosecution that might result from the court's authorization. He contends that under the equitable doctrine of substituted judgment this court can act in Karen Quinlan's best interest by authorizing the cessation of the respirator. He asserts that Karen Quinlan and her family have by virtue of the constitutional right of privacy a right of self-determination which extends to the decision to terminate "futile use of extraordinary medical measures." Also asserted as grounds for granting the sought relief are the constitutional right of free exercise of religious belief and freedom from cruel and unusual punishment.

All defendants . . . [assert] that no constitutional right to die exists and . . . [argue] a compelling state interest in favor of preserving human life.

They all, essentially, contend that since Karen Quinlan is medically and legally alive, the court should not authorize termination of the respirator—that to do so would be homicide and an act of euthanasia.

The doctors suggest that the decision is one more appropriately made by doctors than by a court of law, and that under the circumstances of this case a decision in favor of plaintiff would require ascertainment of quality-of-life standards to serve as future guidelines.

The prosecutor, if plaintiff is granted the relief sought, requests a declaratory judgment "with regard to the effect of the homicide statutes and his duty of enforcement."

The hospital also seeks a declaratory judgment that the criteria outlined by the Ad Hoc Committee of the Harvard Medical School to Examine the Definition of Brain Death be sanctioned as the ordinary medical standards for determination of brain death . . .

The case presented is:

Given the facts that Karen Quinlan is now an incompetent in a persistent vegetative state; that at the outset of her unconsciousness her parents placed her under the care and treatment of Dr. Morse, and through him, Dr. Javed and St. Clare's Hospital, urging that everything be done to keep her alive, and that the doctors and hospital introduced life-sustaining techniques, does this court have the power and right, under the mantle of either its equity jurisdiction or the constitutional rights of free exercise of religion, right of privacy or privilege against cruel and unusual punishment, to authorize the withdrawing of the life-sustaining techniques?

I pause to note the scope of my role. I am concerned only with the facts of this case and the issues presented by them. It is not my function to render an advisory opinion. In this age of advanced medical science, the prolongation of life and of organ transplants, it is not my intent, nor can it be, to resolve the extensive civil and criminal legal dilemmas engendered.

The absence of specific legal precedents does not delimit the scope of my determination . . .

. . . Plaintiff invokes the inherent power of an equity court as the protector and general guardian of all persons under a disability. He urges that under the doctrine of *parens patriae* the court, as representative of the sovereign, may intervene "in the best interests" of Karen Quinlan and allow her to die a natural death . . .

Equity speaks of conscience. That conscience is not the personal conscience of the judge. For if it were, the compassion, empathy, sympathy I feel for Mr. and Mrs. Quinlan and their other two children would play a *very* significant part in the decision. It is a judicial conscience––"a metaphorical term, designating the common standard of civil right and expediency combined, based upon general principles, and limited by established doctrines to which the court appeals, and by which it tests the conduct and right of the suitors" . . . The rationale behind not allowing the personal conscience and therefore the noted emotional aspects are that while it may result in a decision based on a notion of what is right for these individuals, the precedential effect on future litigation, particularly in light of the raging issue of euthanasia, would be legally detrimental.

Equity also speaks of morality. The morality involved is that of society––the standards evolve through social advancement in a stabilized community life.

Karen Quinlan is by legal and medical definition alive. She is not dead by the Ad Hoc Committee of Harvard Medical School standards nor by the traditional definition, the stoppage of blood circulation and related vital functions. The quality of her living is described as a persistent vegetative state, a description that engenders total sorrow and despair in an emotional sense. She does not exhibit cognitive behavior (*i.e.*, the process of knowing or perceiving). Those qualities unique to man, the higher mental functions, are absent. Her condition is categorized as irreversible and the chance of returning to discriminate functioning remote. Nevertheless, while her condition is neurologically activated, yet due to the absence of a pre–hospital history and in light of medical histories showing other comatose patients surviving longer coma periods, there is some medical qualification on the issue of her returning to discriminative functioning and on whether she should be removed from the respirator. There is a serious question whether she can live off the respirator and survive (at least two physicians indicated she could not). It is also apparent that extensive efforts to wean her from the respirator created a danger of more extensive brain injury. There is no treatment suggested.

The judicial conscience and morality involved in considering whether the court should authorize Karen Quinlan's removal from the respirator are inextricably involved with the nature of medical science and the role of the physician in our society and his duty to his patient.

When a doctor takes a case there is imposed upon him the duty "to exercise in the treatment of his patient the degree of care, knowledge and skill ordinarily possessed and exercised in similar situations by the average member of the profession practicing in his field" . . . If he is a specialist he "must employ not merely the skill of a general practitioner, but also that special degree of skill normally possessed by the average physician who devotes special study and attention to the particular organ or disease or injury involved, having regard to the present state of scientific knowledge" . . . This is the duty that establishes his legal obligations to his patients.

There is a higher standard, a higher duty, that encompasses the uniqueness of human life, the integrity of the medical profession and the attitude of society toward the physician, and therefore the morals of society. A patient is placed, or places himself, in the care of a physician with the expectation that he (the physician) will do everything in his power, everything that is known to modern medicine, to protect the patient's life. He will do all within his human power to favor life against death.

The attitudes of society have over the years developed a significant respect for the medical profession. Society has come to request and expect this higher duty.

But the doctor is dealing in a science which lacks exactitude . . . a science that has seen significant changes in recent years, a science that will undoubtedly have prodigious advancements in the future, but a science which still does not know the cause of some afflictions and which does not know all the interrelationships of the body functions. In recent years open heart surgery and organ transplantation have made continuation of life possible where the patient is suffering from a fatal disability. The cause of cancer remains to a major extent unknown, but advances have been made in cures and remissions. The brain, the only organ incapable of transplant to date, as Dr. Morse points out, is still, even among neuroanatomists, unknown insofar as the interrelationships of some of its parts and how these parts are controlled.

Doctors, therefore, to treat a patient, must deal with medical tradition and past case histories. They must be guided by what they do know. The extent of their training, their experience, consultations with other physicians, must guide their decision-making processes in providing care to their patient. The nature, extent and duration of care by societal standards is the responsibility of a physician. The morality and conscience of our society places this responsibility in the hands of the physician. What justification is there to remove it from the control of the medical profession and place it in the hands of the courts? Aside from the constitutional arguments, plaintiff suggests because medical science holds no hope for recovery, because if Karen was conscious she would elect to turn off the respirator, and finally because there is no duty to keep her alive.

None of the doctors testified there was *no* hope. The hope for recovery is remote but no doctor talks in the absolute. Certainly he cannot and still be credible, in light of the advancements medical science has known and the inexactitudes of medical science.

There *is* a duty to continue the life-assisting apparatus, if, within the treating physician's opinion, it should be done. Here Dr. Morse has refused to concur in the removal of Karen from the respirator. It is his considered position that medical tradition does not justify that act. There is no mention, in the doctor's refusal, of concern over criminal liability, and the court concludes that such is not the basis for his determination. It is significant that Dr. Morse, a man who demonstrated strong empathy and compassion, a man who has directed care that impressed all the experts, is unwilling to direct Karen's removal from the respirator.

The assertion that Karen would elect, if competent, to terminate the respirator requires careful examination.

She made these statements at the age of 20. In the words of her mother, she was full of life. She made them under circumstances where another person was suffering, suffering in at least one instance from severe pain. Dr. Morse describes her reacting to noxious stimuli—pain—as reflex but not indicative that she is sensing pain as a functioning human being does. The reaction is described as stereotyped, and her reflexes show no adjustment that would indicate she mentally experiences pain.

The conversations with her mother and friends are theoretical ones. She was not personally involved. They were not made under the solemn and sobering fact that death is a distinct choice . . . Karen Quinlan, while she was in complete control of her mental faculties to reason out the staggering magnitude of the decision to be "kept alive," did not make a decision. This is not the situation of a "living will" which is based upon a concept of informed consent.

While the repetition of the conversations indicates an awareness of the problems of terminal illness, the elements involved—the vigor of youth that espouses the theoretical good and righteousness, the absence of being presented the question as it applied to her—are not persuasive to establish a probative weight sufficient to persuade this court that Karen Quinlan would elect her own removal from the respirator.

The breadth of the power to act and protect Karen's interests is, I conclude, controlled by a judicial conscience and morality which dictate that the determination whether or not Karen Ann Quinlan be removed from the respirator is to be left to the treating physician. It is a medical decision, not a judicial one. I am satisfied that it may be concurred in by the parents but not governed by them. This is so because there is always the dilemma of whether it is the conscious being's relief or the unconscious being's welfare that governs the parental motivation.

It is also noted the concept of the court's power over a person suffering under a disability to *protect* and aid the best interests . . . Here the authorization sought, if granted, would result in Karen's death. The natural processes of her body are not shown to be sufficiently strong to sustain her by themselves. The authorization, therefore, would be to permit Karen Quinlan to die. This is not protection. It is not something in her best interests, in a temporal sense, and it is in a temporal sense that I must operate whether I believe in life after death or not. The single most important temporal quality Karen Ann Quinlan has is life. This court will not authorize that life to be taken from her.

A significant amount of the legal presentation to the court has involved whether the act of removing Karen from the respirator constitutes an affirmative act, or could be considered an act of omission. An intricate discussion on semantics and form is not required since the substance of the sought-for authorization would result in the taking of the life of Karen Quinlan when the law of the State indicates that such an authorization would be homicide.

The proceeding brings considerable attention and focus on the physical condition of Karen Quinlan. The results thereof are that in the future the decisions and determinations of the treating doctors and the hospital will be the subject of abnormal scrutiny.

The hospital, through amendment to the pretrial order, seeks a determination of "whether the use of the criteria developed and enunciated by the Ad Hoc Committee of Harvard Medical School on or about August 5, 1968, as well as similar criteria, by a physician to assist him in determination of the death of a patient whose cardiopulmonary functions are being artificially sustained, is in accordance with ordinary and standard medical practice."

The scope of that request is extremely broad. It deals not with the question of Karen Quinlan but a theoretical patient. To the extent that it goes beyond this case, it is a request to make a determination in the abstract and not a proper subject for judicial determination . . .

Counsel for the hospital, in order to avoid the objection that the request deals in an abstraction and therefore constitutes a proscribed advisory opinion, suggests, by letter subsequent to trial, a refinement of the stated issue to refer specifically to Karen Quinlan.

The jurisdiction of the court to deal with such an issue must exist, if at all, under the authority of the Declaratory Judgment Act. Designed to provide judicial declaration of the rights and obligations of parties, the act is a device whereby uncertainty with respect to rights and legal relations may be alleviated . . .

The controversy, however, must have matured and not be something sought in advance of its occurrence . . .

The application is prospective and in advance of the controversy. The doctors do not seek the determination—in fact, they oppose it.

Additionally, just as the matter of the nature and extent of care and treatment of a patient and therefore the patient's removal from a respirator is a medical decision based upon ordinary practice, so, too, is the decison whether a patient is dead and by what medical criteria. Whether Karen Quinlan one day becomes brain–dead and therefore should be removed from the respirator is a decision that will have to be based upon the extant ordinary medical criteria at the time.

a. Right of Privacy—Right of Self Determination.

. . . Plaintiff suggests . . . that the right of self–determination and right of privacy are synonymous. He also suggests the right is exercisable by a parent for his child.

It is not insignificant to this opinion whether the right of self–determination is within the scope of the right of privacy. What is significant is the extent to which it is subject to a compelling state interest . . . and whether the right can be exercised by the parent for his child.

The majority of cases dealing with the refusal of an individual to accept treatment which created an exposure to death involved mature, competent adults . . . None, however, dealt with an incompetent adult, as here, totally unaware of the problem.

The disability places the court in a *parens patriae* circumstance, significantly different from the instance of a competent adult's effort to control his body. This is true in spite of the prior statements of Karen Quinlan concerning dispensing with extraordinary care. For, as indicated, the proofs do not meet a standard clear enough to have the probative weight sufficient to convince the court that Karen Quinlan, in full command of the facts, would favor death.

The judicial power to act in the incompetent's best interest in this instance selects continued life, and to do so is not violative of a constitutional right . . .

The power of the parents to exercise the constitutional right is found lacking on several grounds: First, the only case where a parent has standing to pursue a constitutional right on behalf of an infant are those involving continuing life styles . . .Second, the parents urged Dr. Morse to do everything at the outset to save Karen's life. The parents now ask him to abandon his conscience and allow her life to end . . . [T]he court refused to hold that the right of privacy, being urged through a parent, must be fettered when in conflict with a doctor's duty to provide life–giving care.

There is no constitutional right to die that can be asserted by a parent for his incompetent adult child.

b. Free Exercise.

Religious beliefs are absolute under the Free Exercise Clause but practice in pursuit thereof is not free from governmental regulation . . .

The religious belief here asserted is two–fold: (1) that the discontinuance of extraordinary care to Karen Quinlan is not a mortal sin and (2) to interfere with her natural body functions prevents her from reaching a better life in the hereafter.

The absence of mortal sin contention is based, according to Father Trapasso, on the Papal *allocutio* of November 24, 1957, and Roman Catholic traditions and morals. The impetus of the thought is that it is neither a mortal sin to continue nor discontinue "extraordinary" versus "ordinary" discussions viable legal distinctions. The essence of the contention is that it is optional with the Roman Catholic involved, and to do either does not conflict with the teachings of the Church. It is not a dogma of the Church. It is not a claim "rooted in religious belief." There is no governmental or other interference with religious belief here that is caused by the court's refusal to authorize the termination of the respirator.

The temporal world is what the Free Exercise Clause deals with—not the hereafter. All instances where a religious belief has been freed of attempted governmental interference dealt with *life* styles and *life* circumstances . . .

. . . There is a presumption that one chooses to go on living. The presumption is not overcome by the prior statements of Karen Quinlan. As previously noted, she did not make the statements as a personal confrontation. Additionally, it is not Karen who asserts her religious beliefs but her parents. In those instances where the parental standing to assert the religious belief has been upheld, it dealt with future life conduct of their children, not the ending of life . . .

The right to life and the preservation of it are "interests of the highest order," and this court deems it constitutionally correct to deny plaintiff's request.

c. Cruel and Unusual Punishment.

It is argued that to deny the suspension of the "futile use of extraordinary measures after the dignity, beauty, promise and meaning of earthly life have vanished," is cruel and unusual punishment proscribed by the Eighth Amendment of the United States Constitution . . .

A careful reading of these principles does not support plaintiff here. Continuation of medical treatment, in whatever form, where its goal is the sustenance of life, is not something degrading, arbitrarily inflicted, unacceptable to contemporary society or unnecessary.

The Eighth Amendment has no applicability to this civil action.

Joseph Quinlan applies to be appointed guardian *ad litem* of his daughter's person and property. Karen Quinlan is incompetent and unfit and unable to govern herself as to manage her affairs . . . As next of kin Mr. Quinlan qualifies to be her guardian . . . unless it is shown his appointment would be contrary to Karen's best interest . . . The guardian *ad litem* opposes his appointment.

The responsibility of the guardian over property is to manage the business affairs of the incompetent. There is no reason why Mr. Quinlan should not serve in this capacity.

The responsibility of the guardian over the person of the incompetent is to make the decisions, in this instance, that relate to her welfare, insofar as those decisions are within the person's control. I have ruled that it is a medical decision whether or not Karen should be removed from the respirator. Just as that decision is a medical one, the continued care and treatment of Karen is a medical one. There will be, however, from time to time medical decisions relating to further treatment that will require a guardian's counsel, advice and concurrence. This is reflected by the testimony of Dr. Morse.

Mr. Quinlan impressed me as a very sincere, moral, ethical and religious person. He very obviously anguished over his decision to terminate what he considers the extraordinary care of his daughter. That anguish would be continued and magnified by the inner conflicts he would have if he were required to concur in the day-to-day decisions on the future care and treatment of his daughter. These conflicts would have to offset his decision-making processes. I, therefore, find it more appropriate and in Karen's interests if another is appointed.

For the same reasons, I do not feel Mrs. Quinlan should be appointed.

Daniel Coburn, Esq., who has acted on Karen's behalf throughout this proceeding, is appointed the guardian of her person. Both guardians shall serve without bond in accordance with law and the rules of court, after qualification.

Judgment should be submitted accordingly.

o **Recap of the Case**. From the nursing point of view, one of the most interesting and important aspects of this case is the court's opinion that decisions like those in the *Quinlan* case must be based upon the opinion of medical personnel. The role of practitioners is paramount when decisions are made about termination of life–support systems. Nurses may serve as a catalyst for a consensus opinion among those professionals treating the patient. Such a consensus will be given great weight by the courts.

COURT PERMITS TERMINATION OF
LIFE SUPPORTING TREATMENT IN SOME CASES

The Quinlan case has been followed by a number of similar cases including *Soper v. Storar* and *Eichner v. Dillon*. While it is not entirely clear when a court will permit the termination of life sustaining treatment, it is likely to do so under the following circumstances: 1) the patient is terminally ill or in a "permanent vegetative state," 2) while competent, the patient expressed the desire to forego "extraordinary" treatment, 3) the life sustaining treatment is extremely painful and contributes little or nothing to the longevity of the patient or the patient's ability to engage in continued activity during the remainder of the patient's life.

These two cases were considered together because they raised similar legal questions. Brother Fox was an 83 year old member of the Society of Mary who was in a persistent, vegetative state following cardiac arrest. He was on a respirator with no hope for recovery. John Storar was profoundly retarded and suffering from terminal cancer of the bladder. He required repeated blood transfusions due to uncontrolled bleeding. Guardians were appointed to make decisions concerning medical care for both patients. Fox's guardian asked the court for permission to remove Fox from the respirator. Storar's guardian asked the court to allow her to refuse consent to further blood transfusions.

The court decided that Fox's guardian could remove the respirator, but that Storar's guardian could not refuse further blood transfusions. It is very difficult to determine with precision the reasons for the difference in results in two similar cases. All that can be said is that the court seems to place great stock in declarations by Fox prior to his disability that he wanted life support systems terminated if there was no hope for recovery. Since Storar was incapable of making similar statements, the court seems to rely on the fact that the transfusions did not involve excessive pain.

Soper v. Storar and *Eichner v. Dillon,*
52 N.Y.2d 363, 438 N.Y.S.2d 266, 420 N.E.2d 64 (1981)
New York Court of Appeals

In these two cases the guardians of incompetent patients objected to the continued use of medical treatments or measures to prolong the lives of patients who were diagnosed as fatally ill with no reasonable chance of recovery. *In Matter of Eichner*, Brother Fox, an 83–year–old member of the Society of Mary, was being maintained by a respirator in a permanent vegetative state. The local director of the society applied to have the respirator removed on the ground that it was against the patient's wishes as expressed prior to his becoming incompetent. *In Matter of Storar*, a State official applied for permission to administer blood transfusions to a profoundly retarded 52–year–old man with terminal cancer of the bladder. The patient's mother, who was also his legal guardian, refused consent on the ground that the transfusions would only prolong his discomfort and would be against his wishes if he were competent. In each case the courts below have found that the measures should have been discontinued.

The orders of the lower courts . . . were stayed and the treatments continued pending appeals to the Appellate Division . . . and this court. Nevertheless both of the patients have died, thus rendering these particular controversies moot. However, the underlying issues are of public importance, are recurring in other courts throughout the State and, as these cases illustrate, are likely to escape full appellate review even when the appeals have been expedited. Under those circumstances we may, and often have addressed the issues despite the mootness . . . particularly when, as here, the controlling principles have not been previously identified and discussed by this court . . .

It should be emphasized though, that any guidance we may provide for future classes is necessarily limited. Unlike the Legislature, the courts are neither equipped nor empowered to prescribe substantive or procedural rules for all, most, or even the more common contingencies. Our role, especially in matters as sensitive as these, is limited to resolving the issues raised by facts presented in particular cases.

On the records we have concluded that the order should be reversed in the *Storar* case. In the *Eichner* case the order should be modified and resolved on a narrower ground than relied on by the Appellate Division.

The Eichner Case.

For over 66 years Brother Joseph Fox was a member of the Society of Mary, a Catholic religious order which, among other things, operates Chaminade High School in Mineola. In 1970 Brother Fox retired to Chaminade where he resided with the religious members of the school's staff and continued to perform limited duties. In late summer of 1979 he sustained a hernia while moving some flower tubs on a roof garden at the school. He was then 83 years old and, except for the hernia, was found to be in excellent health. His doctor recommended an operation to correct the condition and to that Brother Fox agreed.

While the operation was being performed on October 1, 1979 he suffered cardiac arrest, with resulting loss of oxygen to the brain and substantial brain damage. He lost the ability to breathe spontaneously and was placed on a respirator which maintained him in a vegetative state. The attending physicians informed Father Philip Eichner, who was the president of Chaminade and the director of the society at the school, that there was no reasonable chance of recovery and that Brother Fox would die in that state.

After retaining two neurosurgeons who confirmed the diagnosis, Father Eichner requested the hospital to remove the respirator. The hospital, however, refused to do so without court authorization. Father Eichner then applied . . . to be appointed committee of the person and property of Brother Fox, with authority to direct removal of the respirator. The application was supported by the patient's 10 nieces and nephews, his only surviving relatives. The court appointed a guardian ad litem and directed that notice be served on various parties, including the District Attorney.

At the hearing the District Attorney opposed the application and called medical experts to show that there might be some improvement in the patient's condition. All the experts agreed, however, that there was no reasonable likelihood that Brother Fox would ever emerge from the vegetative coma or recover his cognitive powers.

There was also evidence, submitted by the petitioner, that before the operation rendered him incompetent the patient had made it known that under these circumstances he would want a respirator removed. Brother Fox had first expressed this view in 1976 when the Chaminade community discussed the moral implications of the celebrated *Karen Ann Quinlan* case, in which the parents of a 19--year--old New Jersey girl who was in a vegetative coma requested the hospital to remove the respirator ... These were formal discussions promoted by Chaminade's mission to teach and promulgate Catholic moral principles. At that time it was noted that the Pope had stated that Catholic principles permitted the termination of extraordinary life support systems when there is no reasonable hope for the patient's recovery and that church officials in New Jersey had concluded that use of the respirator in the *Quinlan* case constituted an extraordinary measure under the circumstances. Brother Fox expressed agreement with those views and stated that he would not want any of this "extraordinary business" done for him under those circumstances. Several years later, and only a couple of months before his final hospitalization, Brother Fox again stated that he would not want his life prolonged by such measures if his condition were hopeless.

In a thoughtful and comprehensive opinion, Mr. Justice ROBERT C. MEADE at the Supreme Court held that under the circumstances Brother Fox would have a common-law right to decline treatment and that his wishes, expressed prior to becoming incompetent, should be honored. The court noted that the evidence of his stated opposition to use of a respirator to maintain him in a vegetative state was "unchallenged at every turn and unimpeachable in its sincerity."

The Appellate Division modified in an exhaustive and wide-ranging opinion by Presiding Justice MILTON A. MOLLEN. The court held that the patient's right to decline treatment was not only guaranteed by the common law but by the Constitution as well. It also found that this right should not be lost when a patient becomes incompetent and, if a patient has not made his wishes known while competent as Brother Fox had done, an appropriate person should be appointed to express the right on his behalf by use of "substituted judgment". The court went on to establish an elaborate set of procedures to be followed by doctors, hospitals, family members, parties and the courts before future applications of this nature may be entertained or granted.

The Storar Case.

John Storar was profoundly retarded with a mental age of about 18 months. At the time of this proceeding he was 52 years old and a resident of the Newark Development Center, a State facility, which had been his home since the age of 5. His closest relative was his mother, a 77-year-old widow who resided near the facility. He was her only child and she visited him almost daily.

In 1979 physicians at the center noticed blood in his urine and asked his mother for permission to conduct diagnostic tests. She initially refused but after discussions with the center's staff gave her consent. The tests, completed in July, 1979, revealed that he had cancer of the bladder. It was recommended that he receive radiation therapy at a hospital in Rochester. When the hospital refused to administer the treatment without the consent of a legal guardian, Mrs. Storar applied to the court and was appointed guardian of her son's person and property in August, 1979. With her consent he received radiation therapy for six weeks after which the disease was found to be in remission.

However in March, 1980 blood was again observed in his urine. The lesions in his bladder were cauterized in an unsuccessful effort to stop the bleeding. At that point his physician diagnosed the cancer as terminal, concluding that after using all medical and surgical means then available, the patient would nevertheless die from the disease.

In May the physicians at the center asked his mother for permission to administer blood transfusions. She initially refused but the following day withdrew her objection. For several weeks John Storar received blood transfusions when needed. However, on June 19 his mother requested that the transfusions be discontinued.

The director of the center then brought this proceeding . . . seeking authorization to continue the transfusions, claiming that without them "death would occur within weeks." Mrs. Storar cross–petitioned for an order prohibiting the transfusions, and named the District Attorney as a party. The court appointed a guardian ad litem and signed an order temporarily permitting the transfusions to continue, pending the determination of the proceeding.

At the hearing in September the court heard testimony from various witnesses including Mrs. Storar, several employees at the center, and seven medical experts. All the experts concurred that John Storar had irreversible cancer of the bladder, which by then had spread to his lungs and perhaps other organs, with a very limited life span, generally estimated to be between 3 and 6 months. They also agreed that he had an infant's mentality and was unable to comprehend his predicament or to make a reasoned choice of treatment. In addition, there was no dispute over the fact that he was continuously losing blood.

The medical records show that at the time of the hearing, he required two units of blood every 8 to 15 days. The staff physicians explained that the transfusions were necessary to replace the blood lost. Without them there would be insufficient oxygen in the patient's blood stream. To compensate for this loss, his heart would have to work harder and he would breathe more rapidly, which created a strain and was very tiresome. He became lethargic and they feared he would eventually bleed to death. They observed that after the transfusions he had more energy. He was able to resume most of his usual activities--feeding himself, showering, taking walks and running--including some mischievous ones, such as stealing cigarette butts and attempting to eat them.

It was conceded that John Storar found the transfusions disagreeable. He was also distressed by the blood and blood clots in his urine which apparently increased immediately after a transfusion. He could not comprehend the purpose of the transfusions and on one or two occasions had displayed some initial resistance. To eliminate his apprehension he was given a sedative approximately one hour before a transfusion. He also received regular doses of narcotics to alleviate the pain associated with the disease.

On the other hand several experts testified that there was support in the medical community for the view that, at this stage, transfusions may only prolong suffering and that treatment could properly be limited to administering the pain killers. Mrs. Storar testified that she wanted the transfusions discontinued because she only wanted her son to be comfortable. She admitted that no one had ever explained to her what might happen to him if the transfusions were stopped. She also stated that she was not "sure" whether he might die sooner if the blood was not replaced and was unable to determine whether he wanted to live. However, in view of the fact that he obviously disliked the transfusions and tried to avoid them, she believed that he would want them discontinued.

The court held that the center's application for permission to continue the transfusions should be denied. It was noted that John Storar's fatal illness had not affected his limited mental ability. He remained alert and carried on many of his usual activities. However, the court emphasized that the transfusions could not cure the disease, involved some pain and that the patient submitted to them reluctantly. The court held that a person has a right to determine what will be done with his own body and, when he is incompetent, this right may be exercised by another on his behalf. In this case, the court found that John Storar's mother was the person in the best position to determine what he would want and that she "wants his suffering to stop and believes that he would want this also."

I

The Appellate Division affirmed in a brief memorandum.

In the *Eichner* case the Supreme Court properly granted the petition. At common law, as CARDOZO noted, every person "of adult years and sound mind has a right to determine what should be done with his own body; and a surgeon who performs an operation without his patient's consent commits an assault, for which he is liable in damages . . . This is true except in cases of emergency where the patient is unconscious and where it is necessary to operate before the consent can be obtained" . . . Even in emergencies, however, it is held that consent will not be implied if the patient has previously stated that he would not consent . . .

Father Eichner urges that this right is also guaranteed by the Constitution, as an aspect of the right to privacy. Although several courts have so held . . . this is a disputed question . . . Neither do we reach that question in this case because the relief granted to the petitioner, *Eichner*, is adequately supported by common–law principles.

The District Attorney urges that the patient's right to decline medical treatment is outweighed by important State interests when the treatment is necessary to preserve the patient's life. We recognize that under certain circumstances the common–law right may have to yield to superior State interests, as it would even if it were constitutionally based . . . The State has a legitimate interest in protecting the lives of its citizens. It may require that they submit to medical procedures in order to eliminate a health threat to the community . . . It may, by statute, prohibit them from engaging in specified activities, including medical procedures which are inherently hazardous to their lives . . . In this State, however, there is no statute which prohibits a patient from declining necessary medical treatment or a doctor from honoring the patient's decision. To the extent that existing statutory and decisional law manifests the State's interest on this subject, they consistently support the right of the competent adult to make his own decisions by imposing civil liability on those who perform medical treatment without consent, although the treatment may be beneficial or even necessary to preserve the patient's life . . . The current law identifies the patient's right to determine the course of his own medical treatment as paramount to what might otherwise be the doctor's obligation to provide needed medical care. A State which imposes civil liability on a doctor if he violates the patient's right cannot also hold him criminally responsible if he respects that right. Thus a doctor cannot be held to have violated his legal or professional responsibilities when he honors the right of a competent adult patient to decline medical treatment.

The District Attorney also urges that whatever right the patient may have is entirely personal and may not be exercised by any third party once the patient becomes incompetent. He notes that although a court may appoint a guardian to manage an incompetent's financial affairs and to supervise his person, some rights have been held to be too personal to be exercised by an incompetent's representative . . . He argues that a right to decline lifesaving treatment conflicts with the patient's fundamental and constitutionally guaranteed right to life (U.S. Const. 14th Amdt.) and to permit a third party to choose between the two means, in effect, that the right to life is lost once the patient becomes incompetent. Finally he urges that if a patient's right to decline medical treatment survives his incompetency, it must yield to the State's overriding interest in prohibiting one person from causing the death of another, as is evidenced by the homicide laws.

The District Attorney's arguments underscore the very sensitive nature of the question as to whether, in case of incompetency, a decision to discontinue life sustaining medical treatment may be made by some one other than the patient . . . However, that issue is not presented in this case because here Brother Fox made the decision for himself before he became incompetent. The Supreme Court and the Appellate Division found that the evidence on this point, as well as proof of the patient's subsequent incompetency and chances of recovery was "clear and convincing." We agree that this is the appropriate burden of proof and that the evidence in the record satisfies this standard . . .

In this case the proof was compelling. There was no suggestion that the witnesses who testified for the petitioner had any motive other than to see that Brother Fox' stated wishes were respected. The finding that he carefully reflected on the subject, expressed his views and concluded not to have his life prolonged by medical means if there were no hope of recovery is supported by his religious beliefs and is not inconsistent with his life of unselfish religious devotion. There were obviously solemn pronouncements and not casual remarks made at some social gathering, nor can it be said that he was too young to realize or feel the consequences of his statements . . . That this was a persistent commitment is evidenced by the fact that he reiterated the decision but two months before his final hospitalization. There was, of course, no need to speculate as to whether he would want this particular medical procedure to be discontinued under these circumstances. What occurred to him was identical to what happened in the *Karen Ann Quinlan* case, which had originally prompted his decision. In sum, the evidence clearly and convincingly shows that Brother Fox did not want to be maintained in a vegetative coma by use of a respirator.

II

In the *Storar* case, of course, we do not have any proof of that nature. John Storar was never competent at any time in his life. He was always totally incapable of understanding or making a reasoned decision about medical treatment. Thus it is unrealistic to attempt to determine whether he would want to continue potentially life prolonging treatment if he were competent. As one of the experts testified at the hearing, that would be similar to asking whether "if it snowed all summer would it then be winter?" Mentally John Storar was an infant and that is the only realistic way to access his rights in this litigation . . . Thus this case bears only superficial similarities to *Eichner* and the determination must proceed from different principles.

A parent or guardian has a right to consent to medical treatment on behalf of an infant . . . The parent, however, may not deprive a child of life saving treatment, however well intentioned . . . Even when the parent's decision to decline necessary treatment is based on constitutional grounds, such as religious beliefs, it must yield to the State's interests, as *parens patriae*, in protecting the health and welfare of the child . . . Of course it is not for the courts to determine the most "effective" treatment when the parents have chosen among reasonable alternatives . . . But the courts may not permit a parent to deny a child all treatment for a condition which threatens his life . . . The case of a child who may bleed to death because of the parents' refusal to authorize a blood transfusion presents the classic example . . .

In the *Storar* case there is the additional complication of two threats to his life. There was cancer of the bladder which was incurable and would in all probability claim his life. There was also the related loss of blood which posed the risk of an earlier death, but which, at least at the time of the hearing, could be replaced by transfusions. Thus, as one of the experts noted, the transfusions were analogous to food—they would not cure the cancer, but they could eliminate the risk of death from another treatable cause. Of course, John Storar did not like them, as might be expected of one with an infant's mentality. But the evidence convincingly shows that the transfusions did not involve excessive pain and that without them his mental and physical abilities would not be maintained at the usual level. With the transfusions on the other hand, he was essentially the same as he was before except of course he had a fatal illness which would ultimately claim his life. Thus, on the record, we have concluded that the application for permission to continue the transfusions should have been granted. Although we understand and respect his mother's despair, as we respect the beliefs of those who oppose transfusions on religious grounds, a court should not in the circumstances of this case allow an incompetent patient to bleed to death because someone, even someone as close as a parent or sibling, feels that this is best for one with an incurable disease . . .

o **Recap of the Cases**. These two cases illustrate the difficulties encountered when courts try to decide whether to remove or terminate life-sustaining treatment. The relevant factors in each case must be identified. Each case must be considered individually. Some of the criteria likely to be considered by courts are: 1) whether the patient is terminally ill or in a permanent vegetative state; 2) whether the patient expressed a desire to forego "extraordinary" treatment before becoming disabled; or 3) whether the life-sustaining treatment is extremely painful and/or contributes little or nothing to longevity or ability to engage in normal activity.

11

"No-Code" Order

PRACTITIONER'S DECISION NOT TO RESUSCITATE UPHELD

When a patient is terminally ill, physicians frequently write a "no code," "no resuscitation," or "do not resuscitate" order in the patient's chart. If such an order is in effect and the patient's heart or breathing stops, the staff will not take steps to revive the patient. While such orders have been written for many years, they have been tested in the courts only recently in such cases as *In the Matter of Shirley Dinnerstein*. Even though the court in *Dinnerstein* upheld "no code" orders, the most accurate statement concerning this area at this time is that there are too few cases to draw definite conclusions about the legality of this type of order.

In the Matter of Shirley Dinnerstein
No. 78–473, Slip. op. (Mass. App. June 30, 1978)
Massachusetts Appeals Court

This case . . . turns on the question whether a physician attending an incompetent, terminally ill patient may lawfully direct that resuscitation measures be withheld in the event of cardiac or respiratory arrest where such a direction has not been approved in advance by a Probate Court.

The patient is a sixty-seven-year-old woman who suffers from a condition known as Alzheimer's disease. It is a degenerative disease of the brain of unknown origin, described as presenile dementia, and results in destruction of brain tissue and, consequently, deterioration of brain function. The condition is progressive and unremitting, leading in stages to disorientation, loss of memory, personality disorganization, loss of intellectual function, and ultimate loss of all motor function. The course of the disease may be gradual or precipitous, averaging five to seven years. At this time medical science knows of no cure for the disease and no treatment which can slow or arrest its course. No medical breakthrough is anticipated.

The patient's condition was diagnosed as Alzheimer's disease in July, 1975, although the initial symptoms of the disease were observed as early as 1972. She entered a nursing home in November, 1975, where her (by that time) complete disorientation, frequent psychotic outbursts, and deteriorating ability to control elementary bodily functions made her dependent on intensive nursing care. In February, 1978, she suffered a massive stroke, which left her totally paralyzed on her left side. At the present time she is confined to a hospital bed, in an essentially vegetative state, immobile, speechless, unable to swallow without choking, and barely able to cough. Her eyes occasionally open and from time to time appear to fix on or follow an object briefly; otherwise she appears to be unaware of her environment. She is fed through a naso–gastric tube, which can cause irritation, ulceration, and infection in her throat and esophageal tract, and which must be removed from time to time, and that procedure itself causes discomfort. She is catheterized and also, of course, requires bowel care. Apart from her Alzheimer's disease and paralysis, she suffers from high blood pressure which is difficult to control; there is risk in lowering it due to a constriction in an artery leading to a kidney. She has a serious, life–threatening coronary artery disease, due to arteriosclerosis. Her condition is hopeless, but it is difficult to predict exactly when she will die. Her life expectancy is no more than a year, but she could go into cardiac or respiratory arrest at any time. One of these, or another stroke, is most likely to be the immediate cause of her death.

In this situation her attending physician has recommended that, when (and if) cardiac or respiratory arrest occurs, resuscitation efforts should not be undertaken. Such efforts typically involve the use of cardiac massage or chest compression and delivery of oxygen under compression through an endotracheal tube into the lungs. An electrocardiogram is connected to guide the efforts of the resuscitation team and to monitor the patient's progress. Various plastic tubes are usually inserted intravenously to supply medications or stimulants directly to the heart. Such medications may also be supplied by direct injection into the heart by means of a long needle. A defibrillator may be used, applying electric shock to the heart to induce contractions. A pacemaker, in the form of an electrical conducting wire, may be fed through a large blood vessel directly to the heart's surface to stimulate contractions and to regulate beat. These procedures, to be effective, must be initiated with a minimum of delay as cerebral anoxia, due to a cutoff of oxygen to the brain, will normally produce irreversible brain damage within three to five minutes and total brain death within fifteen minutes. Many of these procedures are obviously highly intrusive, and some are violent in nature. The defibrillator, for example, causes violent (and painful) muscle contraction which, in a patient suffering (as this patient is) from osteoporosis, may cause fracture of vertebrae or other bones. Such fractures, in turn, cause pain, which may be extreme.

The patient's family, consisting of a son, who is a physician practicing in New York City, and a daughter, with whom the patient lived prior to her admission to the nursing home in 1975, concur in the doctor's recommendation that resuscitation should not be attempted in the event of a cardiac or respiratory arrest. They have joined with the doctor and the hospital in bringing the instant action for declaratory relief, asking for a determination that the doctor may enter a "no–code" order on the patient's medical record without a judicial authorization or, alternatively, if such authorization is a legal prerequisite to the validity of a "no–code" order, that the authorization be given. The probate judge appointed a guardian ad litem, who has taken a position in opposition to the prayers of the complaint . . .

. . . The judge's findings make it clear that the case is hopeless and that death must come soon, probably in the form of cardiac or respiratory arrest. Attempts to apply resuscitation, if successful, will do nothing to cure or relieve the illnesses which will have brought the patient to the threshold of death. The case does not, therefore, present the type of significant treatment choice or election which, in light of sound medical advice, is to be made by the patient, if competent to do so . . . It presents a question peculiarly within the competence of the medical profession of what measures are appropriate to ease the imminent passing of an irreversibly, terminally ill patient in light of the patient's history and condition and the wishes of her family. That question is not one for judicial decision, but one for the attending physician, in keeping with the highest traditions of his profession, and subject to court review only to the extent that it may be contended that he has failed to exercise "the degree of care and skill of the average qualified practitioner, taking into account the advances in the profession."

. . . On the findings made by the judge the law does not prohibit a course of medical treatment which excludes attempts at resuscitation in the event of cardiac or respiratory arrest and that the validity of an order to that effect does not depend on prior judicial approval.

o **Recap of the Case**. The issue of "no code" orders is particularly relevant to nurses in hospitals and long term care facilities. The *Dinnerstein* case upheld practitioners' decision not to resuscitate the patient. As the case law develops further in this area, greater restrictions may be placed by some courts on the power of practitioners to write "no code" orders. For this reason, it is especially important for providers to stay current on cases involving this issue.

Conclusion

As these materials illustrate, the issue of consent to medical treatment is a complex one. As if obtaining consent from a competent adult is not difficult enough, many situations are further complicated by lack of capacity, age, type of treatment, etc. Nevertheless, as Judge Kelleher pointed out in *Wilkinson v. Vesey*, 295 A.2d 676, 690 (R.I., October 20, 1972), obtaining valid consent is "good medicine," "good humanity," "good public relations," and "good medicolegal defense." Consent has a therapeutic value all its own; the informed patient is not so shocked should risks manifest themselves in the course of treatment, and if practitioner-patient rapport is high, patients are much less likely to sue their practitioners.

How to Read a Citation

```
Sample:  Pederson v. Dumonchel,  72  Wash.2d  73,  78,  431  P.2d  973,  977  (1967)
              (1)    \      /    (2)    (4)    (5)  (6)  (7)  (8)  (9)  (10) (11)  (12)
                     (3)
```

Key:

(1)   The name of the plaintiff at the trial court level. The name of the appellant in a case before a court of appeals.

(2)   The name of the defendant at the trial court level. The name of the appellee in a case before a court of appeals.

(3)   The names of the plaintiff and defendant or the appellant and appellee constitute the name of the case.

(4)   Indicates the number of the book in which the case appears.

(5)   Indicates the name of the series of books in which the case appears.

(6)   Designates the page number on which the case begins.

(7)   States the number of the page on which the specific portion of the case referred to by the court begins.

(8)   Many cases are published in more than one series of books. This indicates the number of a second book in which this case appears.

(9)   Indicates the name of another series of books in which this case also appears.

(10)   Designates the page number on which the case begins in the second book in which the case appears.

(11)   States the page number in the second book on which the case begins.

(12)   States the year in which the case was decided.

Glossary

The author relied heavily upon *Black's Law Dictionary*, 5th Edition, West Publishing Co., 1979, to prepare this glossary. Readers should make further use of this excellent resource when necessary.

Actual damages. Compensation for actual injuries or losses such as medical expenses, lost wages, etc.

Affidavit. A written statement of facts given voluntarily under oath.

Allegation. The written statements by a party to a suit concerning what the party expects to prove.

Amended complaint. A corrected or revised version of the document filed in court by the plaintiff to begin a suit.

Amicus curiae. Literally, "friend of the court." Persons or organizations with a strong interest in or views on a suit may ask the court in which the suit is filed for permission to file a brief to suggest a resolution of the case consistent with their views. *Amicus curiae* briefs are often filed in appeals of cases involving a broad public interest such as civil rights cases.

Appellant. The party who appeals the decision of one court to another court.

Appellate brief. Written arguments by attorneys required to be filed with an appellate court stating the reasons why the trial court acted correctly (appellee's brief) or incorrectly (appellant's brief). The contents and form of appellate briefs are often prescribed by the rules of various court systems.

211

Appellate briefs usually contain a statement of issues presented for review by the appellate court, a statement of the case, argument, and a conclusion stating the precise action sought by the party submitting the brief.

Appellate review. Examination of a previous proceeding.

Appellee. The party in a case against whom an appeal is brought. Sometimes also called the "respondent."

Assault. Any conduct which creates a reasonable apprehension of being touched in an injurious manner. No actual touching is required to prove assault.

Assumption of the risk. A defense to plaintiffs' claims based on the theory that plaintiffs may not recover for injuries to which they consent. In order to prove that the plaintiff assumed the risk, the defendant must show that: (1) the plaintiff had knowledge of a dangerous condition, (2) the plaintiff appreciated the nature or extent of the danger, and (3) the plaintiff voluntarily exposed himself to the danger.

Attorney in fact. Any person authorized by another to act in his place either for a particular purpose or for the transaction of business affairs in general. This authority is conferred by a document called a power of attorney.

Battery. An unconsented, actual touching which causes injury.

Borrowed servant rule. A theory of liability or negligence which is used to extend liability beyond the person who actually committed negligent acts to include those who had the right of control over the negligent actions.

Brief. A written statement prepared by an attorney arguing a case in court. A brief contains a summary of the facts of the case, the pertinent laws, and an argument of how the law applies to the facts supporting an attorney's position.

Burden of proof. The requirement of proving facts in dispute on an issue raised between the parties in a case.

Captain of the ship doctrine. This doctrine imposes liability on surgeons in charge of operations for negligence of assistants during periods when those assistants are under the surgeons' control, even though the assistants are also employees of a hospital. This doctrine extends the borrowed servant rule to the operating rooms of hospitals.

Cause of action. The fact or facts which give a person the right to begin a suit.

Common law. As opposed to laws created by legislatures, the common law consists of legal principles based solely on usages and customs of time immemorial, particularly the ancient unwritten law of England.

Complaint. The first document filed in court by the plaintiff to begin a suit.

Conservator. Any individual appointed by a court to manage the affairs of an incompetent person.

Continuance. Adjournment or postponement of a session, hearing, trial, or other proceeding to a subsequent day or time.

Contributory negligence. A defense to a claim of negligence. Any act or omission on the part of the complaining party amounting to a breach of the duty the law imposes on everyone to protect themselves from injury which contributes to the injury complained of by the plaintiff.

Counterclaim. Claim presented by a defendant in opposition to the claim of the plaintiff. If the defendant establishes his claim, it will defeat or diminish the plaintiff's claim.

Cross–complaint. A defendant or cross–defendant (plaintiff) may file a cross–complaint based on: (1) any claim against any of the parties who filed the complaint against him *or* (2) any claim against a person alleged to be liable whether or not the person is already a party to the suit. The claims in a cross–complaint must (1) arise out of the same transaction or occurrence as the original suit *and* (2) must make a claim or assert a right or interest in property or controversy which is the basis for the claim already made.

Cross–defendants. Plaintiffs who, subsequent to suing defendants, are then counter–sued by the defendants. Defendants in a suit brought by defendants.

Cross–examination. The questioning of a witness by an adverse party to test the truth of his testimony or to further develop it.

Declaratory judgment. Provided for in state and federal statutes. A person may seek a declaratory judgment from a court if there is an actual controversy among the parties, and the party asking for the declaratory judgment has some question or doubt about his legal rights. The judgment is binding on the parties both presently and in the future.

Defendant. The person defending or denying; the party against whom a civil lawsuit is brought or the accused in a criminal case.

Defense. A response to the claims of the other party stating the reasons why the claims should not be recognized.

Demurrer. An argument in which the defendant admits the facts in the plaintiff's complaint, but claims that the facts are insufficient to require a response.

Deposition. Device by which one party asks oral questions of the other party or of a witness for the other party before the trial begins. The person who answers questions is called a deponent. The deposition is conducted under oath outside of the courtroom, usually in one of the lawyer's offices. A transcript or word–for–word account is made of the deposition.

Directed verdict. When the party with the burden of proof fails to prove all necessary elements of the case, the trial judge may direct a verdict in favor of the other party, since there can only be one result anyway.

Docket. A list or calendar of cases to be tried during a particular period of time prepared by employees of the court for use by the court and attorneys.

Due process clause. Two clauses in the United States Constitution, one in the Fifth Amendment applicable to the United States Government, the other in the Fourteenth Amendment which protects persons from actions by the states. There are two aspects: (1) procedural, in which a person is guaranteed fair procedures, and (2) substantive, which protects a person's property from unfair governmental interference. Similar clauses are in most state constitutions.

Due process of law. An orderly proceeding in which a person receives notice of the proceeding and the subject matter of the proceeding, and is given an opportunity to be heard and to enforce and protect his rights before a court or person(s) with power to hear and determine the case.

En banc. Full bench. Refers to a session in which all the judges of a court participate in deciding a case, rather than one judge or a regular panel of judges.

Equal protection clause. A provision in the Fourteenth Amendment to the United States Constitution which requires every state to treat individuals in similar circumstances the same in terms of rights and redress of improper actions against them.

Ex parte. On one side only; by or for one party; done for, on behalf of, or on the application of, one party only. A judicial proceeding, order, injunction, etc. is *ex parte* when it is granted at the request of and for the benefit of one party only without notice to any person adversely interested.

False imprisonment. A tort which consists of intentionally confining a person without his consent.

Felony. A crime of a more serious nature. Under federal law and many state statutes, a felony is any offense punishable by death or imprisonment for a term exceeding one year.

Guardian. Any person responsible for taking care of, managing the property of and protecting the rights of another person who, because of youth or lack of understanding, is incapable of managing his own affairs.

Guardian ad litem. A special guardian appointed by a court to prosecute or defend, on behalf of a minor or incompetent, a suit to which he is a party.

Harmless error. Any trivial error or an error which is merely academic because it did not affect important rights of any party to a case and did not affect the final result of the case. Harmless error will not serve as a basis to change a decision of the court.

Implied consent. Signs, actions or facts, or inaction or silence, which indicate that consent is given.

In loco parentis. In the place of a parent; instead of a parent; charged with a parent's rights, duties, and responsibilities.

Infliction of emotional distress. Conduct going beyond that usually tolerated by society which is calculated to cause mental distress *and* which actually causes severe mental distress.

Informed consent. A person's agreement to allow something to happen following a full disclosure of facts needed to make the decision intelligently.

Intent. Design, resolve, or determination which serves as the basis for a person's actions. Intent can rarely be proved directly but may be inferred from the circumstances.

Interrogatories. A tool to elicit information important to a case prior to trial. Interrogatories are written questions about the case submitted by one party to another party or witness. The answers to interrogatories are usually given under oath, i.e. the person answering the questions signs a sworn statement that the answers are true.

Judge a quo. Literally, "from which." A judge of a court from which a case was taken before a decision is made.

Judgment of nonsuit. A decision by a court against plaintiffs when they are unable to prove their cases or refuse or neglect to proceed to trial. A court decision which leaves the issues undetermined.

Judgment notwithstanding the verdict (j.n.o.v.). A judgment entered by order of the court for a party, even though the jury decided in favor of the other party. A motion for directed verdict must usually be made prior to a judgment notwithstanding the verdict.

Jurisdiction. The right and power of a court to decide a particular case.

Jury instructions. Statements made by the judge to the jury regarding the law applicable to the case the jury is considering which the jury is required to accept and apply. Attorneys for both sides usually furnish the judge with suggested instructions.

Justiciable controversy. Courts will only decide justiciable controversies. That is, courts will only decide cases in which there is a real, substantial difference of opinion between the parties as opposed to a hypothetical difference or dispute or one that is academic or moot.

Leave to amend. Permission or authorization given by a judge to any party to a suit to correct or reverse any document filed by the party with the court.

Locality rule. In order to show negligence, according to the locality rule, a plaintiff must prove that the defendant practitioner failed to render care considered reasonable in the same or in a similar geographical location.

Misdemeanor. Criminal offenses less serious than a felony and usually punished by fine or imprisonment other than in a penitentiary. Any criminal offense other than a felony.

Motion for new trial. Request to a judge to set aside a decision already made in a case and to order a new trial on the basis that the first decision was improper or unfair.

Motion for summary judgment. An application made to a court or judge to obtain a ruling or order that all or part of the other party's claim or defense should be eliminated from further consideration. This motion is made when a party believes there is no significant disagreement concerning important facts among the parties <u>and</u> the law supports the position of the party making the motion. A motion for summary judgment may be directed toward all or part of a claim or defense. It may be made on the basis of the pleadings or other portions of the record in the case, or it may be supported by affidavits and a variety of outside material.

Motion to dismiss. An application made to a court or judge to obtain or order that the plaintiff's suit should be eliminated from further consideration by the court or judge. This motion is usually made before a trial is held and may be based on a variety of reasons, such as the insufficiency of the plaintiff's claims, improper service of process of the plaintiff's suit on the defendant, etc.

Motion to intervene/Plea in intervention. A written request to a court to become a party to a case filed in the court based upon an interest in the results of the case.

Negligence. The failure to do something a reasonable person would do or doing something a reasonable person would not do.

Nominal damages. A very small amount of money awarded to plaintiffs in cases in which there is no substantial injury. Nominal damages are awarded to recognize technical invasions of rights or breaches of duty or in cases where the injury is more substantial but the plaintiff fails to prove the amount.

Parens patriae. Literally, "parent of the country." Refers to the role of each state as sovereign and guardian of persons under legal disability. This concept is the basis for activity by states to protect interests such as the health, comfort, and welfare of the people.

Per quod. Literally, "whereby." A phrase used to designate facts concerning the consequences of defendant's actions on the plaintiff which serve as the basis for an award of special damages to the plaintiff.

Petition. A formal, written request to a court asking the court to take certain action regarding a particular matter.

Physician–patient privilege. The right of patients not to reveal or have revealed by their physicians the communications made between patients and physicians. The privilege is established by legislatures in most states and, therefore, varies from state to state. The privilege belongs only to the patient and may be waived by the patient.

Plaintiff. A person who sues in a civil case.

Pleading. The formal, written statements by the parties to a suit of their respective claims and defenses.

Power of attorney. A document authorizing another person to act on one's behalf. The other person is called the attorney in fact. The power of the attorney in fact is revoked on the death of the person who signed the power of attorney. The powers given to the attorney in fact may be general or for special purposes.

Prejudicial error. Any error which substantially affects the legal rights and obligations of a party. A prejudicial error may result in a new trial and the reversal of a decision by the court.

Pre-trial conference. A meeting between opposing attorneys and the judge in a particular case. The purpose of the meeting is to define the key issues of the case, to secure stipulations, and to take all other steps necessary to aid in the disposition of the case. Such conferences are called at the discretion of the court. The decisions made at the conference are included in a written order which controls the future course of the case.

Pre-trial discovery. Any device used by parties prior to trial to obtain evidence for use at trial such as interrogatories, depositions, requests for admission of facts, etc.

Prima facie case. Sufficient evidence presented by the plaintiff upon which a decision that the plaintiff's claims are valid can be reasonably made.

Proximate cause. The dominant cause or the cause producing injury. Any action producing injury, unbroken by any efficient intervening cause, and without which the injury would not have occurred.

Punitive damages. Money awarded to the Plaintiff over and above compensation for actual losses. Punitive damages are awarded in cases where the wrongdoing was aggravated by violence, oppression, malice, fraud, or wickedness. They are intended to compensate for mental anguish, shame, degradation, or to punish or make an example of the defendant.

Remand. To send back. The sending by an appellate court of a case back to a court in which it was previously considered in order to have some further action taken on it.

Request for admissions. Written statements of fact concerning a case which are submitted by the attorney for a party to a suit to the attorney for another party to the suit.

The attorney who receives the request is required to either admit or deny each of the statements of fact submitted. Those statements which are admitted will be treated by the court as established and need not be proved at trial.

Res ipsa loquitur. Literally, the thing speaks for itself. Although the plaintiffs cannot testify to the exact cause of injury, they can prove (1) that the instrument causing injury was in defendants' exclusive control and (2) that the injury they sustained does not normally occur in the absence of negligence. Plaintiffs who prove both of these things can recover damages for negligence even though the exact circumstances of injury are unknown.

Res judicata. A legal principle which says that once a *final* decision is made on a matter, the same question may not be raised at a later date.

Respondent superior. Literally, "let the master say". A basis for extending liability to include the employer for the wrongful acts of employees. This doctrine is inapplicable where injury occurs while the employee is acting outside the legitimate scope of employment.

Re-trial. A new trial of a case which has already been tried at least once.

Stare decisis. Literally, "to abide by or adhere to decided cases." The policy of courts in the United States to apply previously established principles of law to all future cases where the facts are substantially the same, even though the parties to the suit are not the same.

State action. Activity of a state necessary to trigger the protection of the Fourteenth Amendment of the United States Constitution for private citizens.

Statute of limitations. Legislative enactments establishing limits on the right to sue. Statutes of limitations declare that no one may sue unless the suit is filed within a specified period of time after the occurrence or injury which is the basis for the suit.

Stay. A stopping by order of a court. A suspension of the case or some designated proceedings in it. A stay is a kind of injunction with which a court freezes its proceedings at a particular point. It can be used to stop the case altogether or to hold up only some phase of it.

Stipulation. A voluntary agreement between opposing attorneys concerning disposition of a point which alleviates the need for proof of this point or for consideration of this point by the court. This agreement is usually in the form of a written document signed by the attorneys for all of the parties and placed on file as part of the court record.

Third party defendant. A party brought into a suit by the defendant who was not a party to the transaction upon which the suit is based, but whose rights and liabilities may be affected by the suit.

Tort. A private or civil wrong or injury for which a court may award damages. Any civil suit except a suit for breach of contract. Three elements of every tort claim are: (1) existence of a legal duty by the defendant to the plaintiff, (2) breach of this duty, *and* (3) resulting damage to the plaintiff.

Transcript. A word–for–word written record of a trial, hearing, or other proceeding.

Trial. An examination and determination of issues between the parties to a case by a court.

Trial by court or judge. A trial before a judge *only* in contrast to a trial before a judge *and* jury.

Trial court. Judicial examination and determination of issues between the parties in a case.

Vicarious liability. Indirect legal responsibility.

Voir dire. Literally, "to speak the truth." Refers to the preliminary questioning which the court or attorneys conduct to determine the qualifications of a person to serve as a juror in a particular case.

Writ of certiorari. An order of an appellate court used when the court has discretion whether or not to hear an appeal. If the writ is denied, the court refuses to hear the appeal and the decision of the court that previously heard the case remains in effect. If the writ is granted, the appellate court will reconsider the case and perhaps change the decision of the lower court.

Writ of error. A writ issued from an appeals court to a trial court requiring the trial court to send the record of a case to the appeals court for reconsideration. The writ is based on errors of law apparent from the record. It is the beginning of a new suit to reverse a decision of a lower court and is not a continuation of any suit in a lower court.

Writ of habeus corpus. Literally, "you have the body." The primary function of this writ is to force the release of a person from unlawful imprisonment.